Basic Book-keeping for Solicitors

AUSTRALIA AND NEW ZEALAND
The Law Book Company Ltd.
Sydney : Melbourne : Perth

CANADA AND U.S.A.
The Carswell Company Ltd.
Agincourt, Ontario

INDIA
N. M. Tripathi Private Ltd.
Bombay
and
Eastern Law House Private Ltd.
Calcutta and Delhi
M.P.P. House
Bangalore

ISRAEL
Steimatzky's Agency Ltd.
Jerusalem : Tel Aviv : Haifa

PAKISTAN
Pakistan Law House
Karachi

Basic Book-keeping

for

Solicitors

Richard Halberstadt, LL.B. (LOND.)

Solicitor

Fourth Edition

LONDON
SWEET & MAXWELL
1989

First Edition
Second Edition
Third Edition
Second Impression 1987
Fourth Edition

Published by Sweet & Maxwell Ltd.
of South Quay Plaza, 183 Marsh Wall,
Computerset by Promenade Graphics Ltd., Cheltenham
Printed by Richard Clay Ltd., Bungay, Suffolk.

British Library Cataloguing in Publication Data
Halberstadt, Richard
Bookkeeping for Solicitors.—4th ed.
1. Law firms. Accounting
I. Title
657'.2'024344

ISBN 0–421–41370–0

Preface

This book is only concerned with the double-entries to record the dealings which take place in a solicitor's office. It is not concerned in general with prime (or original) entries, which depend so much on individual office practice.

All the illustrations, examples and exercises are fictional. The characters chosen and the sums of money involved have merely been selected so as to provide meat for the accounts. I am well aware, for instance, that in many of the conveyancing examples, although the example involves payment of stamp duty, no stamp duty would normally have been payable or, if in an exceptional case it had been payable, it would not have been of the amount stated in the example. This, I hope, will not detract from the object of the exercise (and of this book) which is not to teach the details of conveyancing but rather how to make the basic double-entries in a solicitor's books of accounts.

I should like to thank all my colleagues who have helped me with the book and particularly Ray Dean, Dai Jones, Lesley King and Malcolm Maddock, for the comments and suggestions they made. I would also like to express my appreciation to the publishers for their assistance and patience. Nevertheless, my greatest thanks must go to my former students. Theirs was the inspiration for the book and they, albeit unknowlingly, provided much of the material. However, they will be pleased to note that this time the mistakes, of which there are bound to be some if not many, are all mine.

I also wish to acknowledge the permission given by The Law Society to use past examination questions. I have, however, had to adapt these questions slightly in order to take account of changes in conveyancing procedure, VAT rates and the examination syllabus. I must point out that the answers to these questions are my own and so, again, any mistakes are mine.

London   Richard Halberstadt
May, 1989

Contents

Section One
THE GENERAL RUNNING OF THE BUSINESS

Section Two
THE HANDLING OF TRANSACTIONS ON
BEHALF OF CLIENTS

Appendix
ANSWERS

HOW TO PASS AN ACCOUNTS EXAMINATION

Much of what is going to follow may seem obvious. The danger is that it will seem so obvious, and not relevant to you, that you will ignore it. Bear in mind that each year a certain number of candidates in Accounts examinations fail, and they probably fail because they have not followed the following rules.

A. PREPARING FOR THE EXAMINATION

1. This will probably be the first examination that you have taken in book-keeping/accounts. It is a practical subject and in the examination you will be asked to draw up accounts. As such it will be very different from an academic university examination. You will not be asked, as at university to "explain" or "discuss"; instead the examination will be concerned with your practical ability, *i.e.* can you do the accounts? In preparing for the examination, therefore, it will not be enough merely to understand the subject. Much of the subject may, in fact, seem very straightforward and obvious merely from reading a textbook and/or watching a tutor explaining (and maybe even doing) the accounts. The crucial point is that you will have to do them yourself. This requires practice.

2. The only way to get sufficient practice is to do exercises. These take time. As a basic rule, it is better to spread out exercises as much as possible rather than cramming them together. "Little and Often" is probably the best advice. Thus, rather than spending three hours one day doing six accounts exercises (each individual exercise lasting about 30 minutes), it is probably better to do one exercise a day, *i.e.* 30 minutes each day, over six days.

3. **How to use this book**
   This is not a book for reading and contemplation; instead, it is more of an exercise book. A good method of study would be:
   (a) read a section through quickly;
   (b) turn to the relevant exercises and do the first one, copying from the example in the text;
   (c) check the answer and if correct, continue to the second exercise, etc.;
   (d) after a few exercises, try the next one without copying from the text;
   (e) when you have done all the exercises in that section, and not before, proceed to the next section.

4. **Do all the exercises in numerical order**
   Do not leave any out. The exercises are graded throughout the book. It is very tempting to try to do the hardest one first but this must be resisted. Master each exercise or group of exercises before proceeding to the next one.

5. **Speed**
   One certain fact about the examination is that you will have a lot to do in the time. This means that you will have to be able to do the accounts quickly. One of the main purposes of the exercises is to build up speed. It is one thing to be able to

1

say: "Oh I can do that—in about 25 minutes"; it is quite another thing to be able to do it in five minutes. A lot of the exercises in this book may seem repetitious. This is deliberate, the idea being that with repetition you will get faster. When doing the exercises, to begin with, concentrate on getting the answers right. However, as you progress, become aware of how long each exercise is taking you. As you get nearer to the examination it is essential to time yourself. As a guide, some of the later questions have time limits suggested.

6. Tidiness

This is often an emotional subject. However, the fact is that it is the students who are tidy that pass accounts examinations. You should work neatly from the very start. If you are naturally a tidy person, you will do this anyway. If, however, you are not naturally tidy, don't put if off. It is a great temptation to do all the preparation work "in rough" and say: "When it comes to the examination, I will do it neatly." You will find this impossible. If you are not by nature tidy, you will be unable suddenly to "switch on" neat work. On the contrary, the strain of an examination can cause even a tidy person to work untidily. The only way that anyone, whether naturally tidy or not, can ensure that they can produce neat work in an examination is to develop the habit beforehand.

Do not crush your written answer to a question into a space the size of a postage stamp; spread it out. From time to time you are bound to make a mistake and wish to alter your answer. If your accounts are all crushed together it will be impossible to make corrections. Furthermore, well-spaced-out work is more pleasing to the eye and will be easier for your examiner to follow. When setting out a column of figures for addition, make sure that the figures are set out with the vertical columns in straight lines. As well as making the work look tidy it will also help to eliminate maths errors.

7. Presentation

Alongside the topic of tidiness is that of presentation. Accounts is the art of presenting financial information. This means that not only is it essential to present the right information (*i.e.* the figures must be correct) but also there is a skill in the way in which the information is presented. This means paying attention to the way the accounts are laid out: which items go on the left and which on the right, the order in which items appear, and, very importantly, "Headings." It is very easy for a beginner to assume that so long as the figures are correct the answer is right and will get full marks. This is not so. If you fail to put the proper headings to the accounts you will lose marks. Again, it is a question of practice. If, all the way through the exercises, you put in the proper headings, by the time you get to the examination it will have become a habit. You will not want to spend time and energy in an examination worrying over what heading to put in; there will be other much more pressing matters to which you will need to devote your mind.

Therefore, when checking your answers, first check that your figures are correct, but secondly (and this is just as important), look critically at your work for tidiness and presentation; if this work had been presented to you by an examination candidate, by your articled clerk, or even by an accountant or bookkeeper employed by you, would you be satisfied with the way in which it was presented?

8. A special word for non-mathematicians

Up to now the advice has all been fairly stern stuff and concerned with "do's" and "don'ts." What about those people who are a little apprehensive about the subject? "But I was never any good at maths" is a cry I hear often. Don't be frightened. You are doing an accounts examination, *NOT* a maths examination, and you do not need to be good at adding up to do accounts. Of course, if you do make mathematical errors your answers will not be right, but generally you will not lose very many marks if your only errors are those of addition and/or subtraction. Tidiness will help here. So often untidiness and mathematical errors go hand in hand. In any event, you are allowed to use a calculator and, if you are at all nervous about your ability to add up and/or subtract swiftly, you should use one.

So often, students who have had bad experiences with maths at a younger age approach accounts with fear and trepidation. If you were not good at maths at school, don't assume you won't be able to do accounts. They are not the same, and you might be in for a pleasant surprise. I know a number of students who hated maths, who assumed they were going to hate accounts as well, but who actually finished up enjoying the subject—even preferring it to such things as The Perpetuity Rule, Capital Gains Tax, and the Rule in *Howe* v. *Lord Dartmouth*!

B. THE EXAMINATION ITSELF

1. Get to the examination in good time. This may seem very obvious and not worth saying, but in every single examination there are some late arrivals. Then, too, there are those who have only just made it and arrive panting, flushed and totally in the wrong frame of mind to cope instantly with an examination. Therefore, plan in advance how to get there, and allow plenty of time for emergencies.

2. **Plan your time in the examination**
   This is probably the most common mistake made by candidates in examinations. As soon as you are given the examination paper, allocate your time between the questions. Allow yourself some time at the beginning to familiarise yourself with the paper and a little time at the end, say five or 10 minutes, to read through your answers. Then, divide the rest of the time rateably between the questions according to the way in which the marks are allocated. When answering a question, *on no account go over the allocated time*. If you do run out of time, stop, and start the next question. You can always come back to the first question at the end.

   Don't waste time if, for example, an account will not balance. It is not uncommon for an examination candidate to be faced with the problem that having done a long, complex, question the Balance Sheet does not balance. What should you do now?—Give up and do the next question, or go back and try to find the reason? The answer is always to go on to the next question. The next one may carry 50 per cent. of the marks. You may find your error quickly, it may take you all the rest of the exam, you may still be looking when the exam ends! It could be that the only thing wrong is a maths error which at the most would have cost you only one mark. However, if you give up the other question, you give up the 50 marks that go with it—all to save one mark! It is not worth it. Finish the whole paper first. Then come back, if there is time, to see what you have done wrong.

3. **Read the examination paper carefully**
   The second most common fault in examinations involves misreading some part of the examination paper.

   Read the general instructions about the paper (usually at the top), and, if there is an answer book, read any instructions on it. Do this BEFORE reading any of the individual questions. It is a good idea, before the examination, to have obtained past copies of exam papers and to familiarise yourself with the instructions given before. In such a case, all you will need to do is check that they are the same, make a note of any changes, and then you can begin to look at the questions.

   The next stage is probably to have a quick read-through of all the questions and then to plan your time (see paragraph 2). You now face the problem of "which question to do first?" Some people just take the questions in their chronological order. Some like to do the most difficult question first, on the basis that they can tackle it when they are fresh. What I have noticed is that, very often, students who have failed an examination say to me that the first question they did was a bad one. This demoralised them and they then went from bad to worse. My own preference is to do the easy question first. There is of course the danger of spending too much time on it, because "I know something about this." If that danger is resisted, then it can be a good policy because it may build up confidence.

Once you have decided on a question, read it through very carefully indeed; read every word. Do not start to draw up any accounts until you have finished reading it through. When you have read it through, check and see precisely which accounts the examiner has asked you to show. These must be presented correctly. All too often, students draw up accounts that they have not been asked to show and omit those that they have been asked to show. If the question says: "Prepare the final accounts," it is not necessary to draw up a Trial Balance, unless the question makes the contrary clear. If the question involves recording dealings with clients and says: "Prepare the entries in the Client Ledger," it is not necessary to show a Cash Sheet, but all necessary Client Ledger accounts should be shown (*e.g.* the Stakeholder Account—being a Client Ledger Account—will have to be shown). If VAT is involved, check what rate of VAT is to be used. For convenience, in this book the standard rate of VAT has been taken as 10 per cent. throughout. Most exams specify the rate you are to use; if your paper does not specify, use the rate in force at the time of sitting the exam.

4. Show all workings

Throughout the examination you will have to make calculations, for example you have to charge a client with VAT. In your answer you should not only show what you think the relevant figure is, but also how you reached it, *i.e.* your calculation. If you do not show any workings and your final figure is wrong, the examiner will probably not know what you have done wrong and will have to make a guess. If your error is a trivial one, a maths error or a transposition of figures (you calculated VAT at 10 per cent. of £340 instead of £430), you will lose very few marks indeed. If, however, you made a serious error involving a lack of understanding of basic principles, you will lose a large number of marks. The danger of showing no workings is that you make a minor slip but, with no workings shown, the examiner assumes you have made a major error and you lose many more marks than you would have done had you shown your workings.

5. In addition to showing workings, or calculations, many candidates are tempted to write essays explaining their answers. In general, this should be unnecessary; the accounts that you produce should speak for themselves. Very occasionally a short note can be helpful. If the question involves a transaction and you decide that it does not need recording, a short note to this effect can help an examiner; he will now know that you knew that no entry was needed, rather than that you did not know what to do and left it out. The two rules to follow are:

    (a) Try to avoid writing notes
    (b) If you have to write one, keep it short.

6. There are a number of errors that should be avoided at all costs. These include:

    (a) putting fixed assets, *e.g.* Premises, on a Profit & Loss Account;
    (b) putting Drawings on a Profit & Loss Account (see page 39);
    (c) debiting a CLIENT ACCOUNT and crediting an OFFICE ACCOUNT or vice versa (see page 83);
    (d) receiving clients' money and putting it into OFFICE ACCOUNT, (see pages 100–103);
    (e) over-drawing CLIENT ACCOUNT, (see page 99).

These are all very serious errors involving the breach of a major accounting principle.

7. **Don't throw away the easy marks**

So often students seem to be devoting all their energy towards some relatively minor point at the expense of basic principles. In order to pass the examination, you must get "the basics" right. Bear in mind that in all examinations some marks are easier to get than others. Probably the easiest marks to get in an Accounts Examination are those for drawing up the right accounts, in the proper form, and with the right headings; getting the right figures is more difficult. Remember too that it is relatively easy to get the first 40–45 per cent. of the marks. The next 10–15 per cent. are a little more difficult to get, the next 15–20 per cent. very difficult to get, and the last 20–25 per cent. impossible for all but the most gifted of persons to get. You do not have to get everything correct in order to pass. You won't fail just because your account doesn't balance. If a safe pass is what you are after, do not waste time on all the little intricacies; concentrate on the basic principles.

8. **Don't panic**

This is where the value of good preparation should show. If you have done sufficient exercises in preparation (including those with a time limit) they should give you confidence. You will have spent many hours doing your practice work. If you have done this properly you should pass. You will have met all the basic principles and practised them many times. Just occasionally, an examiner thinks up a transaction which is slightly different from all the others usually encountered in that exam. On no account give up, saying: "We haven't been taught this—I can't do it." You ought, provided you have mastered them well enough, to be able to work the relevant entries out from basic principles. In any event, remember that the examiner knows that it is different and therefore likely to cause difficulties. This new, or different, item will only be one of several transactions and, on its own, probably will not carry that many marks. It will certainly be in that category where the marks are "very difficult to get." Do not neglect the other items carrying more marks and marks which are easier to get.

The best advice, then, is to prevent panic from starting. You need to plan in advance so that you will not panic on the day. Perhaps what this means is that you should make up your mind that whatever happens you will not panic. However, what if the worst happens and you become aware that you are getting into a panic? The thing to do is to stop, shut your eyes for a minute or two, and rest. Then begin again. Now I realise that this is difficult to do; it is more than likely that what is inducing the panic is the lack of time left in which to complete the paper. The idea of stopping and "wasting some more time" seems abhorrent, but you must. It is far better to do 15 minutes of good work than 20 minutes of muddled work. When you are under pressure and not concentrating well, you are liable to make any number of silly, but disastrous, errors that you would never have made if calm. The most important thing, in this context, is that through your practice work on exercises you should have built up a routine and so, when it comes to this examination, you should plod through your routine methodically and calmly.

9. **Approach the exam questions in a positive way**

Far too many students approach exams in a negative way; they look through the exam paper seeking points which they do not know how to answer. It is true that if the examinations are demanding, it will be a very rare event to be able to go into an examination and answer every single question correctly. However, if you have prepared conscientiously, and the examination is a fair one, the reverse will be true, namely that there should be plenty of material which you can answer. It is better to go into an examination with a positive approach (looking for what you can do) rather than the negative approach. Thus, when reading a question, look out for what you *can* do, and concentrate on the basic principles of the subject.

10. Finally, remember that good exam technique can never be a substitute for inadequate preparation. The fact of the matter is that, although a few students fail because of poor technique, the majority who fail do so because of inadequate preparation.

SECTION ONE

THE GENERAL RUNNING OF THE BUSINESS

Chapter 1

INTRODUCTION

1. The object of bookkeeping is to record information. A bookkeeper's task consists of keeping records (accounts) of all transactions which affect a business so that the information contained in the accounts can be communicated to persons interested in the business. These persons include:

    (a) The owners and/or managers of the business,
    (b) A prospective purchaser of the business,
    (c) Creditors,
    (d) Employees,
    (e) The Inland Revenue and the Commissioners of Customs and Excise.

2. So far as concerns the owners and/or the managers of the business the two chief questions to which they will want answers are:

    (a) Is the business making a profit?
    (b) Is the business solvent?

The first question is answered by looking at a record called a Profit and Loss Account and the second by looking at a document called a Balance Sheet.

3. Whether the business has made a profit (and if so how much) is discovered by deducting the expenses of the business from the income. Basically, therefore, the Profit and Loss Account consists of a list of all the income of the business and list of all the expenses. The latter are then deducted from the former.

Profit and Loss Account

	£
Income	3,000
Expenses	2,000
Profit	1,000

4. Basically a business is insolvent if it is unable to pay its debts (or liabilities). The Balance Sheet lists all the liabilities of the business and all the assets.

Balance Sheet

	£
Assets	XXX
	XXX
	5,000
Liabilities	XXX
	XXX
	5,000

5. Capital

(a) One of the conventions of bookkeeping is that although the proprietors may own the business, for the purposes of bookkeeping they are regarded as an entity separate from the business. They are merely regarded as persons with whom the business deals. The investment made by the proprietors is called "capital" and is a liability of the business. It represents the amount which the business owes to the proprietors and which would be paid to them if the business were wound up.

(b) The first transaction which takes place with most businesses is that the proprietor introduces cash or other assets into the business.

(c) *Example*

Proprietor introduces £1,000 cash in order to start the business. In such a case from the point of view of bookkeeping the proprietor is regarded as a creditor of the business (*i.e.* someone to whom the business owes money). Thus at this stage the business owns £1,000 in cash but owes £1,000 to the proprietor. The Balance Sheet would at this stage look as follows:

Balance Sheet

		£
Assets		
	Cash	1,000
Liabilities		
	Capital	1,000

6. Assets

There are two major kinds of assets: fixed assets and current assets. Fixed assets are those bought for permanent use in the business and are not bought for the purpose of being resold. They are held for the purpose of earning profits and will vary from business to business. Thus the business of a motor trader would have garage premises as fixed assets, whereas the motor cars which are bought for the purpose of re-sale would not be fixed assets. On the other hand, a firm of solicitors who bought a motor car, say for use by one of the partners, would regard the motor car as a fixed asset. The chief current assets of a business are stock, debtors and cash. These are often known as circulating assets because a trader will use his cash to buy stock which he will sell to his customers. These customers will then become debtors who in due course will pay the business in cash. These assets are thus constantly circulating. Those assets which are cash or which can be swiftly converted into cash are known as liquid assets; the most common items are cash and debtors. The trading stock of a business will vary from business to business depending on the trade carried on. What would be a fixed asset for one business will be trading stock for another. Thus a desk would be a fixed asset for a solicitor whereas it would be a current asset for a business dealing in office furniture.

Example (continued)

The business buys a car for £700 cash as a fixed asset. The business still owes the proprietor £1,000 but now owns a car worth £700 and cash of £300.

Balance Sheet

		£
Assets		
	Motor Car	700
	Cash	300
		1,000
Liabilities		
	Capital	1,000

7. **Liabilities**

Liabilities owing to persons other than the proprietor fall into two categories—long-term liabilities and current liabilities. The basic difference between the two is the length of time within which the liability has to be satisfied. The relevant test is whether the liability has to be satisfied in the next accounting period. Thus if the accounts cover a period of 12 months and the liability is payable within the next 12 months it is a current liability, whereas if it is payable in more than a year's time it is a long-term liability. A bank overdraft which is repayable on demand is a current liability whereas a special bank loan repayable in five years would be a long-term liability.

Example (continued)

A friend of the proprietor lends the business £500 cash, to be repaid in two years. The business now owes £1,500 (£1,000 to the proprietor, £500 to the friend) and owns a car worth £700 and cash of £800.

Balance Sheet

		£
Assets		
	Motor Car	700
	Cash	800
		1,500
Liabilities		
	Capital	1,000
	Loan	500
		1,500

The business then buys stock of £300 from A Supplier, payment to be made in one month's time. This will mean an additional asset will be held (stock worth £300) but there will be an additional liability to A Supplier for £300.

Balance Sheet

		£
Assets		
	Motor Car	700
	Stock	300
	Cash	800
		1,800
Liabilities		
	Capital	1,000
	Loan	500
	A Supplier	300
		1,800

8. The basic formula for the Balance Sheet is:

$$\text{LIABILITIES} = \text{ASSETS}$$

The two parts of the Balance Sheet should always be equal, however many transactions have taken place. The assets may change, but this will not alter the total of the assets. For example, the business may own £1,000 in cash and later purchase some furniture for £400—the total of the assets still equals £1,000 but, instead of a single item of cash, the business now owns furniture worth £400 and cash of £600. On the other hand the total of the assets may increase (or decrease) but the liabilities of the business will always increase (or decrease) proportionately. Thus the business may borrow £5,000 from the bank. The result will be that the assets will increase by this figure but the liabilities will also increase by the same amount owed to the bank.

9. Accounting principles or conventions

(a) When determining what entries to make in a set of accounts accountants observe various principles or "concepts."

(b) *The going concern concept.* It is assumed that the business is continuing its activities in the foreseeable future. This may be relevant when valuing the assets of a business. If the assets are valued on the basis that the business is a going concern a very different figure may be reached from the one which would have been reached if the assets had been valued on the basis that the business was being discontinued.

(c) *The consistency concept.* This means that similar accounting policies should be applied from one year to the next. Thus if one method of valuation is followed in the first year of business a similar method should be followed in the second and subsequent years. This could be relevant when it comes to valuing stock in hand or work in progress at the end of a financial period. If a different method of valuation is used from year to year then the accounts produced over a series of years will be misleading.

(d) *The prudence concept.* This means that only profits which have been realised should be included in the accounts. On the other hand liabilities and losses likely to arise but not yet realised should be taken into account. Thus if there is doubt a loss should be included, a profit should be omitted. This is particularly relevant when considering the depreciation or appreciation of fixed assets after they have been purchased (see *post*, Chap. 6).

(e) *The accruals concept.* All income and expenses in the accounting period to which the accounts relate should be taken into account, without regard to the date of receipt or payment (see *post*, Chap. 6).

Chapter 2

BASIC PRINCIPLES OF DOUBLE-ENTRY

1. Account

An account is a record, *i.e.* a written report of events or transactions that have occurred. A business will need to keep a whole set of accounts to record all the dealings in which the business engages. There will need to be a separate account (or record).

  (a) for each person with whom the business deals, to record the dealings with that person;
  (b) for each type of asset (or thing) owned by the business, to record dealings with that asset;
  (c) for each type of transaction which determines the size of the profit (or loss) eventually made by the business. These transactions can be sub-divided into transactions which produce *income* (or a profit) for the business, and those which produce an *expense* (or a loss).

2. Transaction

A business transaction involves a transfer of values. The value may be money, goods, or services. Money may be paid to a creditor or received from a debtor, a shop may sell goods to a customer or buy goods from a wholesaler, a hairdresser may cut a customer's hair, or a solicitor may give legal advice to a client. The transactions are always recorded in terms of money. Thus if a shop sells a pair of shoes to a customer for £10, the accounts will record that the sale was worth £10 (and not that it was a sale of two shoes).

3. The two aspects of a transaction

Every business transaction has two aspects or two sides to it. If the proprietor introduces £1,000 cash into the business, the business will hold assets of £1,000 but will also owe the proprietor the same amount. In this case the assets have increased by £1,000 but the liabilities have also increased by the same amount. If the business then buys fixed assets for £600, cash will decrease but the fixed assets will increase.

4. Ledger

Originally the accounts of a business were kept in a book which was called a Ledger and each page in the Ledger was called a Folio. Nowadays the accounts are too many to be kept in a single book but the name of the Ledger still remains.

5. An account, or folio, is divided into two halves: a left-hand side and a right-hand side. The left-hand side of the page is called the debit side and the right-hand side is called the credit side.

6. Whenever a transaction takes place two entries are made (hence the name the "double-entry" system). One entry is made on the left-hand side of an account (*i.e.* an account is debited) and another entry is made on the right-hand side of an account (*i.e.* an account is credited). Usually the two entries are made on different accounts, although sometimes they are made on the same account.

7. Thus the accounting equation is realised namely that THE SUM TOTAL OF ALL THE LEFT-HAND ENTRIES (*i.e.* DEBITS) ALWAYS EQUALS THE

13

SUM TOTAL OF ALL THE RIGHT-HAND ENTRIES (*i.e.* CREDITS). At first it may be useful to avoid thinking in terms of debits and credits and merely to think in terms of left-hand entries and right-hand entries. It is important to realise that these words debit and credit are being used in a technical sense to mean the left-hand side of an account and the right-hand side of an account. They must not be confused with the normal use of such words in everyday language. A common error is to think of a debit as "a bad thing" and a credit as "a good thing." Thus if money is received one might think of only crediting an account. What has to be realised is that when "a good thing" happens (*e.g.* money is received) two entries have to be made, *i.e.* a debit AND a credit.

8. AT ALL TIMES THE BASIC RULE OF BOOKKEEPING MUST BE BORNE IN MIND NAMELY *FOR EVERY DEBIT ENTRY THERE MUST BE A CORRESPONDING CREDIT ENTRY*, (and vice versa).

9. **Cash**

The account to record dealings with cash is called "The Cash Account." This account is common to all businesses. It will record all the receipts of cash and all the payments of cash. As stated above, the account is divided into two halves. All the receipts are traditionally recorded on the left-hand side of the page (*i.e.* debits) and all the payments are recorded on the right-hand side of the page (*i.e.* credits).

Thus, *so far as the Cash Book is concerned*:

DEBIT RECEIPTS
CREDIT PAYMENTS

Example 1
Cash of £800 is received from Alice.

(a) *The First Entry*

DEBIT (*i.e.* left-hand side) the Cash Account

Cash
----
800 |

(b) *The Second Entry*
This can be worked out from the First Entry. Since that was a DEBIT (*i.e.* a left-hand entry), it follows that the other entry must be a CREDIT (or right-hand entry). The money was received from Alice and therefore an account must be kept to record all the dealings with her. The entry is therefore made on that account as follows:

CREDIT the account of Alice

Alice

| **800**

Example 2
Cash of £70 is paid to Bill.

(a) *The First Entry*

CREDIT (*i.e.* right-hand side) the Cash Account

<u>Cash</u>
|
| 70

(b) *The Second Entry*

This can be worked out from the First Entry. Since that was a CREDIT (right-hand entry), it follows that the other entry must be a DEBIT (left-hand entry). The money was paid to Bill and therefore an account must be kept to record all the dealings with him. The entry is therefore made on that account as follows:

DEBIT the account of Bill.

<u>Bill</u>
70 |

10. Purchases and sales of trading stock

(a) All businesses which deal in goods will need to record their dealings with their trading stock. What their trading stock is will vary from business to business (*e.g.* a motor dealer would have motor cars as his trading stock whereas a furniture shop would have furniture). Solicitors do not deal in goods but these transactions are useful as an illustration of basic bookkeeping principles.

(b) By convention, instead of having a single account to record dealings with trading stock, traders have two separate accounts, one to record all the purchases and another to record all the sales.

(c) The purchases are all entered on the left-hand side of the Purchases Account (*i.e.* DEBIT) and the sales are all entered on the right-hand side of the Sales Account (*i.e.* CREDIT).

(d) *Illustration 1*

The business buys goods worth £30 from Charles.

1. *The First Entry*

DEBIT (*i.e.* left-hand side) the Purchases Account

<u>Purchases</u>
30 |

2. *The Second Entry*

As the First Entry was on the DEBIT (or left-hand side) of the Purchases Account it follows that there must be another entry on the CREDIT (or right-hand side) of another account. The goods were bought from Charles and it follows that the relevant account will be the account of Charles. The entry therefore is:

CREDIT the account of Charles

<u>Charles</u>
| 30

(e) *Illustration 2*

The business sells goods worth £80 to Diana.

1. *The First Entry*

CREDIT (*i.e.* right-hand side) the Sales Account.

Sales	
	80

2. *The Second Entry*

As the first entry was on the CREDIT (or right-hand side) of the Sales Account it follows that there must be another entry on the DEBIT (or left-hand side) of another account. The relevant account will be an account in the name of Diana. The entry is therefore:

DEBIT the account of Diana

Diana	
80	

11. Purchases, sales and cash—examples

(a) May 1. The business buys goods worth £50 from Edward, payment to be made on June 1. This is known as a purchase on credit terms. In this sense the word "credit" is not being used in its technical bookkeeping sense but in its everyday language sense. It means that the goods do not have to be paid for until a later date. The double-entry is:

DEBIT the Purchases Account.
CREDIT the account of Edward.

Purchases		Edward	
50			50

If one looks at the account of Edward this shows that the business has bought goods worth £50 from him and thus the business owes £50 to Edward.

(b) June 1. The business pays Edward the £50. The double-entry is:

CREDIT the Cash Account.
DEBIT the account of Edward.

Cash		Edward	
	50	50	50

If one looks now at the account of Edward it will be seen that the two sides of his account are equal. The technical phrase for this is that the account "balances." This must be correct because the business previously owed £50 to Edward, it has now paid Edward the amount due, and so there is no money owing to him.

(c) July 1. The business sells goods worth £60 to Fred, payment to be made on

August 1. This is known as a sale on credit, *i.e.* the goods do not have to be paid for until a later date. The entries are:

CREDIT the Sales Account
DEBIT the account of Fred

Sales		Fred	
	60	**60**	

If one looks at the account of Fred this shows that the business sold goods worth £60 to him and thus Fred owes £60 to the business.

(d) August 1. The business receives the £60 in cash from Fred. The entries are:

DEBIT the Cash Account
CREDIT the account of Fred

Cash		Fred	
60		60	**60**

If one looks now at the account of Fred it will be seen that the two sides balance. The business was previously owed £60 by Fred, he has now paid the amount due, and so there is nothing owed by him to the business.

12. Summary

(a) *Receipt of Cash*

DEBIT the Cash Account
CREDIT the account of the person from whom the money was received.

(b) *Payment of Cash*

CREDIT the Cash Account
DEBIT the account of the person to whom the money was paid.

(c) *Purchase of trading stock*

DEBIT the Purchases Account
CREDIT the account of the person from whom the goods were bought.

(d) *Sales of trading stock*

CREDIT the Sales Account
DEBIT the account of the person to whom the goods were sold.

13. Exercises
Assume that all purchases and sales are on credit

(1) Record the following dealings with Alice
Receive Cash £1, £2, £3. Pay Cash £6, £7, £8. Receive £10, £11, £12. Pay £13, £14, £15. Receive £16, £17. Pay £18, £19, £20.
(2) Record the following dealings with Bill and Carol
  (a) Buy goods from Bill £21, £22, £23. Sell goods to Bill £26, £27, £28. Buy goods from Bill £31, £32, £33. Sell goods to Bill £34, £35, £36.
  (b) Buy and sell goods from and to Carol as follows:
  Buy £41. Sell £42. Buy £43. Sell £44. Buy £45.

(3)　(a)　Record dealings with Dick
　　　　　Buy goods £51. Pay Dick £51 cash. Buy goods £52. Pay £52. Buy goods
　　　　　£53. Pay £53.
　　　(b)　Record dealings with Ellen.
　　　　　Sell goods £56. Receive cash from Ellen £56. Sell goods £57.
　　　　　Receive £57. Sell goods £58. Receive £58.
(4)　Record the following dealings
　　Buy goods £61 from Fred. Sell goods £62 to George. Pay cash £63 to Fred.
　　Receive £64 from George. Buy goods £65 from Fred. Sell goods £66 to
　　George. Pay £67 to Fred. Receive £68 from George. Buy £69 from Fred. Sell
　　£70 to George.

Chapter 3

DOUBLE-ENTRY—FURTHER STEPS

A. BALANCING

1. This accounting technique is used on two occasions:

(a) At the foot of each page of an account.
(b) At the end of each accounting period.

2. When one reaches the bottom of a page one does not merely turn over and start a fresh page. Instead, the entries are stopped a line or two before the end of the page so that the account can be balanced and then only the balance is carried forward to start off the new page.

3. At the end of each accounting period a trial balance has to be prepared (see p. 24). Before the trial balance is drawn up each account has to be balanced.

4. **Procedure**

(a) The entries on the account of Alice are as follows:

Alice

Cash	15	Purchases	25
Cash	30	Purchases	40

(b) There are three steps.

Step 1
Add to the lighter side the amount needed to make both sides equal.

Alice

Cash	15	Purchases	25
Cash	30	Purchases	40
Balance	**20**		

N.B. This is one part of a double-entry. It is often known as the "Balance *carried* down." It is most important to realise that there therefore needs to be a corresponding entry somewhere in the system (see Step 3).

Step 2
Insert the totals of both sides which should now be equal. This is not a double-entry.

Step 3
The corresponding entry for Step 1 above is now made below the total.

Alice

Cash	15	Purchases	25
Cash	30	Purchases	40
Balance	20		
	—		—
	65		65
	—		—
		Balance	**20**

This entry is known as the "Balance *brought* down."

(c) The balance is called a debit or credit balance according to the side on which it is brought down (*i.e.* the entry made in step 3 above). Thus in the example above there is a credit balance (*i.e.* it has been brought down on the right-hand—credit side).

B. LAYOUT

5. **Illustration**

DR[2]   Cash Account No. 10[1]   CR[2]

Date[3]	Details[4]	Fo[5]	Amount[6] £	Date[3]	Details[4]	Fo[5]	Amount[6] £
May 1	Margaret	2	300 —				

(1) The account is headed with the name of the account and the number.
(2) The account is divided into two halves. The left-hand side is the debit side and this can be shown by the letters DR in the top left-hand corner. The right-hand side is the credit side and this can be shown by the letters CR in the top right-hand corner.[1]
(3) The first column on each of the two sides is for the date of the transaction.
(4) The second column on either side is for details of the transaction. Note that this is the broadest of the columns. Here one enters sufficient information about the transaction to communicate to the reader what is involved. One of the items of information which should normally be given is the name of the account where the other entry appears. Thus if some money is received from Margaret the name of Margaret appears in the details so suggesting that the other entry is on the account for Margaret.
(5) The narrowest of the columns is that headed "Fo." This is an abbreviation for folio number. It is used to provide a cross-reference primarily for the purposes of an audit. Thus this could show the number of the account where the corresponding entry appears, *e.g.* the number of Margaret's account might be 2.
(6) The last of the columns is that for the amount of money involved in the transaction. Note that one does not need to write the pound sign each time. It is sufficient to enter the pound sign once only on each side at the top of the columns.

---

[1] These letters "DR" and "CR" are not normally shown.

6. Alternative presentation of an account

Date	Details	Fo	Debit	Credit	Balance
			£	£	£

(a) Instead of dividing the account into two sides with four columns either side for the date, the details, the folio reference and the amount, this layout uses six columns. There is only one date column, one details column, and one folio reference column. Then there is a column for the debits and a column for the credits. One of the interesting features of the alternative layout is that the final column is for the balance.

(b) *Illustration 1*
Cash of £100 is received from Charles. The entry in the Cash Account using this layout is as follows:

Cash No. 10

Date	Details	Fo	Debit £	Credit £	Balance £
Feb. 1	Charles	3	100	—	100

(c) *Illustration 2*
Cash of £60 is paid to Diana. The Cash Account would now look as follows:

Cash No. 10

Date	Details	Fo	Debit £	Credit £	Balance £
Feb. 1	Charles	3	100	—	100
Feb. 2	Diana	4	—	60	40

(d) The advantage of this is that the account will always show the current balance. It may happen from time to time that an account shows an unusual balance. For instance one would hope that normally the Cash Account would have a debit balance (*i.e.* showing cash in hand). On occasions, however, there may be an overdraft at the bank and there would therefore be a credit balance on the Cash Account (see *post*, p. 30).

(e) *Illustration 3*
Pay Edward £150 cash.

Cash No. 10

Date	Details	Fo	Debit £	Credit £	Balance £
Feb. 1	Charles	3	100	—	100
Feb. 2	Diana	4	—	60	40
Feb. 3	Edward	5	—	150	110CR

(f) If an account which should normally have a credit balance happens at some time to have a debit balance (*e.g.* of £40) then the figure is shown as follows: 40^{DR}

C. TYPES OF ACCOUNT

7. Accounts can be grouped into three different types:

(a) Personal
(b) Real
(c) Nominal

8. Personal accounts

(a) These accounts record dealings with persons. There will be a separate personal account for each person with whom the business deals. An example of a personal account is the Capital Account. This is the personal account of the proprietor of the business and should show, at any time, the amount owing to him.

Example
Proprietor introduces £5,000 cash. The double-entry is:

DEBIT the Cash Account
CREDIT the Capital Account

Cash		Capital	
5,000			5,000

(b) A person who owes money to the business is known as a debtor and his account should show a debit balance.

Example
Goods are sold to Alice for £100 and thus Alice owes the business this amount. The double-entry is:

CREDIT the Sales Account
DEBIT the account of Alice

Sales		Alice	
	100	100	

(c) A creditor is someone to whom the business owes money and his account should show a credit balance.

Example
Goods are bought from Brian for £5,000 and thus the business owes this amount to Brian. The double-entry is:

DEBIT the Purchases Account
CREDIT the account of Brian

Purchases		Brian	
5,000			5,000

9. **Real accounts**

Real accounts record dealings with assets or things owned by the business. There will be a separate account for each type of asset held. Most Real Accounts record dealings with fixed assets, *e.g.* premises, machinery, fixtures and fittings, motor vehicles.

Example
Buy machinery for £8,000 cash. The double-entry is:

CREDIT the Cash Account
DEBIT the Machinery Account

Cash		Machinery	
	8,000	**8,000**	

Real Accounts should show a debit balance.

10. **Nominal accounts**

Nominal accounts record dealings with intangibles: expenses and income. An example of an income account for a trader would be the Sales Account. This is a nominal account because its purpose is to record the income derived from the sales of the trading stock. The chief income account of a solicitor is called the Costs Account, which records the earnings of a solicitor from charging clients with costs for acting on their behalf. (See *post*, p. 32.) Examples of expense accounts include wages, rent and rates, lighting and heating, postages and telephones.

Example 1—Expenses
Pay wages £340. The double-entry is:

CREDIT the Cash Account
DEBIT the Wages Account

Cash		Wages	
	340	**340**	

Example 2—Income
Sell goods to Charles for £200. The double-entry is:

CREDIT the Sales Account
DEBIT the account of Charles

Sales		Charles	
	200	**200**	

Expense accounts should usually have a debit balance. Income accounts should usually have a credit balance.

11. **Summary of balances**

(a) *Personal Accounts*

Debtors: should have a DEBIT balance
Creditors: should have a CREDIT balance

(b) *Real Accounts*

Assets: should have a DEBIT balance

(c) *Nominal Accounts*

Expenses: should have a DEBIT balance
Income: should have a CREDIT balance

12. Exercises

(1) The proprietor introduces £10,000 cash by way of capital into the business. The business buys premises for £8,000 cash. The business buys trading stock from X for £400 on credit. The business sells stock to Y for £600 on credit. The business buys stock from X for £700 on credit. The business sells stock for £900 cash. The business pays X £470. The business receives £60 from Y. The business pays wages of £100. From this information prepare the double-entries and balance the accounts.

(2) (a) Albert sets up business as a decorator and introduces £5,000 cash into the business.

   (b) The business buys for cash the following fixed assets: furniture and fittings £2,000, van £1,500, tools £400.

   (c) The business pays the following expenses: rent £500, electricity £300, paint £100.

   (d) Albert does various jobs and earns £250 which he receives in cash.

From this information show the double-entries and balance the accounts.

D. TRIAL BALANCE

13. The trial balance is a list of all the accounts together with the balance appearing on each account, the debit balances being listed in one column and the credit balances in another. The totals of the two columns should be equal, or "balance."

14. A trial balance is drawn up at regular intervals. How often this is done depends on the choice of the manager of each business. It can be done monthly, weekly, or even daily, if this is what the manager requires.

15. A major purpose of preparing a trial balance is to check the accuracy of the accounts. Another purpose is as a preliminary step for the preparation of final accounts (see p. 37).

16. Provided the system has been maintained accurately the sum total of all the debits should always equal the sum total of all the credits. Further, if each account is balanced properly, the total of all the debit balances should still agree with the total of all the credit balances. It is however important to realise that not all bookkeeping errors are revealed by a trial balance. The following will not be revealed:

(a) *Errors of omission.* Obviously if the bookkeeper omits to enter a transaction altogether, the total of all the debits and the credits will be equal but the accounts will be inaccurate because they fail to record the particular transaction.

(b) *Errors of commission.* Such an error occurs where the correct amount is posted to the wrong account, *e.g.* £100 of goods were bought from A and the Purchases account is debited with £100 but the corresponding credit of £100 is entered on the account of B (instead of A). The debits will still equal the credits but the accounts will incorrectly show that the firm owes B £100.

(c) *Errors of principle.* Such an error occurs where a transaction is dealt with in a fundamentally incorrect manner, *e.g.* money spent on an expense is incorrectly posted to an account recording the purchase of fixed assets. This error is similar to an error of commission in that an entry is made on an incorrect account. The difference is that if an error of principle is not corrected, the final accounts will be inaccurate, *e.g.* expenses will be stated incorrectly and so will the fixed assets. On the other hand with an error of commission, if the error is not corrected the Profit and Loss Account and Balance Sheet will still be correct (*e.g.* in the previous paragraph the total creditors figure will be accurate—it is only the details of the creditors which will be wrong).

(d) *Errors of original entry.* This type of error occurs where the entries are made on the correct accounts but the wrong figure is inserted. Thus if £50 is received from C and is entered on the accounts of Cash and C as £500.

(e) *Compensating errors.* This type of error occurs where two or more errors are made which cancel each other out. Thus the Cash Account shows that £80 was paid to F and £30 was paid to G but these were incorrectly entered as £60 paid to F and £50 to G on the accounts of F and G. The two errors would thus cancel each other out and the Cash Account would come out correctly but the accounts of F and G would be inaccurate.

17. Method of preparing a trial balance

(a) Balance each individual account (see p. 19).
(b) Prepare the trial balance.

This is done by heading a piece of paper with the date at which the trial balance is drawn up. Each account is then listed and the appropriate balance put in the appropriate column. It is important to realise that the trial balance is not an account, *i.e.* no double-entries are involved. It is merely a list of existing balances.

18. Illustration

At the end of January the balances on the accounts of a trader are as follows:

Capital (credit) £20,000, Debtors (debit) £500, Creditors (credit) £4,000, Premises (debit) £15,000, Machinery (debit) £8,000, Cash (debit) £20, Wages (debit) £600, Rates (debit) £30, Income (credit) £150.

The Trial Balance would look as follows:

Trial Balance as at 31st December

	DR £	CR £
Capital		20,000
Debtors	500	
Creditors		4,000
Premises	15,000	
Machinery	8,000	
Cash	20	
Wages	600	
Rates	30	
Income		150
	24,150	24,150

19. **Exercises**

(1) Buy goods on credit from X for £50. Sell goods on credit to Y for £100. Receive £70 from Y. Pay X £40. Sell goods on credit to Z for £180. Buy goods on credit from X for £230. Cash Sale £42. Receive £120 from Z. Pay X £190.

Prepare the accounts to record the above, including a trial balance.

(2) February 1. D decides to start a business and puts in capital of £5,000. February 2. D buys stock from S Ltd. on credit for £10,000 and for cash £4,000. February 3. D sells goods to A for cash £13,000 and on credit for £1,000, and to B on credit for £2,000. February 10. D pays S Ltd. February 11. A pays D the amount due. February 12. B pays D £1,500.

Prepare the accounts of D. to record the above, including a trial balance.

(3) Sally starts a business. On March 1 she puts in capital of £1,500 and borrows £3,000 from X.

March 1. Sally pays one year's rent for premises £500.
March 1. She buys fixtures and fittings for cash £750.
March 1. She buys stock for cash £1,500.
March 8. She sells stock for cash £2,000.
March 8. She pays electricity bill £25.
March 8. She pays wages £150.
March 8. She buys stock on credit from Tom £2,000.
March 9. She sells stock for cash £4,000.
March 9. She sells stock to Rachel on credit £500.
March 10. She pays Tom £1,500.
March 10. She sells stock to Rachel on credit £250.
March 20. Rachel pays £750.

Prepare the accounts to record the above, including a trial balance.

(4) January 1. Commence business with capital of £2,000 cash.
January 2. Pay rent £100, for furniture £200.
January 3. Buy goods from A £600.
January 4. Sell goods to X £500.
January 4. Buy goods from B £700.
January 5. Pay wages £10.
January 8. Sell goods to X £300.
January 9. Pay A £500.
January 10. Receive £490 from X.
January 10. Pay B £600.
January 11. Buy goods from A £800.
January 12. Pay wages £10.

From the above prepare the accounts, including a trial balance.

(5) Enter the following transactions in the books of account of N. Nott, and extract a trial balance at the end of the month.

September 1. Started business with £5,000 cash.
September 1. Paid rent £700.
September 1. Bought fixtures for £1,200 cash.
September 5. Bought goods for £800 cash.
September 8. Cash sales £130.
September 11. Sold goods on credit to O. Penn £230.
September 15. Cash sales £240.
September 16. Bought a motor van paying £900.
September 17. O. Penn paid his account.
September 19. Bought goods for cash £300.
September 22. Bought goods on credit from R. Street for £420.

(6) Prepare a trial balance from the following figures:

Capital £2,200. Rent £620. Furniture £250. Rates £35. Sundry Expenses £12. Purchases £3,100. Sales £2,800. Debtors £915. Creditors £840. Cash £908.

(7) Prepare a trial balance as at December 31 from the following details:

Capital £40,000. Loan £10,000. Rates £3,000. Premises £28,000. Motor Vehicles £13,000. Fixtures £1,800. Wages £14,000. Purchases £30,000. Sales £50,000. Postages and Telephones £900. Lighting and Heating £2,800. Creditors £4,500. Debtors £8,600. Cash £2,400.

Chapter 4

THE BOOKS KEPT BY A SOLICITOR

A. THE BOOKS

Books of Double-Entry	*Other Books*
Cash Book	Bills Delivered Book
Petty Cash Book	Journal
Clients' Ledger	
Private Ledger	
Nominal Ledger	

B. THE BOOKS OF DOUBLE-ENTRY

Obviously even with a medium-sized business there would be too many accounts to keep them all in the same book (or ledger). The accounts therefore are kept in a series of books which amount in effect to sub-divisions of the Ledger.

1. Cash Book (C.B.)

(a) One needs to distinguish between money passed through the bank account and money kept in cash on the premises. In order to do this there will need to be two cash accounts, one to deal with the cash in the bank and the other to deal with the petty cash kept on the premises. The first Cash Account (Cash in Bank) is kept on its own in the Cash Book and the second (Cash in Hand) in another separate book—the Petty Cash Book.

(b) *Money paid directly into the bank account*
All business receipts should be banked promptly. Money received should be handed immediately to the Cashier. Each day he should pay all the money received into the bank and have in his possession a copy of the paying-in slip. From this slip the double-entries can be made up, *i.e.*

DEBIT the Cash Book.
CREDIT the account of the person from whom the money is received. (See *post* p. 83).

(c) *Money paid out by cheque*
The Cashier will also be responsible for all payments by cheque. He would therefore write out all the cheques (and the counterfoils). From the counterfoils the double-entries can be made up, *i.e.*

CREDIT the Cash Book
DEBIT either the account of the person to whom the money was paid (see *post*, p. 84) or the relevant account in the Nominal Ledger in respect of expenses or fixed assets (see *post*, p. 32).

29

(d) *Overdraft*

The balance in the Cash Book should normally be a debit balance representing cash in the Bank. If, however, the solicitor has an overdraft at the bank the balance on the Cash Book would be a credit balance.

Illustration

March 1 There is a nil balance in the solicitor's bank account.
March 2 The solicitor receives £10 from Albert, as a loan.
March 3 The solicitor pays £30 on rent, thus overdrawing the bank account.

Cash Book

2 March	Albert	10	3 March	Rent		30
	Balance c/d	**20**				
		30				30
			3 March	Balance b/d		**20**

Albert		Rent	
	Cash 10	Cash 30	

(e) *Dishonour of cheque*

When a solicitor receives notification that a cheque received and paid into the bank has been dishonoured the entries are as follows:

CREDIT the Cash Book
DEBIT the account of the person from whom the money was received.

Illustration

May 1   A cheque for £400 is received from Charles and paid into the bank.
May 10 The bank notifies you that the cheque has been dishonoured.

Cash Book

1 May	Charles	400	10 May	Charles Dishonoured Cheque	**400**

Charles

10 May	Cash Cheque Dishonoured	**400**	1 May	Cash You	400

2. Petty Cash Book (P.C.B.)

Whoever handles the small items of petty cash expenditure, whether the Cashier or some other person, he will keep a separate book—the Petty Cash Book. The system most commonly adopted for the handling of the petty cash is known as the imprest system. At the start of each week the person handling the petty cash is given a float (the imprest amount). Whenever a petty cash payment is made, a petty cash voucher has to be completed and, if necessary, signed by a person in authority. Petty cash is only handed out in exchange for a completed voucher. The virtue of such a system is that at any time the petty cash in hand plus completed vouchers should equal the imprest amount. At the start of each week the float is restored to the imprest amount by reference to the completed petty cash vouchers in the possession of the person handling the petty cash.

Withdrawing the float (the imprest amount) from the bank

CREDIT the Cash Book
DEBIT the Petty Cash Book

Example
£20 is withdrawn out of the bank for petty cash.

Cash		Petty Cash	
	Petty Cash **20**	Cash **20**	

During the week the petty cashier hands out money in exchange for completed petty cash vouchers. These petty cash vouchers constitute the authority for the payments and from them the appropriate double-entries can be made.

CREDIT the Petty Cash Book
DEBIT the appropriate Ledger Account

Example
Pay £5 in respect of Postages out of Petty Cash.

Petty Cash		Postages	
	Postages 5	Petty Cash 5	

3. Clients' Ledger (C.L.)
A solicitor will need at least one ledger account for each client to record his dealings with that client. This will be a personal account. All these accounts will be kept in the Clients' Ledger (for entries see *post* Chapter 12).

4. Private Ledger (P.L.)
This contains any account that a solicitor wishes to keep private. This will probably include

    (a) Capital Account (see p. 22)
    (b) Drawings Account (see *post* p. 37)
    (c) Costs Account (see *post* p. 32)

5. Nominal Ledger (N.L.)

    (a) This ledger contains all the remaining accounts. It is sometimes known as the General Ledger. The accounts most commonly kept in this ledger will be accounts recording expenses and perhaps fixed assets.
    (b) *Expenses*
        Examples of such accounts will be Wages and Salaries, Rent and Rates, Lighting and Heating. Entries will normally be made on these accounts when the particular expense is paid.

Illustration

The solicitor pays wages of £550.

Cash			Wages & Salaries	
	550		550	

These accounts should show a debit balance.

(c) *Fixed Assets*

Examples of such accounts will include Premises, Fixtures and Fittings, Machinery and Equipment. Entries will normally be made on these accounts when the asset is paid for.

Illustration

The solicitor buys and pays £670 for Fixtures and Fittings

Cash			Fixtures & Fittings	
	670		670	

Real accounts will normally show a debit balance. (If a fixed asset is bought but not paid for until later see *post*, p. 34.)

C. OTHER BOOKS

6. Bills and the Bills Delivered Book

(a) When a solicitor sends a bill to a client charging the client with costs a copy of the bill should be kept. From this document an entry can be made in a formal Bills Delivered Book. However, the Solicitors' Accounts Rules 1975 (S.A.R.) Rule 11(3) provides that it is sufficient to maintain a file containing copies of all the bills which have been sent out. This is the most simple method to adopt. Whether a formal book is maintained or simply a file of copy bills sent out, Rule 11 provides that the record must distinguish between profit costs and disbursements.

(b) From the copy of each bill (or the Bills Delivered Book) the bookkeeper can make up the appropriate double-entries in the ledgers, *i.e.*

CREDIT the Costs Account (in the Private Ledger)
DEBIT the account of the appropriate client (in the Clients' Ledger)

(c) The Costs Account is the main income account of a solicitor. It may be helpful to think of this account as the solicitors' equivalent of a Sales Account. Thus the entries are all on the credit side.

(d) *Example*

June 1 Send a bill to Alice for £800 Costs

CREDIT Costs Account
DEBIT the Ledger Account of Alice

Costs			Alice	
	Alice **800**		Costs **800**	

July 1. Receive the amount due from Alice

DEBIT the Cash Book
CREDIT the Ledger Account of Alice

Cash		Alice	
Alice **800**		Costs 800	Cash **800**

7. Journal

(a) This is sometimes used as a preliminary step (called an Original Entry or a Prime Entry) before making the double-entries.
(b) If used at all, it can be used for the following transactions:
  (i) Correction of errors;
  (ii) Bad debts;
  (iii) Depreciation of assets and other closing adjustments (see *post*, Ch. 6);
  (iv) Transfers when preparing final accounts (see *post*, Ch. 5);
  (v) Transfers of clients' money (see *post* Ch. 13);
  (vi) Purchase of fixed asset on credit.
(c) Correction of errors.

Illustration
(i) £50 received from Alice was incorrectly posted to Bill

Cash	Bill
50	**50**

(ii) The error is corrected as follows:
DEBIT the account of Bill (*i.e.* the account on which the incorrect entry was made).
CREDIT the account of Alice (*i.e.* the one on which the entry should have been made).

Bill		Alice	
50	50		**50**

The entry of the debit on the account of Bill is the correct way of eliminating an error. The same result could have been achieved by crossing out the incorrect entry, but the method used above is the proper one to adopt.
(d) *Bad Debts*
The writing-off of bad debts is a common experience of all businesses. Thus every business needs to keep an account to record this—the account usually being called "The Bad Debts Account." It is a nominal account and records the expense to the business of having to write off various debts as bad.
The events will begin with a customer or client owing the business a sum of money, *e.g.* A. B. Client owes the business £50 (*i.e.* he is a debtor).

A.B. Client	
Balance 50	

The customer or client then defaults in payment. Maybe he is made bankrupt (or where he is a company the company is wound-up) or maybe the proprietor of the business decides that it will not be worth the trouble and expense of attempting to enforce the payment. In any event the decision is made to write this off as a bad debt. The entries are:

(i) *The first entry*
CREDIT the account of the customer or client. The result is that this account is now closed. The customer or client is no longer shown as owing the money.

(ii) *The second entry*
DEBIT the Bad Debts Account. This now records the writing-off of the bad debt as a business expense.

(iii) *Illustration*
The debt of £50 due from A. B. Client is written-off.

A.B. Client			Bad Debts	
Balance	50	Bad Debts **50**	A.B. Client **50**	

(See also *post* p. 136).

(e) *Purchase of fixed asset on credit*

Illustration
A solicitor buys some machinery for £1,000 from A. Supplier on credit. The entries are:

DEBIT the real account
CREDIT a ledger account in the name of the supplier. This will probably be kept in the Nominal Ledger (not the Clients' Ledger because the supplier is not a client as such).

Machinery		A. Supplier	
1,000			**1,000**

(f) The layout of the Journal and the way entries in it are made depend entirely upon the accounting system in use in each particular office. Basically however, the Journal is a list of the relevant events (*e.g.* writing-off of bad debts) and indications of which account to debit and which account to credit. It is not necessary to keep this book at all subject to one very important qualification. When a solicitor has to transfer clients' money from the Ledger Account of one client to another client (see *post*, p. 109), it is compulsory under Rule 11 (S.A.R.) to make a preliminary entry (or Prime Entry). If the solicitor maintains a journal then this book is the convenient one to use. If however the solicitor does not maintain a journal then some other record needs to be kept. In such a case the book is often known as a Transfer Book. Again there is no prescribed layout for the book. Basically all it contains is a list of the transfers which are made.

8. Exercises

(1) Prepare a trial balance from the following figures:
Capital £60,000. Salaries £42,000. Postages £1,020. Rates £4,160. Furniture and Fittings £11,000. Premises £33,000. Debtors £3,000. Creditors £2,400. Cash in Bank £180. Cash in Hand £40. Costs £32,000.

(2) Prepare a trial balance from the following figures:
Capital £30,000. Loan from George £15,000. Costs £46,500. Interest Received £300. Fixtures and Fittings £24,000. Machinery and Equipment £17,100. Motor Cars £12,000. Salaries £19,200. Rent and Rates £18,000. Light and Heat £2,600. Interest Paid on Loan £2,400. Bad Debts £580. Debtors £620. Bank Overdraft £4,210. Creditors £490.

Chapter 5

FINAL ACCOUNTS

A. TRANSFERS

1. An important bookkeeping technique used when preparing Final Accounts is a transfer. It is similar to the technique of balancing (see *ante* page 19). However, instead of bringing down the balance (be it debit or credit) the balance is transferred to another account.

2. *Illustration*
   Account A looks as follows:

A	
15	25
30	40

3. *Step 1*
   Add to the lighter side of the account *from* which the transfer is being made the amount to make both sides equal.

A	
15	25
30	40
20	
65	65

4. *Step 2*
   The corresponding entry is made on the account *to* which the transfer is to be made (*i.e.* Account B).

B	
	20

B. PRELIMINARY STEPS

5. Before the Final Accounts are prepared a trial balance is drawn up so as to check the accuracy of the accounts and to facilitate the preparation of the Final Accounts.

6. *Drawings*

   (a) It is customary for the drawings of the proprietor to be recorded on a separate account from the Capital Account so as to reduce the number of entries on the Capital Account.

Example
Proprietor withdraws £50 in cash.

Cash		Drawings	
	50	**50**	

N.B. Drawings should have a DEBIT balance.

(b) At the end of the period the total of the Drawings Account is transferred to the Capital Account.

Example
At the end of the period the solicitor's drawings total £1,500.

Drawings			Capital	
Balance 1,500	Capital **1,500**		Drawings **1,500**	

(c) Various closing adjustments are made on some of the nominal accounts (see Chapter 6).

C. THE PROFIT AND LOSS ACCOUNT

7. The object of this account is to ascertain the net profit of the business. It is important to realise that this is an account and the normal rules of double-entry apply. Thus if the Profit and Loss Account is debited, some other account must be credited.

8. The basic rule is: TRANSFER ALL NOMINAL ACCOUNTS TO THE PROFIT AND LOSS ACCOUNT.

9. Income accounts

(a) These are transferred to the Profit and Loss Account and will appear there on the credit side.

(b) *Illustration*

There is a balance of £6,000 on the Costs Account to be transferred to the Profit and Loss Account. The entries are therefore

DEBIT the Income Account
CREDIT the Profit and Loss Account

Costs			Profit and Loss	
Profit **6,000**	Balance 6,000			Costs **6,000**
& Loss				

10. Expenses

(a) These are transferred to the debit side of the Profit and Loss Account.

(b) The basic steps are:

CREDIT the Expense Account
DEBIT the Profit and Loss Account

(c) *Illustration*
  There is a £4,000 balance on the Wages Account to be transferred to the Profit and Loss Account.

Wages			Profit & Loss	
Balance 4,000	Profit **4,000**		Wages **4,000**	
	& Loss			

11. Drawings are not an expense of the business and they are NOT transferred to the Profit and Loss Account.

12. The resulting balance on the Profit and Loss Account is the net profit (or loss) and this is transferred to the Capital Account.

Illustration

Profit & Loss			Capital	
Wages 4,000	Costs 6,000		Net	
Net			Profit **2,000**	
Profit **2,000**				
6,000	6,000			

13. The heading
  The Profit and Loss Account is always headed "Profit and Loss Account for the . . . . . . " and then follows the period that it covers (*e.g.* " . . . . . . year ending 31st December . . . . . . "). It is important to realise that this account shows the results achieved by a business over a period (be it a week, a month, six months or a year).

14. Thus the Profit and Loss Account of a firm of solicitors for the year ending December 31, 19XX might look as follows:

Messrs. A & B — Solicitors

Profit and Loss Account for the year ended 31st December 19XX

	£		£
Rent and Rates	1,000	Costs	5,500
Salaries	3,000	Miscellaneous	
		Income	500
Net Profit	2,000		
	6,000		6,000

15. Vertical presentation
  This form of presentation is the one commonly used today, especially when companies publish their accounts which have to be read by persons unfamiliar with accounting techniques. Instead of listing the income and expenses side by side, they are listed one above another as follows:

Messrs. A & B — Solicitors
Profit and Loss Account for the year ended 31st December 19XX

Income		£	£
	Costs	5,500	
	Miscellaneous Income	500	
			6,000
Less *Expenses*			
	Salaries	3,000	
	Rent and Rates	1,000	
			4,000
Net Profit			2,000

D. THE BALANCE SHEET

16. This is a statement listing all the remaining balances on the accounts. It is important to realise that the balance sheet is not an account. It is not debited or credited and there are no balancing double-entries. Technically, all the liabilities (being credits) should be listed on the right-hand side of the balance sheet and all the assets (being debits) should be listed on the left-hand side. Unfortunately, as a result of an historical accident, the balance sheet in Great Britain used to be presented the other way round (continental countries presented it the correct way round).

17. The actual presentation of a balance sheet is most important and this includes the order in which the items are listed. There is a choice of two orders:

(a) The order of permanence;
(b) The order of liquidity.

18. The order of permanence is the one most commonly used. The assets are listed starting with the most permanent asset, or the most difficult one to turn into cash, and thus the fixed assets will be listed before the current assets. On the liabilities side capital is listed at the top of the balance sheet, long-term liabilities are listed in the middle, and current liabilities are listed at the end. Thus a balance sheet presented in the order of permanence used to appear as follows:

Balance Sheet as at 31st December 19XX

Capital		*Fixed Assets*		£
	21,000	Premises		10,000
		Furniture & Fittings		6,000
Long Term Liabilities		Machinery		4,000
Loan from X	500	Motor Cars		1,200
				21,000
Current Liabilities		*Current Assets*		
Creditors	250	Debtors	350	
		Cash	200	550
	21,750			21,750

19. The order of liquidity is the reverse of the order of permanence. If this order were adopted cash would be at the top of the list of assets, and land and buildings would be at the bottom. Similarly, on the liabilities side, current liabilities would

be listed at the beginning, long-term liabilities listed in the middle and capital listed at the end.

20. **Vertical presentation**

(a) The balance sheet is still composed of the 5 major blocks: Capital, Long-Term Liabilities, Current Liabilities, Fixed Assets, and Current Assets. However, instead of listing the blocks side by side, one group on the left and one on the right, they are listed one on top of another. Thus taking the illustration shown, the balance sheet would *at this stage* look as follows:

Balance Sheet as at 31st December 19XX

LIABILITIES	£	£
Capital		21,000
Loan from X		500
Creditors		250
		21,750
ASSETS		
Fixed Assets		
Premises	10,000	
Furniture & Fittings	6,000	
Machinery	4,000	
Motor Cars	1,200	21,200
Current Assets		
Debtors	350	
Cash	200	550
		21,750

N.B. THE ASSETS COULD BE LISTED FIRST AND THE LIABILITIES SECOND.

(b) However, another alteration in presentation is also made. Instead of showing the Current Liabilities in the list of liabilities it is shown as a deduction from Current Assets. The balance sheet today therefore looks as follows:

Balance Sheet of A and B Solicitors as at 31st December 19XX

CAPITAL EMPLOYED	£	£
Capital		21,000
Loan from X		500
		21,500
EMPLOYMENT OF CAPITAL		
Fixed Assets		
Premises	10,000	
Furniture & Fittings	6,000	
Machinery	4,000	
Motor Cars	1,200	
		21,200
Current Assets		
Debtors	350	
Cash	200	
	550	
Less *Current Liabilities*		
Creditors	250	
Net Current Assets		300
		21,500

(c) One advantage of this is that the balance sheet shows the difference between Current Assets and Current Liabilities, known as Working Capital or Net Current Assets. This is a most important figure when it comes to analysing the results of the business and determining its relative success or failure.

21. Capital

It is customary not merely to show the final balance on the Capital Account but to show all the detailed movements. Thus if at the beginning of the period the balance on the Capital Account had been £10,500, the net profit earned over the period in question was £12,000 and the drawings for the same period were £1,500 the information in the balance sheet in respect of Capital would appear as follows:

Capital

		£	£
Balance as at 1st January		10,500	
Plus	Net Profit	12,000	
		22,500	
Less	Drawings	1,500	21,000

22. Clients' money

(a) A solicitor is in a special position in that he handles money on behalf of clients (clients' money). The Solicitors Accounts Rules 1975 require him to keep records of dealings with clients' money separate from records of his ordinary business dealings (for details see *post*, Chap. 10). This has an effect on the final accounts of a solicitor's business in the Balance Sheet. As the solicitor will be holding money on behalf of clients in a separate bank account (clients' bank account) there will therefore be at least two separate figures for Cash in Bank on the balance sheet, namely: "Cash in Bank (Office Account)," "Cash in Bank (Client Account)." In the balance sheet there will therefore need to be a balancing item for the Cash in Bank (Client Account) namely "clients' money held on behalf of clients and due to them."

(b) Thus, taking the balance sheet above, if the solicitor held £50,000 on behalf of clients in CLIENT ACCOUNT the balance sheet would look as follows:

Balance Sheet of A & B Solicitors as at 31st December 19XX

CAPITAL EMPLOYED	£	£
Capital		
Balance as at 1st January	10,500	
Plus Net Profit	12,000	
	22,500	
Less Drawings	1,500	21,000
Loan from X		500
		21,500

EMPLOYMENT OF CAPITAL
   Fixed Assets
  Premises   10,000
  Furniture and Fittings 6,000
  Machinery   4,000
  Motor Cars   1,200

                21,200

   Current Assets
  Debtors   350
  Cash   200

          550
Less *Current Liabilities*
  Creditors   250

 Net Current Assets   300
 Client Account
  Cash in bank   50,000
Less Amount owing to clients 50,000   —

                21,500

23. *Exercises*

Use the vertical method of presentation throughout

(1) Prepare a Profit and Loss account from the following figures:

Costs £7,000. Administration Expenses £3,000. Financial Expenses £2,000. Miscellaneous Expenses £500.

(2) Prepare a Profit and Loss account for the six months ending March 31 from the following information:

Costs £32,000. Salaries £15,000. Stationery £500. Postages and Telephones £1,600. Fares £700. Rent £2,000. Electricity £200. Rates £300. Sundry Expenses £130.

(3) Prepare a Profit and Loss account for the six months ending December 31 from the following figures:

Costs £19,000. Commissions Received £200. Salaries £9,000. Postages and Telephones £600. Fares £400. Rates £100. Rent £900. Electricity £800. Interest Paid £80. Interest Received £500. Investment Income £300. Sundry Expenses £320.

(4) Prepare a Balance Sheet from the following figures:

Capital £1,000. Cash £600. Fixed Assets £700. Loan £300.

(5) Prepare a Profit and Loss Account and Balance Sheet from the following information:

Costs £210. Administration Expenses £100. Financial Expenses £40. Miscellaneous Expenses £20. Fixed Assets £700. Capital £1,000. Loan £300. Drawings £200. Debtors £700. Creditors £400. Cash £150.

(6) From the following Trial Balance of a solicitor you are required to draw up a Profit and Loss Account for the year ended December 31 and a Balance Sheet as at that date.

Trial Balance as at 31st December

	£	£
Costs		19,157
Rent & Rates	854	
Light & Heat	422	
Wages	3,164	
Insurances	105	
Premises	50,000	
Fixtures & Fittings	11,000	
Vans	10,166	
Debtors	3,672	
Creditors		1,206
Cash at Bank	3,347	
Drawings	2,400	
Motor Expenses	1,133	
Capital		65,900
	86,263	86,263

(7) From the following information prepare a Profit and Loss Account and Balance Sheet for the year ending December 31: Capital as at January 1 £50,000. Drawings £18,000. Costs £41,000. Salaries and Wages £7,000. Rates £3,800. Lighting and Heating £4,100. Furniture and Fittings £18,000. Commission received £3,000. Stationery £5,000. Postages and Telephones £2,400. Loan from A. Friend £10,000. Interest on loan £1,200. Bad Debts £500. Bank overdraft £1,000. Premises £30,000. Machinery and Equipment £13,000. Debtors £4,000. Creditors £2,000.

(8) Prepare a Profit and Loss Account and Balance Sheet for the year ending December 31 from the following information: Costs £12,000. Investment Income Received £2,500. Salaries £8,000. Postages and Telephones £700. Rates £50. Rent £900. Fares £150. Light and Heat £250. Bank Charges £100. Audit Fees £700. Sundry Expenses £200. Furniture and Fittings £9,400. Capital £25,000. Drawings £2,800. Machinery £12,200. Investments £3,000. Debtors £1,780. Creditors £1,200. Cash in Bank (Office Account) £470. Cash in Bank (Client Account) £8,100. Amount Owing to Clients (Client Account) £8,100.

Chapter 6

CLOSING ADJUSTMENTS

A. THE ACCRUAL CONCEPT

1. The calculation of the net profit of a business is based on the difference between revenue and expenses. The revenue of a business is not the same as the amount of income actually received in the period. Similarly the amount of expenses is not necessarily the same as the amount of cash actually paid out on expenses in the same period. Account has to be taken of liabilities which have accrued due and which have not yet been paid and also of income which has accrued due but not yet received. This is known as the Accrual Concept. The bookkeeping entries up to the Trial Balance are based on income received and expenses paid. Several adjustments therefore have to be made to the accounts before the Profit and Loss Account can be drawn up.

B. DEPRECIATION

2. Fixed assets are shown in the accounts at book value, which is usually cost price. However, this is most unlikely to be the current market value of the asset, particularly after some time has elapsed since it was purchased. Most of the fixed assets will have gone down in value since purchase as a result of wear and tear and/or age. Obsolescence can also cause depreciation. Assets can also become inadequate because of size; the business has grown to such an extent that the machinery in question is too small to be able to cope economically with the size of turnover involved.

3. Depreciation can only be recorded accurately in retrospect after the fixed asset has been disposed of. Nevertheless, the entries in respect of depreciation are made annually in advance of the asset being disposed of and therefore it must be understood that these entries are merely estimates. There are several methods of spreading the effective cost of a fixed asset over its life. Although these are beyond the scope of this book an illustration may help to understand the principles involved. The simplest one is known as the straight-line method of depreciation. Immediately the asset is purchased an estimate is made of its effective life and of what its value would be at the end of that life. The formula is then:

$$\frac{\text{Cost Price} - \text{Residual Value}}{\text{Effective Life}}$$

Illustration 1
A machine is bought for £5,000 and it is estimated that it will last six years. It is also estimated that at the end of those six years the machine will be worth £1,400.

$$\frac{£5,000 - £1,400}{6} = £600$$

45

The result therefore is that if the entries for depreciation are made each year, assuming the estimate to be correct, the accounts will approximately show what the asset is worth from time to time. It must be emphasised however, that this is a rough and ready method of calculating depreciation and that the true value of the asset may be substantially different.

4. In order to record the depreciation of fixed assets a new account is opened called Depreciation Account. The entries are:

DEBIT the Profit and Loss Account
CREDIT the Depreciation Account

Profit and Loss		Depreciation	
600			**600**

5. The balance on the Depreciation Account will always be a credit balance and this will therefore have to be reflected in the Balance Sheet. Technically the Depreciation Account showing a credit balance should be listed on the left-hand side of the Balance Sheet. However a more helpful method of presentation is adopted by showing it as a deduction on the right-hand side from the cost price of the relevant fixed assets.

Illustration 1 (cont . . .)

Balance Sheet

Fixed Assets	£	
Machinery	5,000	
less Depreciation	600	
		4,400

6. The consequence of this is that the Balance Sheet shows approximately the current value of the fixed assets. Note that in the following year the Profit and Loss Account will show the depreciation for that year only (*i.e.* £600) whereas the Balance Sheet will show the total depreciation for the two years (*i.e.* £1,200).

Illustration 2
The machine is depreciated in the second year by a further £600.

Profit and Loss (Year 2)		Depreciation	
Depreciation **600**		Balance	600
		Profit &	
		Loss	**600**

Balance Sheet

Fixed Assets		
Machinery	5,000	
Less Depreciation	1,200	
		3,800

7. Where several different types of fixed asset are depreciated there will be a separate Depreciation Account for each type of fixed asset.

Illustration

There is a balance of £5,000 on the Fixtures Account and £4,000 on the Motor Cars Account. The fixtures are to be depreciated by 10 per cent. and the motor cars by 25 per cent.

Fixtures		Motor Cars	
Balance 5,000		Balance 4,000	

Depreciation (Fixtures)		Depreciation (Motor Cars)	
	Profit & Loss **500**		Profit & Loss **1,000**

Profit & Loss	
Depreciation (Fixtures 500) (Motor Cars 1,000) **1,500**	

8. Some fixed assets, *e.g.* freehold land, may appreciate in value. It is however the practice not to record increases in the values of fixed assets until the fixed assets are actually sold. This is as a result of the concept of Prudence (see *ante*, page 12).

9. When an asset is sold a new account is opened called the Assets Disposal Account. The entries are as follows:

(a) Transfer the cost of the asset to the Assets Disposal Account.

CREDIT the Fixed Asset Account
DEBIT the Assets Disposal Account

Illustration

A machine originally bought for £5,000 is sold for £4,000.

Machinery		Assets Disposal	
Balance 5,000	Assets Disposal **5,000**	Machinery **5,000**	

(b) Record the receipt of the cash, *i.e.*

DEBIT Cash Book
CREDIT the Assets Disposal Account

Cash		Assets Disposal	
Assets Disposal **4,000**		Machinery 5,000	Cash **4,000**

(c) The next step is to transfer the amount of depreciation, if any, which has been entered into the accounts in respect of the fixed asset from the Depreciation Account to the Assets Disposal Account, *i.e.*

DEBIT the Depreciation Account
CREDIT the Assets Disposal Account

Illustration (cont . . .)

The machine had previously been depreciated by £1,200 (*i.e.* there is a credit balance of £1,200 on the Depreciation Account).

Depreciation		Assets Disposal	
Assets Disposal **1,200**	Balance 1,200	Machinery 5,000	Cash 4,000
			Depreciation **1,200**

(d) The balance of the Assets Disposal Account will now show the discrepancy, if any, between the estimated depreciation and the depreciation which has actually been incurred. This balance should be transferred to the Profit and Loss Account for the relevant period.

Illustration (cont . . .)
In this transaction there has been a surplus of depreciation of £200 so that according to the accounts the business has made a profit of £200 on the disposal of the machinery. The entries would therefore appear as follows:

Profit and Loss		Assets Disposal			
Profit on		Machinery	5,000	Cash	4,000
disposal		Profit	**200**	Depreciation	1,200
of machine	**200**				
			5,200		5,200

C. BILLS DUE AND UNPAID

10. As has been said before, the amount of expenses to be shown in the Profit and Loss Account is not necessarily the same as the amount of expenditure actually incurred in the period. One has to take into account not only expenses paid but also expenses which have been incurred and which remain unpaid at the end of the period.

11. *Illustration*

In a calendar year the total amount paid in respect of telephones is £330. However, the last telephone bill was paid in respect of the period up until the end of November and it is estimated that the expenditure on telephones actually incurred in December is £30. Thus, assuming that the estimate is correct, the total expenditure on telephones for the year will come to £360. This needs to be recorded in the accounts.

12. **The double-entries**
There are four steps.

(a) DEBIT the account concerned with the amount of the closing adjustment.
(b) Insert the total on both sides of the account.
(c) CREDIT the account below the totals with the amount of the closing adjustment.
(d) Transfer the difference between the two sides above the totals to the Profit and Loss Account.

13. *Illustration*

(a) *Step 1*

Telephones		
Balance	330	
Outstanding account	**30**	

(b) *Step 2*

Telephones			
Balance	330		
Outstanding account	30		
	360		**360**

(c) *Step 3*

Telephones			
Balance	330		
Outstanding account	30		
	360		360
		Outstanding account	**30**

N.B. This is the corresponding entry for Step 1.

(d) *Step 4*

Telephones			
Balance	330	Profit & Loss	**360**
Outstanding account	30		
	360		360
		Outstanding account	30

Profit and Loss	
Telephones **360**	

14. The result is as follows:

    (a) The Profit and Loss Account will show the true expense for the full year rather than the amount actually paid.

    (b) The relevant account will end the period with a credit balance brought down. When the Balance Sheet is drawn up this credit balance will need to be listed on it. Thus one of the current liabilities in the Balance Sheet will be bills due but unpaid (see *post*, page 56).

D. PAYMENTS IN ADVANCE

15. This is the reverse of bills due and unpaid. Some expenses may be paid in advance. Thus the rates may be paid in October and cover the period from October 1, to March 31. If the accounts are made up for the period ending December 31, then the proportion (*i.e.* one-half) is attributable to the current period.

16. *Illustration*

    In a year the total amount actually paid in respect of rates is £1,000. However, as at December 31, it is discovered that £250 had been paid in advance.

Thus, the true annual rates bill is only £750. This needs to be recorded in the accounts.

17. **The double-entries**

There are four steps:

(a) CREDIT the account concerned with the amount of the closing adjustment.
(b) Insert the total on both sides of the account.
(c) DEBIT the account below the totals with the amount of the closing adjustment.
(d) Transfer the difference between the two sides above the totals to the Profit and Loss Account.

18. *Illustration*

(a) *Step 1*

Rates			
Balance	1,000	Paid in advance	**250**

(b) *Step 2*

Rates			
Balance	1,000	Paid in advance	250
	1,000		**1,000**

N.B. Note that the totals will be £1,000 (*i.e.* the amount of the heavier side) and that a space has been left for a further entry on the credit side above the totals (see Step 4).

(c) *Step 3*

Rates			
Balance	1,000	Paid in advance	250
	1,000		1,000
Paid in Advance	**250**		

N.B. This is the corresponding entry for Step 1.

(d) *Step 4*

Rates				Profit & Loss	
Balance	1,000	Paid in advance	250	Rates **750**	
		Profit & Loss	**750**		
	1,000		1,000		
Paid in Advance	250				

19. The result is as follows:

(i) The Profit and Loss Account will show the true expense for the full year rather than the amount actually paid.

(ii) The relevant account will end the period with a debit balance brought down. When the Balance Sheet is drawn up this debit balance will need to be listed on it. Thus one of the current assets in the Balance Sheet will be accounts paid in advance (see *post*, page 56).

E. WORK IN HAND

20. At the end of the year the Costs Account will show the total of the bills sent out to clients. It will not show the work done by the firm for which no bill has yet been sent. If the accounts are to be accurate they should record the total of all work done during the year whether or not a bill has been delivered to the client. Work in hand therefore needs to be recorded in the accounts.

21. *Illustration*

The bills sent out during the year total £36,000. In addition the firm has done work for which no bill has as yet been sent out totalling £4,000. The result is that the total amount of work done by the firm during the year is £40,000.

22. **The double-entries**

There are four steps.

(a) CREDIT the Costs Account with the adjustment.
(b) Insert the total on both sides.
(c) DEBIT the Costs Account below the totals with the adjustment.
(d) Transfer the difference between the two sides above the totals to the Profit and Loss Account.

23. *Illustration*

(a) *Step 1*

Costs		
	Balance	36,000
	Work in hand	**4,000**

(b) *Step 2*

Costs		
	Balance	36,000
	Work in hand	4,000
40,000		**40,000**

(c) *Step 3*

	Costs		
	Balance	36,000	
	Work in hand	4,000	
40,000		40,000	
Work in hand	**4,000**		

N.B. This is the corresponding entry for Step 1.

(d) *Step 4*

	Costs				Profit & Loss		
Profit & Loss **40,000**	Balance	36,000				Costs	**40,000**
	Work in Hand	4,000					
40,000		40,000					
Work in hand	4,000						

24. The result is as follows:

(a) The Profit and Loss Account will show the work actually done during the year rather than the amount of bills sent out.

(b) The Costs Account will end the period with a debit balance brought down. When the Balance Sheet is drawn up this debit balance will need to be listed on it. Thus the first current asset in the Balance Sheet of a solicitor's business will be Work in Hand (see *post*, page 56).

F. STOCKS

25. Accounts such as the Stationery Account will at the end of the period show the amount of cash actually paid for stationery rather than the amount of stationery used. Probably there will be some stationery left over in *e.g.* the stationery cupboard. This needs to be recorded in the accounts.

26. A firm has paid £8,000 for stationery over the year but at the end of the year £200 worth of stationery is left over in the stock cupboard. Thus the firm has used stationery to the value of £7,800.

27. **The double-entries**
There are four steps as follows:

(a) CREDIT the account with the adjustment.
(b) Insert the totals.
(c) DEBIT the account with the adjustment below the totals.
(d) Transfer the difference between the two sides above the totals to the Profit and Loss Account.

28. *Illustration*

   (a) *Step 1*

Stationery	
Balance 8,000	Stock **200**

   (b) *Step 2*

Stationery	
Balance 8,000	Stock 200
8,000	**8,000**

N.B. Note that the totals will be £8,000 (*i.e.* the amount of the heavier side) and that a space has been left for a further entry on the credit side above the totals (see Step 4).

   (c) *Step 3*

Stationery	
Balance 8,000	Stock 200
8,000	8,000
Stock **200**	

N.B. This is the corresponding entry for Step 1.

   (d) *Step 4*

Stationery		Profit & Loss	
Balance 8,000	Stock 200	Stationery **7,800**	
	Profit		
	& Loss **7,800**		
8,000	8,000		
Stock 200			

29. The result is as follows:

   (a) The Profit and Loss Account shows the stationery used during the year.
   (b) The Stationery Account will end the period with a debit balance brought down. When the Balance Sheet is drawn up this balance will need to be listed on it. Thus, the second current asset in the Balance Sheet will be Stocks (see *post*, page 56).

G. BAD DEBTS

30. The balance on the Bad Debts Account at the end of a period shows the amount of bad debts written off. At the end of the period, however, it is probable that some of the outstanding debtors will eventually prove to be bad. Some provision needs to be made for them.

31. *Illustration*

In the year the amount of bad debts written off amounted to £70. At the end of the year £180 was still owing from debtors. It is estimated that of these debtors £20 worth will turn out to be bad. If this is correct it means that the number of bad debts incurred with the firm during the year will have amounted to £90.

32. **The double-entries**

There are four steps as follows:

(a) DEBIT the Bad Debts Account with the provision.
(b) Insert the totals.
(c) CREDIT the Bad Debts Account below the totals with the provision.
(d) Transfer the difference between the two sides above the totals to the Profit and Loss Account.

33. *Illustration*

(a) *Step 1*

Bad Debts

Balance	70	
Provision	**20**	

(b) *Step 2*

Bad Debts

Balance	70		
Provision	20		
	90		**90**

(c) *Step 3*

Bad Debts

Balance	70		
Provision	20		
	90		90
		Provision	**20**

N.B. This is the corresponding entry for Step 1.

(d) *Step 4*

Bad Debts			
Balance	70	Profit & Loss	**90**
Provision	20		
	90		90
		Provision	20

Profit & Loss		
Bad Debts	**90**	

34. The result is as follows:

(a) The Profit and Loss Account will show the bad debts incurred during the year rather than the bad debts written off.[1]

(b) The Bad Debts Account will end the period with a credit balance brought down and when the Balance Sheet is drawn up this balance will need to be listed on it. Technically, it should be listed (as a credit) with the Current Liabilities but for convenience it is listed among the Current Assets as a *deduction* from Debtors. The reason for this is that the final figure for Debtors will show not just the amount owing from the debtors but the amount which the business expects to collect from them.

35. *Recovery of debt previously written off as bad.* It may happen that a debt which has previously been written off is unexpectedly recovered from the debtor. If this happens the simplest procedure is:

DEBIT the Cash Book
CREDIT the Bad Debts Account

Illustration
There is a balance of £100 on the Bad Debts Account representing the following bad debts written off:– R £10, S £20, T £30, U £40.
Today the £10 is unexpectedly received from R.

Cash		
Bad Debts (R)	**10**	

Bad Debts			
Balance	100	Cash (R)	**10**

36. *Illustration*
The trial balance of Vicky, a solicitor, is as follows:

Trial Balance

	DR £	CR £
Capital		2,000
Income (Costs)		4,500
General Expenses	3,100	
Rates	450	
Telephone	160	
Stationery	100	
Bad Debts	70	
Debtors	180	
Creditors		150
Cash	90	
Fixed Assets	2,500	
	£6,650	£6,650

[1] No entry is made, at this stage, on any particular debtor's account. Such an entry is only made if and when a decision is made to write off the debt due from that debtor (see *ante*, p. 34).

The Profit and Loss Account and Balance Sheet without making any closing adjustments would therefore look as follows:

Profit and Loss Account

	£		£
General Expenses	3,100	Income	4,500
Rates	450		
Telephone	160		
Stationery	100		
Bad Debts	70		
N.P.	620		
	4,500		4,500

Balance Sheet

EMPLOYMENT OF CAPITAL		£	£
Fixed Assets			2,500
Current Assets			
Debtors		180	
Cash		90	
		270	
Current Liabilities			
Creditors		150	
Net Current Assets			120
			2,620

CAPITAL EMPLOYED		
Capital	2,000	
Net Profit	620	
	—	2,620

The following closing adjustments need to be made: Telephone bill due and unpaid £40. Rates paid in advance £10. Stationery stock in hand at the end of the period £30. Provision for estimated bad debts £20. Work in hand £500. Depreciation on fixed assets £100.

With these closing adjustments the Final Accounts would look as follows:

Profit and Loss Account

	£		£
General Expenses	3,100	Costs	5,000
Rates	440		
Telephone	200		
Stationery	70		
Bad Debts	90		
Depreciation	100		
N.P.	1,000		
	5,000		5,000

Balance Sheet

EMPLOYMENT OF CAPITAL	£	£	£
Fixed Assets			
Balance		2,500	
less Depreciation		100	2,400
Current Assets			
Work in hand		500	
Stationery stock		30	
Debtors	180		
less Provision	20	160	
Prepayments		10	
Cash		90	
		790	
Current Liabilities			
Creditors	150		
Accounts Outstanding	40	190	
Net Current Assets			600
			3,000
CAPITAL EMPLOYED			
Capital		2,000	
Net Profit		1,000	3,000

37. *Exercises*

Note: When calculating depreciation
    (a) in the year in which an asset is purchased provide a full year's depreciation, irrespective of date of purchase.
    (b) in the year in which an asset is sold provide no depreciation.

(1) On June 30, there is a balance of £7,000 on the Furniture Account and £2,100 on the Library Account. It is decided to depreciate the Furniture by 18 per cent. and the Library by 5 per cent. Show the entries to record this.

(2) The balances on the Motor Cars and the Depreciation (Motor Cars) Accounts at January 1, were £8,000 and £800 respectively. Another car was bought on March 1 for £9,000. At December 31, it was decided to provide for depreciation on the Motor Cars at 10 per cent. p.a. Show the entries to record this.

(3) As at January 1, Alice owned two machines originally purchased for £12,000 and £4,000 respectively. Depreciation is calculated at 10 per cent. p.a. of the original cost price and the first machine (held for two years) has been depreciated by £2,400 and the second by £400. On April 30, the first machine was sold for £10,000 and a new machine bought for £15,000. Show the double-entries to record the above, including depreciation up to December 31.

(4) As at December 31, there was a balance of £1,400 on the Electricity Account. It is estimated that electricity consumed but not yet charged for as at that date amounts to £150. Show the Electricity Account.

(5) A firm has a combined Rent and Rates Account. As at December 31, there is a balance on the account of £1,000. The rent of £3,000 p.a. however, is paid in arrears on March 1, each year. On October 30, the rates for the period from October 1, to March 31, amounting to £200 were paid. Show the entries in the Rent and Rates Account as at December 31, including any necessary closing adjustments.

(6) The balance on the Stationery Account as at the end of the year was £520 and there was a stock of £33 in the stationery cupboard. Show the entries in the Stationery Account to record this.

(7) The balance on the Costs Account as at March 31, was £15,000. Work in Hand is estimated at £200. Show the entries in the Costs Account to record this.

(8) Show the entries in the Costs Account to record the following information: Bills sent out during the year £21,000. Work in Hand at the start of the year £1,300. Work in Hand at the end of the year £1,900.

(9) Write up the Bad Debts Account from the following information: Write off Carol as a Bad Debt £40. Write off Dick £70. As at the end of the year it is estimated that there will be further Bad Debts amounting to £20.

(10) Write up the Bad Debts Account from the following information: Write Offs £800. Received from Edward, a debtor previously written off, £31. Provision for estimated Bad Debts at the end of the year £60.

(11) From the following information prepare a Profit and Loss Account and Balance Sheet for the year ending December 31: Costs £24,000. Rent and Rates £2,562. Light and Heat £1,701. Wages £9,492. Insurances £473. Bad Debts £440. Capital as at January 1, £44,695. Drawings £7,200. Creditors £13,618. Premises £32,000. Fixtures and Fittings £20,000. Depreciation on Fixtures and Fittings £4,000. Debtors £11,016. Cash in Bank £1,429.

The following closing adjustments need to be made: Work in hand £3,471. Rent paid in advance £150. Account outstanding in respect of Light and Heat £435. Estimated provision for Bad Debts £50. The fixtures and fittings are to be depreciated by a further 20 per cent. of cost.

(12) From the following information prepare a Profit and Loss Account and Balance Sheet for the year ending December 31: Costs £60,000. Wages £42,750. Rates £600. General Expenses £19,940. Insurances £485. Stationery £2,300. Interest Received £17,500. Postages £525. Premises £30,600. Furniture £15,000. Depreciation on Furniture £5,000. Machinery and Equipment £32,000. Depreciation on Machinery £20,500. Disposal of Machinery £3,300. Capital as at January 1, £60,000. Drawings £8,000. Debtors £20,780. Cash in Bank (Office Account) £1,610. Creditors £24,290. Suspense £10,000. Bad Debts £6,000.

The following closing adjustments need to be made: Work in hand £17,500. Stationery Stock as at December 31, £200. Provision for estimated Bad Debts £1,040. General Expenses accrued due but unpaid £1,620.

You are given the following information in respect of machinery and equipment. On March 31, equipment was sold for £3,300. This equipment was originally bought for £7,000 some three years ago and had been depreciated by £4,200 as at January 1. New equipment was purchased on March 31, for £10,000 and although an entry was properly made in the Cash Book the double-entry was made on a suspense account. As at the end of the year depreciation on the machinery and equipment is to be calculated at 20 per cent. No further depreciation is to be done in respect of the equipment sold on March 31, but the new equipment is to be depreciated for the full year.

The furniture is to be depreciated by a further £3,000.

Chapter 7

PARTNERSHIP ACCOUNTS

1. The first thing to grasp is that the principles are the same as for the accounts of a sole practitioner. The accounts used are the same and the variations are only of a small nature.

2. **Capital**

As there is now more than one proprietor of the business, separate Capital Accounts are needed for each proprietor.

Example

John and Kate are in partnership and introduce £5,000 and £4,000 respectively in cash into the business.

Cash	
Capital John 5,000	
Capital Kate 4,000	

Capital John		Capital Kate	
	Cash 5,000		Cash 4,000

3. **Current Accounts**

(a) The drawings of a sole practitioner are transferred at the end of the year from Drawings Accounts to Capital Account. In the accounts of a partnership, drawings are not transferred to Capital but are instead transferred to a Current Account. There will be a separate Current Account for each partner.

Example

At the end of the first year of business John's drawings amount to £6,000 and Kate's drawings amount to £5,000.

Drawings John	
Balance 6,000	To Current A/C **6,000**

Drawings Kate	
Balance 5,000	To Current A/C **5,000**

(b) A similar procedure is adopted with the earnings of the partners *e.g.* net profit. Instead of being credited to the Capital Account of each partner net profit is credited to the Current Account of each partner (see below).

(c) The result is that the Capital Account shows the amount of money which each individual proprietor has invested permanently in the business. The Current Account shows the amount which a partner is at any time entitled to withdraw from the business.

4. The daily entries in the accounts, *e.g.* payment of expenses, receipt of income, are all the same up to and including the preparation of the Profit and Loss Account. However, after the expenses and income have all been recorded in the normal way in the Profit and Loss Account, there is an extension to the Profit and Loss Account known as the Appropriation Account. This is not a separate account but is in fact a continuation of the Profit and Loss Account.

(a) After the expenses and income have all been entered in the Profit and Loss Account the net profit (or loss) can be ascertained.

DEBIT the Profit and Loss with the net profit
CREDIT the Appropriation Account

N.B. The entries are reversed if there is a net loss.

Illustration

	Profit & Loss		
Expenses	2,000	Income	3,000
N.P.	**1,000**		
	3,000		3,000
		N.P.	**1,000**

(b) *Partners' salaries.* It may be agreed that the partners are to be paid salaries before any resulting profit or loss is shared between them. If this is so the entries are:

DEBIT the Profit and Loss Account
CREDIT the Current Account of each individual partner.

Illustration

Profit & Loss (Appropriation)			Current Account Paul	
Partners Salaries		N.P. 1,000	Salary	**40**
Paul	**40**			
James 50	90			

(c) *Interest on Capital Account.* It may also be agreed that the partners are to be entitled to interest on the amount standing to the credit of their Capital Account. If this is so the relevant entries are:

DEBIT the Profit and Loss Account
CREDIT the Current Account of each individual partner

Illustration

Profit & Loss (Appropriation)			Current Account Paul	
Partners Salaries		N.P. 1,000	Salary	40
Paul	40		Interest	**60**
James 50	90			
Interest on Capital				
Paul	**60**			
James 70	130			

(d) The resulting balance (profit or loss) can then be transferred to the Current Accounts of each individual partner in the agreed profit-sharing ratio.

Illustration

Profit & Loss (Appropriation)			Current Account Paul		
Partners Salaries			N.P. 1,000	Salary	40
Paul	40			Interest	60
James	50	90		N.P.	**390**
Interest on Capital					
Paul	60				
James	70	130			
Share of Profit					
Paul	**390**				
James	390	780			
		1,000	1,000		

5. Sometimes during a year there is a change in the way in which profits are shared. This may occur because a partner retires, a new partner is admitted, or the existing partners decide to vary their existing profit-sharing agreement. In such circumstances a Profit and Loss Account is drawn up for the full year but there will be two Appropriation Accounts: one for the period before the change, and the other for the period after the change, the full year's net profit being divided proportionately between the two Appropriation Accounts.

Illustration

Vicky and Sarah share profits equally. On March 31 they decide to alter their profit-sharing ratio to Vicky 2: Sarah 1. Their accounts for the year ending December 31 show Income £200,000. Expenses £160,000.

Profit and Loss for the year ending 31st December 19XX

	£
INCOME	200,000
less EXPENSES	160,000
NET PROFIT	40,000

Appropriation Account for the 3 months ending 31/3/XX

	£	£
Vicky ($\frac{1}{2}$)	5,000	
Sarah ($\frac{1}{2}$)	5,000	10,000

Appropriation Account for the 9 months ending 31/12/XX

	£	£
Vicky ($\frac{2}{3}$)	20,000	
Sarah ($\frac{1}{3}$)	10,000	30,000
		40,000

6. *Exercises*

(1) Prepare a Profit and Loss Account (including an Appropriation Account) from the following figures:

Income £100,000. Expenses £88,000. The net profit is to be divided between the three partners as follows: A : 2, B : 1, C : 1.

(2) Prepare a Profit and Loss Account (including an Appropriation Account) from the following figures:

Income £75,000. Expenses £63,000. There are two partners, A and B. A has a capital account balance of £6,000 and B has a capital account balance of £4,000 and each partner is to be entitled to interest on capital of 12 per cent. In addition A is to be entitled to a salary of £2,000 and B to a salary of £2,500. Any resulting profit is to be shared in the proportion A : 2, B : 1.

(3) Prepare a Profit and Loss Account (including an Appropriation Account) from the following figures:

Income £9,000. Expenses £11,000. There are two partners, A and B. A is to be entitled to interest on capital of £150 and B is to be entitled to £50. A is to receive a salary of £800. Any resulting profit is to be shared between the two partners equally.

(4) A, B and C were in partnership and shared profits in the ratio 2 : 1 : 1. Last year the firm made a net profit of £10,000. Exactly half-way through the year A retired and D was admitted as a new partner, the new profit-sharing ratio being B : 2; C : 2; D : 1. As from A's retirement, the firm agreed to pay the new partners 10 per cent. per annum on the balance outstanding on their capital accounts, which were B : £8,000; C : £6,000; D : £6,000. Prepare the Profit and Loss Account.

(5) A, B and C are in partnership sharing profits 2: 1 : 1. A and B receive interest on capital at 10 per cent. per annum. C receives a salary of £400. Prepare a Profit and Loss Account and Balance Sheet from the following figures:

Capital: A : £3,000; B : £2,000; C : £2,000. *Current Accounts*: (Credit) A : £100; B : £200; C : £300. *Expenses*: Salaries £200, General Expenses £560, Rent and Rates £300, Financial Expenses £40. *Drawings*: A : £1,900; B : £1,200; C : £1,600. *Costs*: £5,000. *Work in Hand*: £1,000. *Debtors*: £600. *Creditors*: £200. *Cash*: £400. *Fixed Assets*: £6,000.

(6) Prepare a Profit and Loss Account and Balance Sheet for the year ending December 31, from the following information:

At the beginning of the year A and B were in partnership sharing profits equally. In addition each was entitled to a salary, A : £2,000; B : £3,000. At the end of March C was admitted as a partner and as from that date the profit-sharing arrangements were that each partner was entitled to receive interest at 8 per cent. per annum on the balance of his capital account. As at that date the balances on the capital accounts were A : £40,000; B : £40,000; C : £4,000. In addition any resulting net profit was to be shared in the ratio A : 2; B : 2; C : 1. As at the end of the calendar year the balances on the remaining accounts were as follows:
Fixed Assets £70,000. Costs £185,000. Expenses £170,000. Debtors £17,000. Creditors £9,000. Loan from D (repayable in 7 years) £5,000. Cash £1,000. Drawings: A : £12,000; B : £10,000; C : £3,000. Work in Hand is estimated at £15,000.

(7) The balances on the ledger accounts of Grace Leslie & Co., Solicitors, on 30/5/80 were:

	£	
Wages and Salaries	12,560	
Costs	22,960	
Rent and rates	2,870	
Office expenses	3,680	
Insurance and other commissions received	470	
Library	2,750	
Furniture and Fittings	5,600	
Bank balances: Office Account	850	
Client Account	11,240	
Outstanding costs owing from clients	830	
Petty cash balance	50	
Agency expenses paid	730	
Clients ledger balances	11,240	
Capital Accounts: Grace	5,000	
Leslie	2,500	
Current Accounts: Grace	190	Debit
Leslie	820	Debit

The partners share profits equally.

Work in progress is estimated at £7,500. Depreciation of 20 per cent. p.a. is charged on furniture and fittings and £1,000 per year is written off the Library. Rent of the firm's premises is payable in advance and the rent of £350 for the quarter commencing June 1, has been paid.

Prepare the firm's Profit and Loss Account and Balance Sheet for the 6 months ending 30/5/80.

(8) Alpha and Beta practise in partnership as solicitors, sharing profits 3 : 1. From the following information prepare their final accounts for the 6 months ending December 31, 1979.

	£
Costs	24,000.00
Investment Income Received	200.00
Deposit Interest Received	4,000.00
Insurance Commission Received	500.00
Salaries	10,000.00
Rent and Rates	5,500.00
Light and Heat	1,200.00
General Expenses	4,600.00
Deposit Interest Paid	200.00
Capital Accounts: Alpha	3,000.00
Beta	1,000.00
Drawings Accounts: Alpha	4,000.00
Beta	1,800.00
Fixtures and Fittings	5,200.00
Depreciation on Fixtures and Fittings	2,400.00
Investments	1,600.00
Debtors	1,500.00
Cash at Bank — Clients' Account	70,000.00
Cash at Bank — Office Account	500.00
Creditors	1,000.00
Amount due to clients	70,000.00

Depreciation of £800 is to be charged on the Fixtures and Fittings.

[Time limit: 1 hour]

(9) Wendy and Tom are in partnership sharing profits in the ratio 2 : 1. As at December 31, the balances on the accounts are as follows: Capital Accounts—Wendy £40,000, Tom £20,000. General Expenses £376,200. Drawings—Wendy £21,500, Tom £13,300. Freeholds £30,000. Fixtures £18,000. Depreciation on Fixtures £3,400. Library £14,000. Depreciation on Library £3,200. Motor Cars £16,500. Depreciation on Motor Cars £3,500. Debtors £122,000. Creditors £200,000. Disposal of Car £3,800. Costs £340,000. Cash in bank £2,400.

Work in hand is estimated at £80,000. On May 1, a motor car was disposed of for £3,800. This car had been depreciated by £3,500 since its purchase for £7,500. On the same date as this old motor car was sold a new car was purchased for £9,000 and this new one is to be depreciated by 20 per cent. Fixtures are to be depreciated by £3,600 and Library by 20 per cent. of cost.

From the above figures prepare a set of Final Accounts for the year ending December 31.

[Time limit: 1 hour]

7. Revaluation

(a) From time to time the partners may wish to revalue the assets of the business. In general this is most likely to occur:
   (i) if they change the ratio in which they share profits
   (ii) when a new partner is admitted to the firm
   (iii) when one of the existing partners leaves the firm.
(b) The reason for this is that, unless there is some agreement to the contrary, if the business is sold and the sale price of the assets exceeds their book values, then any resulting profit or loss is shared between the partners in their profit sharing ratios as at the date of sale.

Illustration

Paul and James are in partnership sharing profits equally. The book value of their fixed assets is £6,000 (*i.e.* they originally paid £6,000 for them) although their current market value is now £27,000. They decide to admit Alexander as a partner. Under the new agreement any one partner can serve a notice on the other partners determining the partnership immediately (this is known as a partnership at will); all profits are to be shared by the partners equally. A day later, Alexander gives due notice terminating the partnership agreement. As a result, all the partnership assets have to be sold and they therefore realise £27,000. The partnership has made a profit on the disposal of the fixed assets of £21,000, in which profit Alexander is entitled to share, and thus he would receive £7,000 of the profit made on the sale of those assets in circumstances when the increase in value really ought to belong to Paul and James.

(c) In order to cope with such a situation the assets of the business can be revalued at the date the change in the partnership takes place, so that the assets are stated in the accounts at their current value. The resulting increase in value is shared between the existing partners (*i.e.* Paul and James) in their old profit sharing ratio.
(d) In order to record this a new account is opened called a Revaluation Account.
(e) Asset increasing in value.
   (i) The double-entry is:

DEBIT the Asset Account with the increase in value
CREDIT the Revaluation Account

(ii) *Illustration*

Premises appearing in the accounts at a book value of £6,000 are revalued at £27,000, *i.e.* an increase of £21,000.

Premises		Revaluation	
Balance 6,000			Premises **21,000**
Revaluation **21,000**			

(iii) The result is that the new balance on the Premises Account is the current market value of £27,000.

(f) Asset decreasing in value.

  (i) The double-entry is

CREDIT the Asset with the decrease in value
DEBIT the Revaluation Account

(ii) *Illustration*

Machinery which appears in the accounts at a book value of £3,000 is revalued at £2,000, *i.e.* a decrease of £1,000.

Machinery		Revaluation	
Balance 3,000	Revaluation **1,000**	Machinery **1,000**	Premises 21,000

(iii) The result is that the new balance on the Machinery Account is its current market value, *i.e.* £2,000.

(g) The resulting profit or loss on the revaluation has to be shared between the old partners.

  (i) The first stage is to balance the Revaluation Account.

Illustration

Revaluation			
Machinery	1,000	Premises	21,000
Balance	**20,000**		
	21,000		21,000
		Balance	**20,000**

(ii) Unless otherwise agreed, this resulting profit or loss is transferred to the Capital Accounts of the old partners in their old profit sharing ratio, *i.e.*

DEBIT the Revaluation Account
CREDIT the Capital Accounts of the old partners

The surplus of £20,000 is to be transferred to the Capital Accounts of Paul and James equally.

Revaluation

Machinery	1,000	Premises	21,000
Balance	20,000		
	21,000		21,000
Paul	**10,000**	Balance	20,000
James	**10,000**		
	20,000		

Capital Paul			Capital James	
Balance	5,000		Balance	5,000
Revaluation	**10,000**		Revaluation	**10,000**

8. **Goodwill**

(a) If the partners have been in business for some time then it is possible, if they were to sell the business, that they could get a higher price for it by selling all the assets of the business together as a going concern rather than selling each asset separately for its current market value. Thus although Paul and James could sell each individual asset and realise a total of £30,000, if they were to sell the whole business as a going concern they may be able to realise £80,000. This extra £50,000 over and above the market value of the fixed assets is known as goodwill.

(b) It is not normally the practice to record goodwill in the accounts of a business. However, when there is a change among the partners in a partnership, it may sometimes be agreed that the goodwill of the business is to be valued and this value entered into the accounts of the partnership. There are many different ways of valuing goodwill which are beyond the scope of this book but it must be emphasised that the question of whether or not goodwill is to be valued and, if so, what value is to be placed on it is in all cases one for agreement between the partners.

(c) If the partners decide to value goodwill a new account is opened called the Goodwill Account and the entries are as follows:

DEBIT the Goodwill Account
CREDIT the Revaluation Account

(d) *Illustration*

Paul and James instead of merely revaluing the premises at £27,000 and the Machinery at £2,000 also value the Goodwill at £50,000.

Goodwill			Revaluation			
Revaluation	**50,000**		Machinery	1,000	Premises	21,000
					Goodwill	**50,000**

(e) The result is that the new surplus on the Revaluation is £70,000 which has to be transferred to the Capital Accounts of Paul and James equally, thus increasing their Capital Accounts to £40,000 each.

Revaluation

Machinery	1,000	Premises	21,000
Balance	70,000	Goodwill	50,000
	71,000		71,000
Paul	35,000	Balance	70,000
James	35,000		
	70,000		70,000

(f) Another result is that there is a new asset, Goodwill, which appears in the firm's books and which will have to be shown on the Balance Sheet:

EMPLOYMENT OF CAPITAL
Fixed Assets

Premises	27,000	
Machinery	2,000	29,000
Goodwill		50,000

9. *Exercises*

(1) Alice and Bill are in partnership sharing profits in the ratio Alice : 3; Bill : 1. Their fixed assets are Freeholds £15,000; Machinery £8,000. They decide to revalue their assets as follows: Freeholds £52,000; Machinery £5,000. Show the entries to record this.

(2) Carol, Dick, and Elaine are in partnership sharing profits in the ratio 3 : 3 : 2. Fred is admitted as a partner. He introduces £3,000 capital in cash. The assets of the old firm previously appearing in the Balance Sheet at a value of Freeholds £12,000; Fixtures £3,000; Investments £5,000, are revalued as follows: Freeholds £32,000; Fixtures £2,000; Investments £7,000. It is agreed that the profit on this revaluation is to be shared between the old partners equally. Show the entries in the firm's books to record the above.

(3) George, Helen and Ian are in partnership sharing profits in the ratio George : 3; Helen : 2; Ian : 1. The balances on the accounts as at December 31, are as follows:

Capital. George £15,000, Helen £12,000, Ian £11,000.
Current Accounts. George £1,000, Helen £800, Ian £200.

Premises £10,000; Fixtures and Fittings £11,000; Motor Cars £9,000; Debtors £21,000; Cash £12,500; Creditors £23,500.

George retires on December 31. The Motor Cars are transferred to George at their book value and of the Debtors of £21,000, £7,000's worth are also transferred to George. The Fixtures and Fittings are revalued at £5,000 and the Premises are revalued at £40,000. George is paid the amount due to him in cash in respect of the balances on his Capital and Current Accounts.

Show the entries in the Revaluation Account, and the Capital Account of George to record the above and also show the Balance Sheet of the new firm as at the following January 1.

(4) Jane and Kevin are in partnership sharing profits equally. They have also agreed to pay interest on Capital Account at the rate of 12 per cent. per annum. They decide to admit Lorna as a new partner on July 1. She is to introduce capital in cash of £5,000 and as from July 1, all three partners are to be entitled to interest on capital at 12 per cent. per annum, Lorna is to be entitled to a salary of £8,000 per annum and any resulting profit or loss is to be shared between the three partners in the ratio Jane : 2; Kevin : 2; Lorna : 1.

As at June 30, the balances on the Capital Accounts of Jane and Kevin were £45,000 each and it was agreed that the following fixed asset would be revalued: Premises, which at that date had a Balance Sheet value of £40,000, would be revalued at £70,000; the Balance Sheet value of the remaining assets would not be altered.

As at December 31, the balances on the accounts other than Premises and the Capital Accounts are as follows: Income (for the year ending December 31) £200,000. Expenses £137,000. Machinery £15,000. Motor Cars £10,000. Current Assets (including Cash) £40,000. Current Liabilities £5,000. Current Accounts: Jane £500 (credit); Kevin £400 (credit); Lorna nil. Drawings: Jane £27,050; Kevin £26,850; Lorna £5,000.

From the above information prepare a Profit and Loss Account for the year ending December 31, together with a Balance Sheet as at that date.

Chapter 8

BANK RECONCILIATION

1. It is essential that the owner of any business should have an accurate record of the balance in his bank account. If the business has an overdraft it is advisable to keep the overdraft as low as possible so as to reduce the amount of interest payable; on the other hand if the business has large sums of money with the bank it might be possible for some of this money to be invested and so make more money for the business. Only if the business has up to date and accurate records of the state of the bank account can any decision be made. For these reasons a solicitor should obtain regular bank statements from his bank and check them with his Cash Book.

2. As mentioned in Chapter 5 (p. 42), a solicitor holds money on behalf of clients (clients' money) in a separate bank account (clients' bank account). The solicitor must check his Cash Book for clients' money with a bank statement for the clients' bank account at least every three months under Rule 11 S.A.R. It is also provided that a reconciliation statement must be kept in the relevant Cash Book or some other suitable place.

3. It is unlikely that the balance shown in the Cash Book will agree with the balance shown in the bank statement. There are several reasons why this may be so.

   (a) *Errors*. Mistakes may have been made by the bank, or by the solicitor when making up his Cash Book. For instance the solicitor may have received a cheque for £15 but the bookkeeper made a transposition of figures and entered the amount in the accounts as £51 instead.
   (b) *Bank charges*. The first indication that a solicitor may have of the bank charges made by the bank will be the inclusion of this item in the bank statement. The solicitor will therefore need to write the appropriate entry into his Cash Book and make up the balancing entry.
   (c) Credit transfer payments, receipts of dividends, interest, etc., will be shown on the bank statement but may not have been entered into the Cash Book. If so the relevant double-entries should be made forthwith.
   (d) Standing orders may have been paid by the bank and again no entry of these may have been made in the books.
   (e) *Late credits*. There may be amounts paid into the bank which have not yet been noted on the bank statement. Thus, if the solicitor paid items into the bank by means of the night safe system late one evening, these will have been received by the bank too late for it to include on the bank statement prepared that day.
   (f) *Unpresented cheques*. Payments by cheque are recorded in the Cash Book as soon as the cheques are sent out. The cheques are not recorded by the bank until they are received by the bank for payment. Cheques may therefore have been sent out by the solicitor to third persons and still be in the post, or the recipients have received the cheques but not yet banked them, or the recipients have banked the cheques but those cheques have not yet passed through the banking system.

4. There are two basic steps to take:

(a) Correct the Cash Book.
(b) Prepare the bank reconciliation statement.

5. **Correcting the Cash Book**
Any items appearing in the bank statement but not entered in the Cash Book (or entered incorrectly) should be dealt with.

Example

You despatched a cheque for £19 but by mistake this was entered into the Cash Book as £17. The Cash Book must therefore be credited an extra £2. In addition you should also check the corresponding entry to see whether that too was entered incorrectly.

6. **The Bank Reconciliation Statement**

(a) *Procedure*
  (i) The statement should be headed with the date.
 (ii) Insert the balance as per the bank statement.
(iii) Deduct unpresented cheques.
(iv) Add late credits.

(b) *Example*
The bank statement shows a credit balance of £200. The solicitor has unpresented cheques of £100 and late credits of £50. This means that when unpresented cheques are eventually received by the bank the balance should be reduced to £100 but when the late credits are received and noted by the bank this should then increase the balance to £150. Accordingly the bank reconciliation statement should look as follows:

	£
Bank Reconciliation Statement as at	
Balance as per bank statement	200
Less: Unpresented Cheques	100
	100
Plus: Late Credits	50
	150

(c) If the whole procedure has been carried through correctly the resulting figure should show the balance as per the Cash Book. If it does not then an error has been made.

7. *Exercises*

(1) Prepare a bank reconciliation from the following figures: balance as per bank statement £500; unpresented cheques £100; late credits £50.

(2) Prepare a bank reconciliation statement from the following figures: Overdraft as per bank statement £400; unpresented cheques £50; late credits £100.

(3) From the following information prepare a bank reconciliation statement. The Cash Book shows a balance of £500. The bank statement shows a credit balance of £300 and bank charges of £60. Unpresented cheques amount to £140 and late credits to £280.

(4) From the following information prepare a bank reconciliation statement. The Cash Book shows that the account is overdrawn by £40. The bank statement shows a credit balance of £50 and bank charges of £18. Unpresented cheques amount to £124 and late credits to £16.

(5) On December 31, the Cash Book showed cash in hand of £3,000. The bank statement as at the same date shows a balance of £4,000. However, the bank statement revealed bank charges of £40 and a standing order paid of £200 which had not been entered into the Cash Book. You also discover that on the debit side of the Cash Book an item which should have been entered as £70 was incorrectly entered as £10 and further that there is a mistake in addition which resulted in the debit side total being £100 too heavy. Unpresented cheques amount to £1,550 and late credits to £270. From this information prepare a bank reconciliation statement and also show the adjustments which would appear in the Cash Book.

(6) The balance on December 31, of the Cash Book shows an overdraft of £1,000. The bank statement as at that date reveals an overdraft of £2,000, bank charges of £500, interest paid on overdraft of £250. Unpresented cheques amounted to £130 and late credits amounted to £40. A cheque for £50 had been entered as a payment in the Cash Book instead of as a receipt. A cheque received for £140 had been dishonoured with no corresponding entry in the Cash Book. A cheque drawn for £800 was entered in the Cash Book as £600. Owing to an error of addition the credit side had been undercast by £100. From this information show the adjustments in the Cash Book and a bank reconciliation statement.

(7) On December 31, the bank statement of Pearse & Co. (Office a/c) showed an overdraft of £6,000.

The Bank Statement showed that the following items had not been recorded in the Cash Book:
  (i) Bank charges: £520
  (ii) Bank interest paid: £700
  (iii) Direct debits: £4,320
Unpresented cheques amounted to £368, and late credits to £42.

For the above show the adjusted Cash Book and a bank reconciliation statement.

(8) The Cash Sheet of Jones, shows a debit balance of £878 as at March 31, 1975, but when the bank statement for that month is received, it shows that Jones has an overdraft of £227. Jones cannot understand how the discrepancy has arisen and as he now has to meet a payment for £324 he requests that you investigate the position. It is ascertained that all receipts are banked and all payments are made by cheque.

The bank statement shows the following entries:

Paleonthian Bank Limited Profligo Branch

Account: Jones		Payments £	Receipts £	Balance £
March	1 1975 balance forward			692 Cr.
	3 623	145		547 Cr.
	6 624	296		251 Cr.
	10 credits		189	440 Cr.
	13 625	316		124 Cr.
	15 standing bankers order	60		64 Cr.
	21 credits		338	402 Cr.
	22 627	261		141 Cr.
	24 cheque returned	49		92 Cr.
	25 Giro direct transfer		126	218 Cr.
	28 629	76		142 Cr.
	31 631	200		58 Dr.
	31 626	169		227 Dr.

The Cash Sheet for Jones for the month of March 1975, shows:

Cash Sheet

Date		Details	DR £	CR £	Balance £
1975					
March	1	Balance	251		251
	7	Cash	153		404
	8	B Ltd.	36		440
	9	SR Ltd.		316	124
	14	GP		169	45 Cr.
	17	DP Ltd.	85		40
	18	FG		261	221 Cr.
	19	LM	49		172 Cr.
	20	Cash	177		5
		XYZ Ltd.	27		32
	22	PCD		42	10 Cr.
	25	JKO Ltd.		76	86 Cr.
	26	PTR	33		53 Cr.
	28	PDG		54	107 Cr.
	29	JNQ	101		6 Cr.
	30	DBM Ltd.	678		672
		Wages etc.		200	472
	31	Cash	235		700
		YU	500		1,207
		KZ		89	1,118
		KLO		240	878

Prepare the bank reconciliation statement for Jones, and effect any other accounting entries in the Cash Sheet you deem necessary so that the books accurately reflect the above transactions and accord with normal accounting practice.

(Part II Qualifying Examination August 1975.)

[Time limit: 30 minutes]

(9) The Cash Sheet of Smith shows a debit balance of £1,756 as at December 31, 1979, but the bank statement as at that date, shows an overdraft of £454. All receipts are banked and all payments are made by cheque.

The Cash Sheet for Smith for the month of December, 1979, shows:

Cash Sheet

Date		Details	DR £	CR £	Balance £
1979					
Dec.	1	Balance	502		502
	6	Cash	306		808
	9	T Ltd.	72		880
	10	BA Ltd.		632	248
	13	GK		338	90 Cr.
	15	Z Ltd.	170		80
	17	RS		522	442 Cr.
	18	GG	98		344 Cr.
	21	Cash	354		10
		BBN	54		64
		DCP		84	20 Cr.
	23	OKJ Ltd.		152	172 Cr.
	25	TF	66		106 Cr.
	27	DPN		108	214 Cr.
	28	ND	202		12 Cr.
	30	LKJ	1,356		1,344
		Salaries		400	944
	31	Cash	470		1,414
		POY	1,000		2,414
		ZK		178	2,236
		LKO		480	1,756

The bank statement shows the following entries:—

Crando Bank Limited

1979			Payments £	Receipts £	Balance £
Dec.	1	Balance forward			1,384 Cr.
	2	323	290		1,094 Cr.
	5	324	592		502 Cr.
	9	Credits		378	880 Cr.
	13	325	632		248 Cr.
	14	Standing bankers order	120		128 Cr.
	21	Credits		676	804 Cr.
	21	327	522		282 Cr.
	23	Cheque returned	98		184 Cr.
	27	Giro direct transfer		252	436 Cr.
	28	329	152		284 Cr.
	31	331	400		116 Dr.
	31	326	338		454 Dr.

Prepare a statement for Smith, reconciling the balance in the Cash Sheet with that shown on the bank statement, and effect any other accounting entries in the Cash Sheet you deem necessary, so that the books accurately reflect the above transactions and accord with normal accounting practice.

(Part II Qualifying Examination February 1980.)

[Time limit: 25 minutes]

Chapter 9

REVISION EXERCISES

[Time limit for each question: 1 hour.]

(1) The Trial Balance of Jones, a practising solicitor, shows the following position:

Trial Balance at December 31, 1980

	DR £	CR £
Profit Costs, less work in hand 31.12.79		72,946
Sundry Rents		1,000
Interest Received		1,532
Capital Account		38,161
Drawings	15,234	
General Expenses	49,769	
Due from clients	11,428	
Due to clients		94,620
Creditors		1,143
Fixtures, Furniture and Library at cost	4,000	
Accumulated depreciation on Fixtures, Furniture and Library to 31st December 1979		2,000
Motor cars at cost	8,300	
Accumulated depreciation on Motor Cars to 31st December 1979		1,900
Cash at Bank — Clients' Account	94,620	
Lease at cost	14,000	
Cash at Bank — Office Account	15,927	
Petty Cash Balance	24	
	£213,302	£213,302

For many years it has been the business policy of Jones, to charge depreciation at the following rates on the cost price of the assets:

Fixtures, Furniture and Library 15 per cent. per annum
Motor Cars   25 per cent. per annum

The amount shown for Motor Cars in the Trial Balance, includes the cost of a car (£4,000) which was purchased on July 1, 1980, another car being sold by Jones on the same day, for £1,350. The latter car had been purchased by Jones on January 1, 1979, for the sum of £2,000. The proceeds of sale of the car were inadvertently credited to Capital Account, and no further adjustment has been made in Motor Cars Account with regard to that sale.

On December 31, 1980, General Expenses which are outstanding and not yet accounted for, amount to £628, whilst the value of work in hand and stock of stationery amounts to £2,348 and £74 respectively. An adjustment is to be made in respect of rates and insurances which have been paid in advance, and which amount to the sum of £695. Amounts paid in respect of stationery, rates and insurances, are included in General Expenses.

From the above information, prepare a Profit and Loss Account for the year ended December 31, 1980, together with a Balance Sheet as at that date.

(Solicitors Final Examination Winter 1981)

(2) April, Blossom & Co., are solicitors; the partnership consists of Jones and Smith who share profits and losses as to Jones two-thirds and Smith one-third. Each partner is entitled to interest on his capital in the firm, and Smith is entitled, in addition, to a partnership salary of £5,000 per annum.

The following Trial Balance is prepared from the firm's books for the year ended June 30, 1976.

Trial Balance at June 30, 1976

	DR	CR
Profit Costs		£83,567
Interest Receivable		1,469
Administration Expenses	£43,176	
General Expenses	16,059	
Cash at Bank — Office Account	1,356	
Petty Cash Balance	14	
Capital Accounts:		
Jones		15,000
Smith		5,000
Current Accounts:		
Jones		2,300
Smith		1,200
Drawings — Jones	14,500	
Smith	9,000	
Library	1,456	
Furniture	2,795	
Depreciation of furniture		470
Motor Cars	13,030	
Depreciation on motor cars		5,580
Lease	6,000	
Due from Clients	8,042	
Due to Creditors		842
Cash at Bank — Clients' Account:		
Current Account	6,219	
Deposit Account	84,567	
Amount due to Clients		90,786
	£206,214	£206,214

Jones and Smith are entitled to interest on capital, of £750 and £250 respectively.

At June 30, 1976, bills have been received for Administration Expenses amounting to £1,250, but no action has yet been taken in respect thereof.

Depreciation of £235 is to be provided on Furniture and £1,860 on Motor Cars. The work in progress at June 30, 1976 is valued at £2,126.

From the above information, prepare a Profit and Loss and Appropriation Account for the year ended June 30, 1976, together with a Balance Sheet as at that date.

(Part II Qualifying Examination August 1976).

(3) Olde and Razor are in partnership as solicitors, sharing profits and losses as to Olde two-thirds and Razor one-third. A partnership salary of £12,000 per annum is payable to Razor, and each partner is entitled to interest on capital at the rate of 10 per cent. per annum.

Rustred is admitted into the partnership on July 1, 1985, contributing £30,000 as his share of capital in the firm. The name of the firm is to be Olde, Rustred, Razor & Co., and from the inception of the new partnership, profits and losses are to be shared equally between the partners. The former arrangements for partnership salary and interest on capital are cancelled with effect from July 1, 1985.

The firm's bookkeeper produces the following list of balances, which he has extracted from the firm's books, for the year ended December 31, 1985:

	£
Cash at Bank—Clients Account	
Current Account	72,096
Deposit Account	247,000
Cash at Bank—Office Account	8,642
Due from Clients	45,363
Freehold Land and Buildings	77,000
Motor Cars at cost	32,000
Library, Furniture and Computer at cost	24,000
Provision for depreciation accounts at 1st January, 1985:	
Motor Cars	8,000
Library, Furniture and Computer	12,000
Capital Accounts	
Olde	70,000
Razor	50,000
Rustred	30,000
Drawings	
Olde	36,000
Razor	27,500
Rustred	10,000
Current Accounts	
Olde	7,400 (credit)
Razor	600 (debit)
Profit Costs	310,426
Work in hand at 1st January, 1985	28,115
Interest Receivable	17,427
Administrative and General Expenses	226,327
Bad Debts	750
Petty Cash Balance	85
Due to Clients	319,096
Sundry Creditors	11,129

The following information is relevant:
(a) Depreciation is to be charged (straight line basis) at the following rates:

Motor Cars	25 per cent per annum.
Library, Furniture and Computer	20 per cent per annum.

(b) Work in hand at December 31, 1985, was valued at £32,174.
(c) There are bills outstanding at December 31, 1985, in respect of Administrative and General Expenses, which have not yet been accounted for, and these amount to £1,120.

B|S _ C A|C movements

P|t.

(d) Allowance is to be made, in respect of General Expenses amounting to £315, which have been charged in error to the drawings account of Razor.

(e) Profits are to be allocated between partners on a time basis. (All calculations to be made in months.)

From the foregoing information, prepare a Profit and Loss and Appropriation Account for the year ended December 31, 1985, together with a Balance Sheet as at that date. (Use the vertical form of presentation.)

Movements on partners' current accounts must be shown in detail.

Taxation (including VAT) is to be ignored, for the purpose of the preparation of these Accounts.

(Solicitors' Final Examination. Winter 1986).

(4) Alfred, Basil, and Charles are in partnership sharing profits in the ratio of 3 : 3 : 2. Partners are credited with 5 per cent. per annum interest on the balance of their Capital Accounts. The Balance Sheet at June 30, 1963, showed the partners' Capital Accounts were in credit: Alfred £6,200, Basil £4,400, Charles £3,000.

On December 31, 1963, Alfred retired as a partner but agreed to remain with the firm as a consultant at an annual fee of £600 to be paid in twelve instalments at the end of each month. The partnership agreement provided that on retirement a partner should be entitled to withdraw the balance on his Current Account on the following July 1. The balance on his Capital Account is repayable in five equal instalments. The first instalment is payable on retirement (and this was paid to Alfred) and the remaining balance is to be repaid by four equal instalments without interest, the first of these to be payable on July 1, following retirement. No revaluation of the firm's assets was called for.

On Alfred's retirement, Douglas was admitted to the partnership and introduced £600 capital. It was agreed that the apportionment of profits for the year ended June 30, 1964 should be on a time basis. The new partnership agreement provided that as from January 1, 1964 Basil, Charles, and Douglas should share profits in the proportion of 4 : 4 : 2 and that interest of 5 per cent. per annum should continue to be payable on the balance of their Capital Accounts.

The Trial Balance extracted at June 30, 1964, showed (*inter alia*) the following figures: Income £39,320. Expenses £30,800. Drawings: Alfred £1,200, Basil £2,093 Charles £1,912 Douglas £623. Current Account balances (credit): Alfred £135, Basil £119, Charles £98. Fixed Assets £8,000. Current Assets £11,644. Creditors £3,640.

From the above information, prepare a Profit and Loss Account for the year ended June 30, 1964, together with a Balance Sheet as at that date. Any balance that may be standing on the Current Account of Alfred is to be included in the Current Assets, or Liabilities, as the case may be, of the partnership Balance Sheet.

(Part II Qualifying Examination August 1966—adapted.)

SECTION TWO

THE HANDLING OF TRANSACTIONS ON
BEHALF OF CLIENTS

Chapter 10

INTRODUCTION

A. BASIC PRINCIPLES

1. Solicitors handle both their own business money (office money) and money belonging to clients (clients' money). The Solicitors Accounts Rules 1975 (S.A.R) require a solicitor not only to keep the two sets of money physically separate, but also to record the entries separately in the books of account.

2. To achieve this, the solicitor needs two sets of books:
   (a) one set to record all dealings with clients' money—CLIENT ACCOUNT;
   (b) another set to record all the ordinary dealings in the running of the business (*e.g.* receipt of office money, paying rates, buying stationery)—OFFICE ACCOUNT.

3. THESE TWO SETS OF BOOKS MUST BE KEPT COMPLETELY INDE-PENDENT.
   (a) For every DEBIT in OFFICE ACCOUNT there must be a corresponding CREDIT in OFFICE ACCOUNT and vice versa.
   (b) For every DEBIT in CLIENT ACCOUNT there must be a corresponding CREDIT in CLIENT ACCOUNT and vice versa.

The classic error is to debit CLIENT ACCOUNT and to credit OFFICE ACCOUNT or vice versa.

4. There are four basic sets of entries:
   (a) Receipt of clients' money.
   (b) Receipt of office money.
   (c) Payment of clients' money.
   (d) Payment of office money.

5. To record these a solicitor needs:
   (a) Two Cash Accounts—one for OFFICE ACCOUNT and one for CLIENT ACCOUNT.
   (b) Two personal accounts in respect of each client—one for OFFICE ACCOUNT and one for CLIENT ACCOUNT.

6. **Receipt of clients' money**
   DEBIT Cash Account—CLIENT ACCOUNT
   CREDIT ledger account of client—CLIENT ACCOUNT

Example
Receive £60 clients' money from A. B. Client.

OFFICE A/C BOOKS		CLIENT A/C BOOKS	
Cash	A. B. Client	Cash	A. B. Client
		60–	60–

83

7. **Receipt of office money**
   DEBIT Cash Account—OFFICE ACCOUNT
   CREDIT ledger account of client—OFFICE ACCOUNT

Example
Receive £30 office money from A. B. Client.

OFFICE A/C BOOKS		CLIENT A/C BOOKS	
Cash	A. B. Client	Cash	A. B. Client
30–	30–		

8. **Payment of clients' money**
   CREDIT Cash Account—CLIENT ACCOUNT
   DEBIT ledger account of client—CLIENT ACCOUNT

Example
Pay £50 clients' money to A. B. Client.

OFFICE A/C BOOKS		CLIENT A/C BOOKS	
Cash	A. B. Client	Cash	A. B. Client
		50–	50–

9. **Payment of office money**
   CREDIT Cash Account—OFFICE ACCOUNT
   DEBIT ledger account of client—OFFICE ACCOUNT

Example
Pay £40 office money to A. B. Client.

OFFICE A/C BOOKS		CLIENT A/C BOOKS	
Cash	A. B. Client	Cash	A. B. Client
40–	40–		

10. *Exercises*
    Show all necessary entries.
    (1) (a) Receive £30 clients' money from Alice.
        (b) Pay £20 clients' money to Alice.

    (2) (a) Pay £1,000 office money to Brenda.
        (b) Receive £800 office money from Brenda.

    (3) (a) Receive £70 clients' money from Christine.
        (b) Pay £50 clients' money to Christine.
        (c) Pay £400 office money to Christine.
        (d) Receive £30 office money from Christine.

B. THE BOOKS OF DOUBLE-ENTRY

11. **Cash Books (CB)**

    (a) The Clients' Cash Book—to record dealings with clients' money.
    (b) The Office Cash Book—to record dealings with business money.

12. **Petty Cash Book (PCB)**

Only one petty cash book is needed, namely that to record dealings with office petty cash. Clients' money is not dealt with through the petty cash but, in general, immediately it is received it must be paid into the bank and consequently withdrawals of clients' money are made by cheque.

13. **Clients' Ledgers (CL)**

    (a) Clients' Ledger—CLIENT ACCOUNT
    (b) Clients' Ledger—OFFICE ACCOUNT

14. **Nominal Ledger (NL)**

This contains all the other accounts other than those the solicitor wishes to keep private. However, none of these accounts will involve a dealing with clients' money and therefore only one Nominal Ledger is needed, namely that in OFFICE ACCOUNT. THERE IS NO NOMINAL LEDGER IN CLIENT ACCOUNT.

15. **Private Ledger (PL)**

This contains any account that a solicitor wishes to keep private, *e.g.* Capital Account and Drawings Account. These will not involve any dealings with clients' money and therefore only one Private Ledger is needed namely that in OFFICE ACCOUNT.

16. Instead of having two Cash Books, one for CLIENT ACCOUNT and one for OFFICE ACCOUNT, it is possible to have a single Cash Book with two sets of columns, one set for CLIENT ACCOUNT and the other set for OFFICE ACCOUNT.

17. It is possible to do the same for the Clients' Ledger.

18. The sets of accounts—OFFICE and CLIENT—are still entirely independent. They are only presented in the same book for convenience. Thus, still, for EVERY DEBIT IN OFFICE ACCOUNT THERE MUST BE A CREDIT IN OFFICE ACCOUNT, etc.

19. The other books (Petty Cash Book, Nominal and Private Ledgers) remain unchanged.

Chapter 11

MODERN METHODS OF KEEPING ACCOUNTS

1. The double-entry system of debit and credit outlined so far is based on the assumption that the double-entries are made by hand and are entered by clerks into books. Today some solicitors keep their accounts this way but many use more modern techniques of recording the information.

2. **Manual card system**

(a) Instead of keeping books, with an account on each page of the book, a solicitor may keep the accounts in a series of loose-leaf cards. Each account is on a separate card and the cards are kept in special drawers or cabinets. The layout of these cards is the same as the alternative layout in the traditional Ledger as follows:

Date	Details	Fo	Debit	Credit	Balance
			£	£	£

(See *ante*, p. 21).

(b) A specimen double-entry would look as follows:

£100 is received from Alice.

Cash					
Date	Details	Fo	Debit	Credit	Balance
			£	£	£
	Alice		**100**		

Alice					
Date	Details	Fo	Debit	Credit	Balance
			£	£	£
	Cash			**100**	

3. **Carbon system**

Instead of writing the two entries separately on the two cards (Cash and Alice), the entries are made simultaneously by using a piece of carbon paper. One card is placed on top of the other, with the carbon paper in the middle. The entry is therefore written by hand on the top card and is simultaneously reproduced by means of the carbon on the card underneath.

Illustration

(i) £100 is received from Alice.

(ii) The card of Alice is placed on top of the carbon paper and would therefore look the same as above (paragraph 2(b)), *i.e.*

Alice				
Date	Details	Debit £	Credit £	Balance £
	Cash from Alice		**100**	

(iii) The Cash Card (or Sheet) is placed underneath the carbon and therefore the debit and credit columns of the Cash Sheet have to be reversed, *i.e.*

Illustration

Cash				
Date	Details	Credit £	Debit £	Balance £
	Cash from Alice		**100**	

4. Computer accounts

The precise layout of the accounts varies from system to system according to the type of computer used (this is particularly true in respect of the entries which need to be made to record VAT) but the principles of double entry are the same. Basically most computers use a layout similar to the Manual Card System illustrated above in paragraph 2. A system of computer accounting differs in a number of respects from a system operated manually.

(a) With a computer the entries are made automatically onto cards by the machine. The only function which a human being has to perform is to provide the machine with the relevant information, usually by typing it on a keyboard similar to a typewriter. Thus the operator will instruct the machine to pay George £50 out of clients' money. The machine will then do the rest of the work.

(b) With a manual system the operator will have to do the arithmetic (even if all this means is that the operator uses a calculator) whereas a computer will do all the arithmetic itself automatically.

(c) This therefore means that the balance columns on the manual system have to be calculated by the operator, whereas the balance columns in a computer system are calculated and completed automatically by the machine.

(d) With a manual system the accounts are contained on cards which have to be stored in a cabinet. This is not necessary if accounts are kept on a computer system, when the computer can store all the information inside itself. If the operator wishes to have a copy of the relevant information then the computer can issue a special print-out. However, many solicitors who use a computer still prefer to have the accounts stored on loose-leaf cards, kept in a cabinet, as with a conventional manual system.

(e) An accounts computer can be used for other functions as well as the simple recording of the information. It can be programmed in such a way as to provide special reports, *e.g.* for management. Thus a computer can be programmed to produce at the end of each week a list of all the clients who have been sent bills but who have not yet paid. This would enable the person in charge to keep a check on unpaid bills, issue reminders where necessary, and take any further steps which might be necessary if a client delays paying a bill for an unreasonable length of time.

5. From now on the book will proceed on the basis that the accounts are kept on a computer. However, it is important to realise that the other two systems are fundamentally the same. With a manual card system the accounts will look the same, the only real difference being that each entry has to be made separately and by hand. With a carbon system, the Cash Sheet will be different. Because the entries appear on it via the carbon, the entries have to be the other way round, *i.e.* Credits (Payments) on the left and Debits (Receipts) on the right. The ledger cards, however, (*e.g.* the ledger cards of clients) will look exactly the same as those in the other two systems.

6. Cash in bank—receipts and payments

(a) There will be a Cash Sheet on which will be recorded all the items which formerly would have been recorded in the Cash Book. Whenever money is received and paid into the bank, or payments are made by cheque, the Cash Sheet is used.

(b) *Illustration*

    (i) Receive £100 from Paul.
    (ii) Receive £20 from James.
   (iii) Pay £30 to Paul by cheque.

		Paul		
		DR	CR	BALANCE
(i)	Cash		100	100
(iii)	Cash	30		70

		James		
		DR	CR	BALANCE
(ii)	Cash		20	20

		Cash		
		DR	CR	BALANCE
(i)	Paul	100		100
(ii)	James	20		120
(iii)	Paul		30	90

7. Because a solicitor needs to keep separate records in respect of office money and clients' money, the Cash Sheet will need two sets of columns for credits, debits and balances—one set for OFFICE ACCOUNT, the other set for CLIENT ACCOUNT as follows:

		OFFICE ACCOUNT			CLIENT ACCOUNT		
		DR	CR	BALANCE	DR	CR	BALANCE

8. Petty Cash

(a) When a payment is made out of petty cash, instead of using the Cash Sheet, a new sheet, for petty cash, is used. The layout of this sheet is the same as for the Cash Sheet, except that it contains only one set of columns, namely that for OFFICE ACCOUNT (see *post*, p. 98).

(b) *Illustration*
   £5 is paid out of petty cash to Charles.

Charles							
		OFFICE ACCOUNT			CLIENT ACCOUNT		
		DR	CR	BALANCE	DR	CR	BALANCE
	P. Cash	5		5			

Petty Cash				
		DR	CR	BALANCE
	Charles		5	5

(c) If money is withdrawn from the bank for the petty cash float then the relevant entries are made on the Cash Sheet (payment) and the Petty Cash Sheet (receipt).

Illustration
£30 is withdrawn from the bank for petty cash. Office money is used.

		OFFICE ACCOUNT			CLIENT ACCOUNT		
		Cash					
		DR	CR	BALANCE	DR	CR	BALANCE
	P. Cash Float		**30**				

		Petty Cash		
		DR	CR	BALANCE
	Cash Float	**30**		

9. Clients' Ledger—entries

(a) There will be a separate account or card for each client. There will need to be two sets of columns for debits, credits and balances, one set for OFFICE ACCOUNT, the other set for CLIENT ACCOUNT as follows:

		OFFICE ACCOUNT			CLIENT ACCOUNT		
		DR	CR	BALANCE	DR	CR	BALANCE

(b) *Payments by cheque.*

Illustration
Pay £100 on behalf of Barnaby — office money.

		OFFICE ACCOUNT			CLIENT ACCOUNT		
		Barnaby					
		DR	CR	BALANCE	DR	CR	BALANCE
	Cash	100		100			

The credit entry will appear on the Cash Sheet.

(c) *Payments out of petty cash.*

Illustration
Pay £2 out of petty cash on behalf of Laurence, using office money.

		Laurence					
		OFFICE ACCOUNT			CLIENT ACCOUNT		
		DR	CR	BALANCE	DR	CR	BALANCE
P. Cash		2		2			

The credit entry will appear on the Petty Cash Sheet

(d) *Client Ledger Transfers.* For these transactions a new sheet can be used which may be called a "Transfer Sheet" or a "Journal" (see *post*, p. 109).

10. Nominal Ledger

(a) The cards contained in this Ledger will only require one set of columns, namely that for OFFICE ACCOUNT.
(b) *Payment of expenses.* There will be a separate account (or card) for each type of expense, *e.g.* wages.

Illustration
£400 is paid in respect of wages by cheque.

	Wages		
	DR	CR	BALANCE
Cash	400		400

The credit entry will appear on the Cash Sheet — OFFICE ACCOUNT.

If the expense is paid out of petty cash then the credit entry will be on the Petty Cash Sheet and not the Cash Sheet.

(c) *Purchase of fixed asset.* There will be a separate account (or card) for each type of fixed asset, *e.g.* fixtures and fittings.

Illustration
£500 is paid by cheque in respect of fixtures and fittings.

	Fixtures and Fittings		
	DR	CR	BALANCE
Cash	500		500

The credit entry appears on the Cash Sheet — OFFICE ACCOUNT.

11. **Private Ledger**

(a) Only one set of columns is necessary, namely that for OFFICE ACCOUNT.

(b) *Capital*
When a partner introduces cash as capital then the Capital Account (or card) of that partner is used.

Illustration
A sole practitioner introduces £10,000 capital.

		Capital		
		DR	CR	BALANCE
	Cash		10,000	10,000

The debit entry will appear on the Cash Sheet.

(c) *Drawings.* When the practitioner, or a partner, withdraws money from the business a separate account or card for drawings is used.

Illustration
The practitioner withdraws £200.

		Drawings		
		DR	CR	BALANCE
	Cash	200		200

The credit entry will appear on the Cash Sheet.

Chapter 12

BASIC POSTINGS

A. RECEIPTS

1. The first thing is to decide whether the money received is office or clients' money (see *post*, p. 100).

2. Pay the cheque into the appropriate Bank Account.

3. CREDIT the ledger account or card of the client in either the OFFICE ACCOUNT section or the CLIENT ACCOUNT section, as appropriate.

4. DEBIT the Cash Sheet, in the appropriate section.

Example (1) Receipt of clients' money
Receive £500 clients' money from Laurence.

		Laurence (CL2)					
		OFFICE ACCOUNT			CLIENT ACCOUNT		
		DR	CR	BALANCE	DR	CR	BALANCE
	Cash					**500**	

		Cash					
		OFFICE ACCOUNT			CLIENT ACCOUNT		
		DR	CR	BALANCE	DR	CR	BALANCE
	Laurence				**500**		

Example (2) Receipt of office money
Receive £40 office money from Barnaby.

		Barnaby (CL3)					
		OFFICE ACCOUNT			CLIENT ACCOUNT		
		DR	CR	BALANCE	DR	CR	BALANCE
	Cash		**40**				

Cash							
		OFFICE ACCOUNT			CLIENT ACCOUNT		
		DR	CR	BALANCE	DR	CR	BALANCE
	Barnaby	**40**					

5. If money is received for a client, not from the client himself but from a third person to hold on that client's behalf, the sum is credited direct to the ledger account of the client. DO NOT OPEN AN ACCOUNT FOR THE THIRD PERSON.

Example
Laurence is a plaintiff in an action, which he has just won against Violet. He was awarded £600 damages, which you now receive from Violet to hold on Laurence's behalf.

Laurence (CL2)							
		OFFICE ACCOUNT			CLIENT ACCOUNT		
		DR	CR	BALANCE	DR	CR	BALANCE
	Cash from Violet. Damages.					**600**	

The debit entry will appear on the Cash Sheet.

B. PAYMENTS

Payments by Cheque

6. The first thing is to decide whether to make the payment out of office or clients' money.

    (a) Consider whether the payment is authorised by Rule 7 (SAR).
    (b) Consider whether sufficient clients' money is held for that particular client (see *post*, p. 99).

7. Draw a cheque on the appropriate Bank Account. If the cheque is drawn on the Clients' Bank Account remember Rule 11 (7) (SAR).

8. DEBIT the ledger account or card of the client in either the OFFICE ACCOUNT section or the CLIENT ACCOUNT section, as appropriate.

9. CREDIT the Cash Sheet, in the appropriate section.

Example (1) Payments of clients' money

You hold £500 cleints' money on behalf of Laurence. Pay £100 on his behalf; it is authorised by Rule 7 (SAR).

Laurence (CL2)							
		OFFICE ACCOUNT			CLIENT ACCOUNT		
		DR	CR	BALANCE	DR	CR	BALANCE
	Cash received					500	500
	Cash				**100**		400

Cash							
		OFFICE ACCOUNT			CLIENT ACCOUNT		
		DR	CR	BALANCE	DR	CR	BALANCE
	Laurence				500		
	Laurence					**100**	

Example (2) Payment of office-money

Pay £6 on behalf of Barnaby; you hold no clients' money.

Barnaby (CL3)							
		OFFICE ACCOUNT			CLIENT ACCOUNT		
		DR	CR	BALANCE	DR	CR	BALANCE
	Cash	**6**					

Cash							
		OFFICE ACCOUNT			CLIENT ACCOUNT		
		DR	CR	BALANCE	DR	CR	BALANCE
	Barnaby		**6**				

10. If the money is paid out not to the client himself but to a third person on the client's behalf, the sum is debited on the ledger account of the client. DO NOT OPEN AN ACCOUNT FOR THAT THIRD PERSON.

Example
Pay counsel £80, out of office money, on behalf of A. B. Client.

		A. B. Client (CL1)					
		OFFICE ACCOUNT			CLIENT ACCOUNT		
		DR	CR	BALANCE	DR	CR	BALANCE
	Cash Counsel	**80**		**80**			

The credit entry will appear on the Cash Sheet.

11. *Exercises*
Show Clients' Ledger only.

(1) You act for Alpha. Receive £800 clients' money. Pay £300. Pay £400. Pay £2. Use clients' money.
(2) You act for Beta. Pay £6. Pay £700. Pay £45. Use office money. Receive £300 office money.
(3) You act for Omega. Receive £38 clients' money. Pay £20 and £18 (use clients' money). Pay £16 office money. Receive £9 office money.

Payments out of Petty Cash

12. Office money is used (see *ante*, p. 85).

13. Draw a Petty Cash Voucher to obtain the money.

14. DEBIT the ledger account or card of the client—OFFICE ACCOUNT.

15. CREDIT the Petty Cash Sheet.

Example
Pay £5 petty cash on behalf of A. B. Client.

		A. B. Client (CL1)					
		OFFICE ACCOUNT			CLIENT ACCOUNT		
		DR	CR	BALANCE	DR	CR	BALANCE
	P. Cash	**5**					

Petty Cash				
		DR	CR	BALANCE
A. B. Client			**5**	

16. *Exercises*
Show all entries.

(1) Pay £4 petty cash on behalf of Alpha. Pay £3.20 petty cash on behalf of Beta. Pay £4.60 petty cash on behalf of Gamma.
(2) You act for Delta. Pay £6 petty cash. Receive £18, clients' money. Pay £1.70 petty cash.

C. BALANCES—CLIENT ACCOUNT

17. There is an important proviso to Rule 7 (SAR), the effect of which is that a solicitor must not spend on a client's behalf more clients' money than is held at that time for that particular client.

18. *Example*

(a) Receive £50 from A. B. Client.

A. B. Client (CL1)							
		OFFICE ACCOUNT			CLIENT ACCOUNT		
		DR	CR	BALANCE	DR	CR	BALANCE
	Cash					**50**	**50**

The debit entry will appear on the Cash Sheet.

(b) If the solicitor wished to spend £40 out of clients' money, this would be possible.

Example

A. B. Client (CL1)							
		OFFICE ACCOUNT			CLIENT ACCOUNT		
		DR	CR	BALANCE	DR	CR	BALANCE
	Cash					50	50
	Cash				**40**		**10**

The credit entry will appear on the Cash Sheet.

(c) If, however, the solicitor wished to spend £70 out of clients' money, this could not be done without committing a breach of the Rules.

Example of a breach

A. B. Client (CL1)						
		OFFICE ACCOUNT			CLIENT ACCOUNT	
		DR	CR	BALANCE	DR	CR	BALANCE
Cash						50	50
Cash					**70**		**20**DR

The credit entry will appear on the Cash Sheet.

19. Thus the account of a client (*e.g.* A. B. Client)—CLIENT ACCOUNT—should always have a CREDIT balance; a debit balance means that Rule 7 (SAR) has been broken.

20. *Exercises*

If possible, make all the payments wholly out of clients' money; if this is not possible, make the whole payment out of office money. Do not make the payment partly out of clients' money and partly out of office money.

Show the Clients' Ledger only.

(1) You act for Alan. Receive £100 clients' money. Pay £60. Pay £70.
(2) You act for Brian. Receive £200 clients' money. Pay £30. Pay £400. Pay £50.
(3) You act for Charles. Receive £300 clients' money. Pay £200. Pay £150. Pay £75. Pay £30.
(4) You act for Donald. Receive £400. Pay £100. Pay £350. Pay £150. Pay £40.

D. BALANCES—OFFICE ACCOUNT

21. A similar problem arises when a solicitor receives money from or on behalf of a client: "Is it office or clients' money?" The money received will only be office money if it can be applied

(a) in reimbursement of sums already paid out by the solicitor on the client's behalf out of office money, or
(b) in payment of the solicitor's fees or profit costs charged to the client for acting on his behalf, provided a bill has been sent to the client or the fee has been agreed with the client.

Thus the following receipts would be receipts of office money:

(1) The solicitor has paid £50 out of office money in respect of stamp duty on a conveyance and now receives the money back from the client.
(2) The solicitor has paid £30 out of office money in respect of a court fee and receives the money from the client.

(3) The solicitor sends a bill to a client charging £400 for profit costs and receives a cheque for that sum from the client.

(4) During an interview with a client a fee of £20 is agreed orally and the client immediately gives the solicitor a cheque for this amount.

The following receipts are receipts of clients' money:

(1) Money received from a client in respect of a payment which the solicitor has not yet made but which the solicitor will be making in future on the client's behalf, *e.g.* money received from the client to pay counsel's fees, stamp duty, purchase money on completion in a conveyancing transaction.

(2) Money received "generally on account of costs," where the solicitor has not yet paid out any money from OFFICE ACCOUNT in handling the matter on the client's behalf, and the solicitor has neither agreed a fee with the client nor sent a bill to the client.

Example (1)
Receive £2,000 from A. B. Client generally on account of Costs. This is clients' money.

		A. B. Client (CL1)					
		OFFICE ACCOUNT			CLIENT ACCOUNT		
		DR	CR	BALANCE	DR	CR	BALANCE
Jan 2	Cash					**2,000**	**2,000**

The debit entry will appear on the Cash Sheet.

Example (2)

(a) Spend £50 on behalf of Laurence. No clients' money is held and so office money must be used.

		Laurence (CL2)					
		OFFICE ACCOUNT			CLIENT ACCOUNT		
		DR	CR	BALANCE	DR	CR	BALANCE
Jan 2	Cash	**50**		**50**			

The credit entry will appear on the Cash Sheet.

(b) Now receive partial repayment from Laurence of £30. This is office money.

Laurence (CL2)							
		OFFICE ACCOUNT			CLIENT ACCOUNT		
		DR	CR	BALANCE	DR	CR	BALANCE
Jan 2	Cash	50		50			
Jan 3	Cash		**30**	**20**			

Cash							
		OFFICE ACCOUNT			CLIENT ACCOUNT		
		DR	CR	BALANCE	DR	CR	BALANCE
Jan 2	Laurence		50				
Jan 3	Laurence	**30**					

22. If, therefore, the client owes the solicitor £50 in respect of office money spent on his behalf and gives the solicitor £60, £50 of this will be office money and £10 clients' money. The Rules provide that clients' money must normally be paid into Clients' Bank Account and not Office Bank Account. If all the £60 were paid into the Office Bank Account a breach of the Rules would be committed (*i.e.* £10 clients' money has been paid into OFFICE ACCOUNT contrary to Rule 3 (SAR)).

Example of a breach

Laurence (CL2)							
		OFFICE ACCOUNT			CLIENT ACCOUNT		
		DR	CR	BALANCE	DR	CR	BALANCE
Jan 2	Cash	50		50			
Jan 3	Cash		**60**	**10**CR			

The debit entry will appear on the Cash Sheet.

23. Thus, the account of a client—OFFICE ACCOUNT—should always have a debit balance; a credit balance suggests a breach of Rule 3 (SAR).

24. *Exercises*

Show Clients' Ledger only.

If possible receive all the money wholly into the OFFICE ACCOUNT. If this is not possible, make the receipt wholly into CLIENT ACCOUNT.

  (1) You act for Ethel. Pay £100. Receive £70. Receive £40.
  (2) You act for Fred. Pay £200. Receive £160. Receive £50. Receive £30.
  (3) You act for George. Pay £300. Receive £400. Receive £50. Pay £580 out of office money. Receive £800.

25. SUMMARY

You have probably broken the Rules if:

  (i) You see the ledger account of a client—CLIENT ACCOUNT—with a DEBIT balance.
  (ii) You see the ledger account of a client—OFFICE ACCOUNT—with a CREDIT balance.

E. DELIVERY OF A BILL

26. The charging of costs involves OFFICE ACCOUNT alone:

27. File a carbon copy of bill in the "Bills Delivered Book" file.

28. DEBIT the ledger account of the client—OFFICE ACCOUNT—with the COSTS.

29. A new sheet, called a "Costs Sheet" is used. Thus the balancing entry is CREDIT the Costs Account.

Example

March 5. Deliver a bill to Violet for £160 costs.

		Violet (CL4)					
		OFFICE ACCOUNT			CLIENT ACCOUNT		
		DR	CR	BALANCE	DR	CR	BALANCE
Mar 5	Costs	**160**		**160**			

		Costs		
		DR	CR	BALANCE
Mar 5	Violet		**160**	

30. Note that when a solicitor sends a bill to his client charging the client with the fee (or costs), he will probably also ask the client to reimburse him for payments made (or sometimes to be made) during the transaction on the client's behalf. When delivering the bill DO NOT DEBIT THE LEDGER ACCOUNT OF THE CLIENT WITH THESE PAYMENTS. They are debited when paid out by the solicitor on the client's behalf.

Example
May 1. Pay £2 by cheque on behalf of Jacob.
May 2. Send Jacob a bill charging him £40 costs.
May 9. Receive amount due from Jacob.

Jacob (CL5)								
		OFFICE ACCOUNT			CLIENT ACCOUNT			
		DR	CR	BALANCE	DR	CR	BALANCE	
May								
1	Cash	2		2				
2	Costs	40		42				
9	Cash		42	—				

31. *Exercises*

Show clients' ledger only.

(1) Deliver a bill to Harry for £60 costs. Receive payment.
(2) You act for Ian. Pay £50. Deliver a bill for £40 costs. Receive payment.
(3) You act for Joan. Pay £400. Deliver a bill for £650 costs. Receive payment.
(4) You act for Kate. Pay £80. Deliver a bill for £1,500 costs. Receive payment.

Chapter 13

TRANSFERS

A. BANK TRANSFERS—CLIENT ACCOUNT TO OFFICE ACCOUNT

1. It frequently becomes necessary to transfer a sum of money, which has been correctly paid into the Clients' Bank Account, into the Office Bank Account.

Example

(a) Receive £100 clients' money from A. B. Client.
(b) Send him a bill for £20 costs.

		A. B. Client (CL1)					
		OFFICE ACCOUNT			CLIENT ACCOUNT		
		DR	CR	BALANCE	DR	CR	BALANCE
(a)	Cash					100	100
(b)	Costs	20		20			

2. Rule 7 (SAR). A solicitor is entitled to utilise the clients' money held on A. B. Client's behalf for the payment of this bill. This can be done by Bank Transfer.

3. The Bank will transfer the £20 from the Client's Bank Account to the Office Bank Account, thus reducing the total balance of the former and increasing that of the latter.

Office Bank Account   *Clients' Bank Account*

£20   ←   £20

4. **The double-entries**
There are two steps:

(1) Payment of clients' money.
(2) Receipt of office money.

Step 1. Payment of clients' money
DEBIT ledger account of client—CLIENT ACCOUNT
CREDIT Cash Sheet—CLIENT ACCOUNT

Step 2. Receipt of office money
CREDIT ledger account of client—OFFICE ACCOUNT
DEBIT Cash Sheet—OFFICE ACCOUNT.

Step 1. Payment of clients' money

		OFFICE ACCOUNT			CLIENT ACCOUNT		
	A. B. Client (CL1)						
		DR	CR	BALANCE	DR	CR	BALANCE
(a)	Cash					100	100
(b)	Costs	20		20			
(c)	Cash Transfer				**20**		80

		OFFICE ACCOUNT			CLIENT ACCOUNT		
	Cash						
		DR	CR	BALANCE	DR	CR	BALANCE
(c)	A.B. Client Transfer					**20**	

Step 2. Receipt of office money

		OFFICE ACCOUNT			CLIENT ACCOUNT		
	A. B. Client (CL1)						
		DR	CR	BALANCE	DR	CR	BALANCE
(a)	Cash					100	100
(b)	Costs	20		20			
(c)	Cash Transfer		**20**	—	20		80

		OFFICE ACCOUNT			CLIENT ACCOUNT		
	Cash						
		DR	CR	BALANCE	DR	CR	BALANCE
(c)	A.B. Client Transfer	**20**				20	

5. *Exercises*

Show Cash Sheet and Clients' Ledger.

(1) You act for Alice. (a) Receive £100. (b) Deliver a bill for £20 costs. (c) Transfer the amount due.

(2) You act for Bill. (a) Receive £300. (b) Deliver a bill for £50 costs. (c) Transfer the amount due.

(3) You act for Charles. (a) Receive £600. (b) Pay cheque £70. (c) Deliver a bill for £80 costs. (d) Transfer the amount due.

(4) You act for Dennis. (a) Receive £90. (b) Pay petty cash £10. (c) Deliver a bill for £30 costs. (d) Transfer the amount due.

(5) You act for Ethel. (a) Receive £400. (b) Pay cheque £50. (c) Pay petty cash £6. (d) Deliver a bill for £70 costs. (e) Transfer the amount due.

(6) You act for Frances. (a) Receive £80. (b) Pay by cheque £10. (c) Pay petty cash £1. (d) Deliver a bill for £20 costs. (e) Transfer the amount due.

B. BANK TRANSFERS—OFFICE ACCOUNT TO CLIENT ACCOUNT

6. This becomes necessary where a solicitor has inadvertently committed a breach of the Rules by overdrawing sums held on behalf of a client.

Example 1
Receive £300 from A. B. Client.
Withdraw £400 from Clients' Bank Account on his behalf.

A. B. Client (CL1)							
		OFFICE ACCOUNT			CLIENT ACCOUNT		
		DR	CR	BALANCE	DR	CR	BALANCE
	Cash					300	300
	Cash				400		100 DR

7. IF THE LEDGER ACCOUNT—CLIENT ACCOUNT—HAS A DEBIT BALANCE, THE SOLICITOR HAS COMMITTED A BREACH OF THE RULES, which must be rectified immediately. This is done by withdrawing the appropriate amount from the Office Bank Account and paying it into the Clients' Bank Account. It can be done by a Bank Transfer.

8. The Bank will transfer £100 from the Office Bank Account to the Clients' Bank Account.

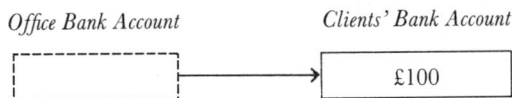

Office Bank Account → *Clients' Bank Account* £100

9. **The double-entries**
There are two steps:

(1) Payment of office money.
(2) Receipt of clients' money.

Step 1. Payment of Office Money
DEBIT ledger account of client—OFFICE ACCOUNT
CREDIT Cash Sheet—OFFICE ACCOUNT

Step 2. Receipt of Clients' Money
CREDIT ledger account of client—CLIENT ACCOUNT
DEBIT Cash Sheet—CLIENT ACCOUNT

Example

Step 1. Payment of Office Money

		OFFICE ACCOUNT			CLIENT ACCOUNT		
		A. B. Client (CL1)					
		DR	CR	BALANCE	DR	CR	BALANCE
	Cash					300	300
	Cash				400		100^{DR}
	Cash Transfer	**100**		100			

		OFFICE ACCOUNT			CLIENT ACCOUNT		
		Cash					
		DR	CR	BALANCE	DR	CR	BALANCE
	A.B. Client Transfer		**100**				

Step 2. Receipt of Clients' Money

		OFFICE ACCOUNT			CLIENT ACCOUNT		
		A. B. Client (CL1)					
		DR	CR	BALANCE	DR	CR	BALANCE
	Cash					300	300
	Cash				400		100^{DR}
	Cash Transfer	100		100		**100**	—

		OFFICE ACCOUNT			CLIENT ACCOUNT		
		Cash					
		DR	CR	BALANCE	DR	CR	BALANCE
	A.B. Client Transfer		100		**100**		

10. *Exercises*
  Show Cash Sheet and Clients' Ledger

  (1) You act for Graham. (a) Receive £40 clients' money. (b) Pay £50 clients' money. (c) Repair the breach.
  (2) You act for Henry. (a) Receive £700. (b) Pay £1,000 clients' money. (c) Repair the breach.
  (3) You act for Ian. (a) Receive £2,000. (b) Pay £2,500 clients' money. (c) Repair the breach.

C. LEDGER TRANSFERS

11. You act for two different clients: Barnaby and Laurence. You receive £600 from Laurence—clients' money.

Laurence							
		OFFICE ACCOUNT			CLIENT ACCOUNT		
		DR	CR	BALANCE	DR	CR	BALANCE
	Cash					600	600

12. You now receive instructions from Laurence to cease holding £500 of this sum on his behalf and to hold it on behalf of Barnaby. This needs a transfer between the two ledger accounts of the two clients.

13. *In the Bank* there is no movement of money at all. Contrast the other two types of transfer (Bank Transfers) where there was a movement of money between the bank accounts.

14. The Double-Entry is:
  DEBIT Laurence—CLIENT ACCOUNT
  CREDIT Barnaby—CLIENT ACCOUNT
  NOTE that there is *no* entry on any Cash Sheet.

15. Under Rule 11 SAR where clients' money is transferred from one client ledger to another client ledger account an entry must be made "in a record of sums transferred." This entry is in addition to the double-entry mentioned above. The way of achieving all the necessary entries is to use a special sheet. This sheet may be called a "Transfer Sheet." The Transfer Sheet is made up in a similar way to the ledger card.

(a) DEBIT the ledger account of the client *from whom* the money is being transferred. The computer will also record this on the Transfer Sheet.

Laurence (CL2)							
		OFFICE ACCOUNT			CLIENT ACCOUNT		
		DR	CR	BALANCE	DR	CR	BALANCE
	Cash					600	600
	Barnaby Transfer				**500**		ͺ100

Transfer Sheet							
		OFFICE ACCOUNT			CLIENT ACCOUNT		
		DR	CR	BALANCE	DR	CR	BALANCE
	Laurence				**500**		

(b) CREDIT the ledger account of the client *to whom* the money is being transferred. Again, the computer will record this on the Transfer Sheet.

Barnaby (CL3)							
		OFFICE ACCOUNT			CLIENT ACCOUNT		
		DR	CR	BALANCE	DR	CR	BALANCE
	Laurence Transfer					**500**	500

Transfer Sheet							
		OFFICE ACCOUNT			CLIENT ACCOUNT		
		DR	CR	BALANCE	DR	CR	BALANCE
	Laurence				500		100
	Barnaby					**500**	500

It should be noted that the double-entry consists of the entries made on the two client ledger cards (*i.e.* Laurence and Barnaby). The entries which appear on the Transfer Sheet are not in this case part of the double-entry at all. They are made in order to comply with Rule 11.

16. *Exercises*

Show Clients' Ledger.

(1) Receive £40 on behalf of John. Transfer £20 to Kevin's account.

(2) Receive £700 on behalf of Lesley. Transfer £400 to Mary's account.

(3) You act for Nick. (a) Receive £300. (b) Deliver a bill for £40 costs. (c) Pay £50 clients' money. (d) Transfer amount due to OFFICE ACCOUNT. (e) Transfer the balance of Clients' Money to the account of Olive—another client. Show Cash Sheet and Clients' Ledger.

(4) You act for Peter, on whose behalf you hold £10 clients' money. Transfer £5 to Robert's account. Transfer £7 to Robert's account—use clients' money and so break the Rules. Repair the breach. Show Cash Sheet and Clients' Ledger.

Chapter 14

REVISION EXERCISES

If possible, make all payments out of clients' money. If it is not possible to make the total payment out of clients' money make the total payment out of office money; do not make a payment partly out of clients' money and partly out of office money. Show Clients' Ledger.

(1) You act for Alice. Pay £300 (cheque). Receive £400. Receive £50. Pay £580 (cheque). Receive £800.

(2) You act for Barbara. Pay £50 (cheque). Deliver a bill (costs £40). Receive payment.

(3) You act for Carol. Pay £1 (cash). Pay £4 (cheque). Deliver a bill (costs £50). Receive payment.

(4) You act for Diana. Receive £100. Deliver a bill (costs £20). Transfer the amount due to OFFICE ACCOUNT from CLIENT ACCOUNT.

(5) You act for Ellen. Receive £200. Pay (cheque) £30. Deliver a bill (costs £40). Transfer the amount due.

(6) You act for Kate. Receive £300. Pay (cash) £4. Pay (cheque) £50. Pay (cheque) £600. Deliver a bill (costs £70). Transfer the amount due.

(7) You act for Mary. Receive £600. Transfer £70 to Sally's account (another client). Pay (cheque) £540. Receive £60. Transfer the amount due to OFFICE ACCOUNT. Show only Mary's account.

(8) You act for Penny. Pay (cheque) £50. Receive £400. Pay (cheque) £7. Pay (cash) £8. Deliver a bill (costs £200). Transfer the amount due to OFFICE ACCOUNT. Transfer the balance to Rachel's account (another client). Show only Penny's account.

Chapter 15

VALUE ADDED TAX

A. THE GENERAL LAW

1. *The charge to tax*

(a) VAT is charged when
   (i) a taxable person,
   (ii) in the course of furtherance of a business carried on by him,
   (iii) makes a taxable supply.

(b) All three conditions must be satisfied, so that no VAT is chargeable if
   (i) the person making the supply is not a taxable person, or
   (ii) the supply is not made in the course or furtherance of a business, or
   (iii) the supply is not taxable.

(c) Thus if a solicitor is a taxable person and in the course of his business he makes a taxable supply to another person (*e.g.* a client), the solicitor must charge that person with VAT. The supply made by the solicitor is called his OUTPUT and the tax charged is called OUTPUT TAX.

2. *Taxable person*

(a) He is a person who
   (i) is registered; or
   (ii) is required to register.

(b) A person is required to register if the value of his taxable supplies exceeds a certain annual figure (which is updated annually).

(c) This is an important definition. Supplies are classified for VAT purposes as being either Taxable or Exempt. In this case the relevant test is the number of Taxable outputs (or supplies) made by a solicitor in a year; any Exempt supplies are ignored. Another point to notice is that the legislation refers to the annual value of the solicitor's output (or turnover), not to his profit.

(d) The result is that a solicitor is taxable if
   (i) he is required to register (*i.e.* if taxable outputs exceed the annual figure) and he does register, or
   (ii) he does not need to register (*e.g.* his taxable outputs are of a small amount) but he has actually registered, or
   (iii) he ought to register (his taxable supplies exceed the annual figure) but he does not actually register.

3. *Business includes any trade, profession, or vocation*

This definition is similar to the definition of "business" for income tax purposes and the effect is that a solicitor's practice is caught by the definition. It is most unlikely that a solicitor will not be a registered person and thus when, in the course of his business, he makes a taxable supply to his clients he will have to charge them with VAT.

4. *Taxable supply*

(a) Any supply other than an exempt supply is taxable.

(b) Supplies may be divided into two categories, taxable and exempt. Taxable supplies may in turn be divided into two further categories: those taxable at the standard rate and those taxable at zero rate.

(c) Supplies taxable at the standard rate.
Basically any supply which is not taxable at zero rate and is not exempt will be taxable at the standard rate.

(d) Zero rate supplies include:
   (i) Books
   (ii) International services
   (iii) Transport.

(e) Exempt supplies include:
   (i) Insurance
   (ii) Postal services
   (iii) Burial and cremation
   (iv) Finance.
   The giving of tax advice is treated as the supply of legal services and not the supply of financial services with the result that it is taxable.

   If a solicitor arranges a loan for a client and makes a specific charge to the client for arranging and negotiating the loan, this is a supply of financial services (*i.e.* exempt).

   If a solicitor places money on deposit with a bank and later the bank pays the solicitor interest on such money, this is treated as a supply of finance by the solicitor to the bank for which the bank pays a fee (*i.e.* the interest) and this is an exempt supply (finance) by the solicitor to the bank.

(f) *Supply*
   (i) If the supplier is a taxable person he must charge VAT on any supply unless the supply is exempt. This will cover supplies of goods or services made by the solicitor in the course of his business, *e.g.* the giving of legal advice (supply of legal services). However, it is not only the supply of legal services which is caught but *ANY* supply made by the solicitor in the course of carrying on his business. Thus it will include the giving of other advice (not legal advice), or the disposal of a fixed asset, *e.g.* sale of an unwanted desk.
   (ii) The word "supply" includes sale, hire-purchase, hire, and exchange.

   Gift of goods
   A gift of goods is taxable but a gift of services is not a supply at all for VAT purposes. Thus if a solicitor makes a gift of goods to a client, VAT is chargeable, whereas if a solicitor performs a service for a client (*e.g.* drafts a will) and makes no charge, then no VAT is chargeable.

   Private use of goods
   If business goods are put to private use outside the business, this is treated as a taxable supply made by the solicitor, *e.g.* the solicitor

   a. uses an asset owned by the firm for private purposes, (*e.g.* takes a desk home),
   b. lends a business asset to a friend,
   c. allows an employee to use an asset of the firm over a weekend.

5. *Offices*

(a) Where a person in the course of carrying on a trade, profession or vocation, accepts any office, any services supplied by him as holder of the office are treated as supplied in the course of a business carried on by him.

(b) The situations in which this is relevant are where a solicitor
  (i) becomes the trustee of a trust, or
  (ii) becomes a director in a company.

(c) The test is whether the solicitor obtained the office as a result of carrying on his practice and it would seem most unlikely that the solicitor could avoid having to charge VAT except in the case of his own private family trusts or companies.

(d) A solicitor also has to charge VAT on oath fees.

6. *Input tax*

(a) In the same way that a solicitor charges output tax to clients on taxable supplies made by him, so too the solicitor is charged with and has to pay VAT on taxable supplies made to him by taxable persons. Thus a solicitor will have to pay VAT on his expenses and on any fixed asset bought by him, provided in both cases that the supply was a taxable supply and the supplier was a taxable person. The supply made to the solicitor is called his INPUT and the tax charged to the solicitor is called his INPUT TAX.

(b) A taxable person is entitled to a credit for input tax paid by him and to deduct that amount from any output tax which he has charged his customers, clients, etc.

(c) Each year is divided into four quarterly periods. At the end of each quarter, the solicitor must account to Customs & Excise for the total output tax in respect of supplies MADE by him less the total input tax in respect of supplies RECEIVED by him.

Illustration. In one quarter, you charge clients £100,000 costs plus VAT of £10,000. You disposed of a surplus machine for £100 plus £10 VAT. You paid, in respect of running expenses of the firm which were subject to VAT, £6,000 plus £600 VAT and bought a new machine for £2,000 plus £200 VAT.

OUTPUT TAX		£	£
	Costs	10,000	
	Machine	10	10,010
INPUT TAX			
	Expenses	600	
	New Machine	200	800
DUE TO CUSTOMS & EXCISE			9,190

(d) Zero-rated supplies.
A person who makes taxable supplies is entitled to deduct all input tax paid in the quarter. For this purpose it is unnecessary to distinguish between zero-rated supplies and standard rated supplies. If it so happens that in any quarter the figure for input tax exceeds the figure for output tax the supplier is entitled to a refund from Customs & Excise. This is likely to occur if a

supplier buys an extremely expensive fixed asset in one period and/or the supplier's outputs are wholly or mainly zero-rated supplies.
  (e) If a supplier makes only exempt supplies then he is not allowed to recover any input tax paid.
  (f) Disallowed inputs.
    In all cases, a supplier is not allowed to claim back any input tax in respect of the following purchases:
      (i) Motor cars;
      (ii) Business entertaining expenses except for reasonable entertainment of overseas customers.

7. *Partial exemption*

  (a) If a solicitor makes only taxable supplies, whether wholly standard or a mixture of standard and zero-rated supplies, he is allowed to deduct all his input tax from his output tax.
  (b) If a solicitor makes only exempt supplies, he is not allowed to deduct any input tax from his output tax.
  (c) If a solicitor makes partly taxable and partly exempt supplies, then he is "partially exempt."
  (d) *De Minimis*
    A partially exempt person may deduct all his input tax as if he only made taxable supplies provided that the value of his exempt supplies is small. In order to determine this there are several different tests, *e.g.* was the value of his exempt supplies less than £200 per month?
  (e) If the solicitor's exempt outputs are above the *de minimis* limit, he will be unable to deduct (and so recover) the total of the input tax which he has paid in a particular quarter. The amount of input tax which he can deduct is basically the proportion which his taxable outputs bear to his total outputs. Thus if, in one quarter, the outputs of a solicitor are made up of 75 per cent. exempt outputs and 25 per cent. taxable outputs then 75 per cent. of the solicitor's input tax is disallowed and he can only deduct 25 per cent. of his input tax from his total output tax.

  Illustration

  OUTPUTS (Excluding VAT)

EXEMPT $\frac{3}{4}$	7,500
TAXABLE $\frac{1}{4}$	2,500
	10,000

  INPUT TAX

TOTAL INPUT TAX	=	4,000
DISALLOWED $\frac{3}{4}$	=	3,000
DEDUCTIBLE $\frac{1}{4}$	=	1,000

  (f) It is, however, possible for a completely different method to be agreed on an individual basis between a business and Customs & Excise.

8. *Value of supply*
  Any price quoted by a supplier to a customer or client is deemed to include VAT unless the supplier makes it clear to the customer or client that the contrary is the case. Thus if a solicitor tells a client that the firm's charges are £100, then the solicitor will have to calculate that sum which, with the addition of VAT, equals £100.

9. *Time—the tax point*

When a solicitor charges a client with VAT, the VAT becomes a debt payable by the client to the solicitor. Similarly the solicitor has to account to Customs & Excise for the VAT and this is a debt owed by the solicitor to Customs & Excise. The importance of deciding the tax point in a transaction is that it fixes the time at which the debt arises between the client and the solicitor, and also the date at which the debt arises between the solicitor and Customs & Excise. Thus if a solicitor is charging a client with £10 VAT, once the tax point has arisen this £10 becomes a debt payable by the client to the solicitor; in turn the solicitor now owes a debt of £10 to Customs & Excise, which the solicitor will have to pay to Customs & Excise at the end of the accounting quarter, subject to any right to deduct and set off input tax.

The rules for determining the timing of the tax point are complex. If a supplier is supplying goods the basic tax point is the date when the goods are made available to the purchaser. A solicitor, however, does not supply goods but services. The basic tax point with services is the time when the services are completed. In practice this is almost impossible to identify. Fortunately, however, there are three alternative tax points.

The first of these is where the supplier issues a tax invoice to the customer or client before the basic tax point arises and the second is where the supplier issues a tax invoice within 14 days after the basic tax point. In the case of solicitors, Customs & Excise have approved a general extension of the 14-day period to 3 months. The effect is that if a solicitor issues a tax invoice to the client at any time during the transaction or within 3 months after the transaction has ended, then the date of the tax invoice will be the tax point.

The third exception is that where a supplier receives payment before the basic tax point arises, then the date that the supplier receives payment is treated as the tax point.

If therefore a solicitor sends all clients a tax invoice at the time of making a charge to them this will fix the tax point as at the date of that invoice. If, however, no tax invoice is sent then the tax point will be the date when the solicitor receives payment.

If there is a continuous supply of services (*e.g.* a solicitor does work for a trust which is billed on a regular basis) the tax point will be the date of each tax invoice or the date when the solicitor receives payment, whichever is the earlier.

10. *VAT invoices*

The VAT invoice is the centrepiece of the administrative system. Whenever a taxable person makes a taxable supply (and so charges VAT) to another taxable person, the supplier must provide the customer or client with a tax invoice within 30 days after the time of the supply. One of the reasons for this is that a taxable person is not allowed to claim a credit in respect of input tax unless he is in possession of a tax invoice addressed to him charging him with the VAT. It should be noticed that there is no obligation to give a tax invoice to a customer or client who is not a taxable person.

Thus a solicitor's firm should ensure that when it is charged with VAT in respect of any supplies to the firm, a tax invoice is received and the original carefully preserved. So far as concerns the outputs of a solicitor's firm, to comply with the law the firm only needs to issue a tax invoice to those clients who are taxable persons and who could claim a tax credit in respect of the VAT charged to them. Having a system where some clients are issued with a tax invoice and some are not could cause administrative difficulties and therefore it may prove simpler to issue all clients with a VAT invoice whether or not they are taxable persons. In addition, if a VAT invoice is issued it will fix the tax point (see above). Finally, a carbon of the VAT invoice should be retained; this carbon will provide evidence of the firm's outputs to substantiate the tax return made to Customs & Excise at the end of the quarter.

VAT invoices must show the following information:

(a) An identifying number.
(b) The solicitor's name, address and VAT registration number.
(c) The time of supply.
(d) The client's name and address.
(e) The type of supply.
(f) A description which identifies the services supplied.
(g) The total charge made, excluding VAT.
(h) The rate of any cash discount offered.
(i) The total VAT payable.

When a solicitor sends a tax invoice to a client the solicitor should describe the type of supply as: "supply of legal services."

11. *Records*

A taxable person must keep records of all transactions connected with his business which affect his tax position and enable him to complete his tax return. Thus a taxable person must keep

(a) a record of all taxable goods and services *received*, both standard and zero-rated supplies, but not exempt supplies.
(b) a record of all supplies *made*, whether standard-rated, zero-rated, or exempt.

If, therefore, the solicitor issues tax invoices in respect of all supplies made by him and keeps a carbon of that invoice, then these carbons will be sufficient records of all the solicitor's outputs, whether taxable or exempt. Similarly in respect of taxable inputs the solicitor should obtain and keep all invoices received. Note that to "issue" a tax invoice, the supplier must give or send it to the customer or client; it is not sufficient simply to prepare it.

At the end of each quarter, a taxable person must make a return not later than one month after the end of the quarter. Before preparing the VAT return the supplier must summarise his records in a "VAT Account" showing

(a) total output tax for the period;
(b) total input tax for the period;
(c) the balance, whether tax payable or tax reclaimed.

B. BASIC ENTRIES

12. When a trader buys and sells goods which are subject to VAT the tax (input or output) is generally recorded, separately from the value of the goods, on an account called "The Customs and Excise Account" or "VAT Account." Thus, if the trader buys goods from A Supplier for £50 plus £5 VAT the entries are:

DEBIT Purchases Account with the value (tax exclusive) of the purchase.
DEBIT Customs & Excise Account with the VAT—input tax.
CREDIT A Supplier with the total (inclusive of VAT).

Example

Purchases		A Supplier	
A Supplier 50		Purchases 50	
		VAT 5	

Customs & Excise	
A Supplier 5	

Similarly, if the trader sells goods to A Customer for £60 plus £6 VAT, the entries are:

CREDIT Sales Account with the value (tax exclusive) of the sale.
CREDIT Customs and Excise Account with the VAT—output tax.
DEBIT A Customer with total (tax inclusive).

Example

Sales		A Customer	
	A Customer 60	Sales 60	
		VAT 6	

Customs & Excise	
	A Customer 6

13. The Customs and Excise Account records the VAT *whenever there is an input or an output* for tax purposes.

(a) Input Tax—DEBIT the Customs and Excise Account.
(b) Output Tax—CREDIT the Customs and Excise Account.

In a solicitor's accounts the Customs and Excise Account is kept in the Nominal Ledger, *i.e.* OFFICE ACCOUNT. *There is no Customs and Excise Account in CLIENT ACCOUNT.*

14. **Inputs**
These arise when a solicitor pays for something (*e.g.* an expense) which is subject to VAT.

DEBIT the appropriate ledger account with the tax exclusive amount.
DEBIT Customs and Excise Account with the VAT—input tax.
CREDIT Cash Sheet—OFFICE ACCOUNT—with total payment.

Example
Pay for stationery £8 plus 80p VAT.

Stationery (NL9)				
		DR	CR	BALANCE
Cash		8–		

Customs & Excise (NL11)				
		DR	CR	BALANCE
Cash Stationery		0–80		

		OFFICE ACCOUNT			CLIENT ACCOUNT		
		DR	CR	BALANCE	DR	CR	BALANCE
	Stationery		8				
	VAT		0–80				

Cash

15. If on making a payment, no input tax deduction is claimed, no entry is made on the Customs and Excise Account and the relevant ledger account is debited with the total payment.

Example (a)
Pay rates £160. There is no VAT on rates.

		DR	CR	BALANCE
	Cash	160–		

Rates (NL7)

Example (b)
Pay £5,500 for a new motor car plus £550 VAT. The input tax on this is disallowed.

		DR	CR	BALANCE
	Cash	6,050–		

Motor Cars (NL21)

16. *Exercises*

(1) Pay £50 plus £5 VAT on telephone bills. Pay £40 plus £4 VAT for type-writer. Pay £30 plus £3 VAT on stationery.

(2) Pay £5 on train fare, pay £4 on postage stamps, pay £10 on water rates, pay £8 interest on bank loan. There is no input tax payable in respect of any of these items. Pay £7 plus 70p VAT for entertaining a client—the VAT is disallowed as an input.

17. *Outputs*

A solicitor normally has a tax point for output tax when he sends a bill to a client charging the client with the costs.

Example

Charge A. B. Client £70 costs.

		A. B. Client (CL1)					
		OFFICE ACCOUNT			CLIENT ACCOUNT		
		DR	CR	BALANCE	DR	CR	BALANCE
	Costs	70–		70–			

18. The double-entry for the VAT is:

DEBIT the ledger account of client—OFFICE ACCOUNT
CREDIT Customs and Excise Account.

Example

Record the VAT output tax of £7.

		A. B. Client (CL1)					
		OFFICE ACCOUNT			CLIENT ACCOUNT		
		DR	CR	BALANCE	DR	CR	BALANCE
	Costs	70–					
	VAT	7–		77–			

	Customs & Excise (NL11)			
		DR	CR	BALANCE
	A. B. Client		7–	

C. PAYMENTS ON BEHALF OF A CLIENT—METHODS OF TREATMENT

19. During the course of a transaction, a solicitor often makes payments on behalf of a client and obtains re-imbursement from the client usually at a later date. These payments may be:

(a) *taxable* (*i.e.* when the solicitor makes the payment it is subject to VAT, *e.g.* counsel's fees); or

(b) *non-taxable* (*i.e.* not subject to VAT, *e.g.* court fees).

20. For VAT purposes, there are two ways of dealing with such payments:

(a) the Principal Method

(b) the Agency Method.

(a) *The Principal Method*

In this case, the original supplier is deemed to supply the goods or services to the solicitor. The solicitor is then deemed to supply the goods or services to the client. Thus, if the relevant item involved the purchase of tools, the ironmonger would be deemed to sell the tools to the solicitor who would be deemed to resell them to the client.

(b) *The Agency Method*

In this case, the original supplier is deemed to supply the goods or services direct to the client. All the solicitor does is to pay the supplier's bill on the client's behalf. Thus, the ironmonger would be deemed to sell the tools direct to the client. The solicitor merely pays the ironmonger's bill (as the client's agent) and gets re-imbursement from the client.

21. **Non-taxable payments**

An item is subject to VAT if a taxable person in the course of his business makes a taxable supply. Thus, a payment made by a solicitor will not be taxable in any one of the three following cases:

(a) Supply to the solicitor by an *unregistered supplier* (*i.e.* not registered for VAT).

(b) Supply to the solicitor by a supplier but supplied *not in the course of the business*.

(c) Supply to the solicitor of an *exempt supply*.

If the solicitor adopted the Principal Method for (a) or (b) above, the solicitor would not pay VAT to the supplier but when he claimed re-imbursement from the client he would have to charge the client with VAT. This is because the solicitor would be a taxable person who would make a taxable supply in the course of his business.

Example

An unregistered supplier supplies services to you for £150—no VAT (supplier not registered). You now, in turn, re-sell the services to the client for £150. You must add VAT, *i.e.* the total amount due from the client would be £150 plus VAT £15 = £165.

If the solicitor adopted the Agency Method, the solicitor would pay no VAT to the supplier and would merely claim re-imbursement of the sum paid on behalf of the client.

Example

As above. You would pay the supplier £150 and would obtain re-imbursement of this sum only (no VAT) from the client.

In either event then the solicitor ought to use the Agency Method and not the Principal Method so as to save the client money.

With item (c)—an exempt supply—if the solicitor adopted the Principal Method the solicitor would pay no VAT to the supplier but, this time, when claiming re-imbursement from the client would not have to charge VAT. Although a taxable person and in business, the solicitor is now making an *exempt supply* to the client. This does, however, mean that the solicitor has an output for VAT purposes and it is an exempt one. Because of the system for disallowing a proportion of input tax as a deduction from output tax in respect of partially exempt traders, it is in the solicitor's interest to avoid exempt outputs as far as possible. If the Agency Method is used, the solicitor has no input or output (the supply is deemed to be made direct to the client) and so the solicitor again always ought to use the Agency Method. Customs & Excise permit solicitors to treat payments on an agency basis provided certain conditions are satisfied, namely:

(a) the solicitor acted as the agent of the client when paying the third party; and
(b) the client actually received and used the services provided by the third party (this condition usually prevents the solicitor's own travelling and subsistence expenses, telephone bills, postage, and other payments being treated on the agency basis) (see *post*, page 158)); and
(c) the client was responsible for paying the third party; and
(d) the client authorised the solicitor to make the payment on his behalf; and
(e) the client knew that the services paid by the solicitor would be provided by a third party; and
(f) the outlay is separately itemised when the solicitor invoices the client; and
(g) the solicitor recovers only the exact amount paid to the third party; and
(h) the services which the solicitor pays for are clearly additional to the supplies which the solicitor makes to the client.

In most cases, there should be no problem with treating payments made to third parties as being made as the agent of the client; the solicitor will be able to debit the client with the precise amounts paid out and to exclude these amounts when calculating any VAT due on the solicitor's supply to the client. (It should be noticed that if a solicitor treats a payment on the agency basis, the solicitor must keep evidence (such as a copy invoice) to enable the solicitor to show that he was entitled to exclude the payment from the value of his own supplies to the client.) However, it is sometimes the practice for all or some of the costs incidental to a supply to the client, such as travelling expenses, to be treated as disbursements and shown or charged separately on the bill/invoice issued to the client. Thus sometimes solicitors send bills to clients showing their profit costs (or fees) and under "Disbursements" list items such as "Postages, fares, and telephone calls."

Illustration	£
COSTS	100
DISBURSEMENTS	
Postages and fares	20
	120

Where these costs have been incurred by the solicitor in the course of making his own supply to the client, they must be included in the value of that supply when VAT is calculated, with the result that VAT will be charged on the total amount including those incidental costs (see *post*, page 158).

22. CONCLUSION

With non-taxable payments always use the Agency Method, except for incidental costs, *e.g.* postages, fares, and telephones.

23. Taxable payments—Agency Method

A feature of the VAT system is that a registered supplier can claim a deduction for input tax if he has a tax invoice *addressed to him* charging him with VAT. Thus, if a solicitor receives a tax invoice from a supplier, which tax invoice is addressed to the client, the solicitor will be unable to claim any input tax deduction in respect of VAT. In such a case if the solicitor decided to use the Principal Method, although he would not be able to claim any input tax deduction because the tax invoice was not addressed to him, the solicitor would still have an output for VAT purposes and have to charge the client VAT. The Principal Method is thus inappropriate and the solicitor should always use the Agency Method.

24. Taxable payments—Principal Method

When a solicitor receives a tax invoice from a supplier addressed to him, the client is unable to claim any input tax deduction in respect of it (the invoice being addressed to the solicitor). If the solicitor used the Agency Method in such a case, the solicitor would also be unable to claim the input tax as a deduction. If, however, he used the Principal Method, the solicitor would claim an input tax deduction when paying the supplier, and he would then have an output (with output tax) when charging the client. He would now have to send his own tax invoice for the item resold to the client, which invoice would be addressed to the client, and thus the client in an appropriate case could now claim a deduction for the VAT.

Example

Supplier sends you a bill for £250 plus VAT (*i.e.* a total of £275). You pay the supplier and claim £25 input tax deduction. You then charge the client with the item: £250 plus VAT (*i.e.* £275). This means you have an output of £25 and send the client a tax invoice in respect of it.

If the supply to the client was in respect of the client's business, *e.g.* collection of bad debts, and the client is a taxable person, he will want to claim the input tax deduction in respect of it. In such a case, therefore, the Principal Method must be used. In order to avoid any problems of classification and to achieve a uniform practice, it is suggested that the solicitor should always use the Principal Method where the supplier's invoice is addressed to the solicitor. In addition, before the Agency Method could be used the eight conditions set out in paragraph 21, above, would have to be satisfied. Finally, the solicitor must keep evidence not only to show that he was entitled to exclude the payment from the value of his own supplies to the client, but also to show that he did not reclaim input tax on the supply by the third party. This would probably be administratively very difficult to do if he did not use the Agency Method in such cases.

25. CONCLUSION

If the supplier's tax invoice is addressed to the *client*, use the *Agency Method*.
If the supplier's tax invoice is addressed to the *solicitor*, use the *Principal Method*.

D. PAYMENTS—DOUBLE ENTRIES—INPUTS

26. Non-taxable payments

(a) Method of treatment: Agency Method.
(b) Office or clients' money may be used.

(c) DEBIT ledger account or card of client—OFFICE or CLIENT ACCOUNT, as appropriate.
(d) CREDIT the Cash Sheet.

Example
Pay court fees £7 on behalf of A. B. Client.

		OFFICE ACCOUNT			CLIENT ACCOUNT		
		DR	CR	BALANCE	DR	CR	BALANCE
	Cash Court fees	7–		7–			

A. B. Client (CL1)

The credit entry will appear on the Cash Sheet.

27. Taxable payments. Supplier's invoice addressed to client

(a) Method of treatment: Agency Method.
(b) Office or clients' money may be used.
(c) DEBIT ledger account or card of client—OFFICE or CLIENT ACCOUNT, as appropriate—with TOTAL PAYMENT. There is no entry on the Customs & Excise Account because on the Agency Method the solicitor is not claiming any input.
(d) CREDIT the Cash Sheet.

Example
Pay surveyor's fee £40 plus VAT, Agency Method, on behalf of A. B. Client.

		OFFICE ACCOUNT			CLIENT ACCOUNT		
		DR	CR	BALANCE	DR	CR	BALANCE
	Cash Survey fee	44–		44–			

A. B. Client (CL1)

The credit entry will appear on the Cash Sheet.

28. Taxable payments. Invoice to solicitor

(a) Method of treatment: Principal Method.
(b) OFFICE MONEY ONLY MUST BE USED. Since the solicitor is using the Principal Method his business will be claiming the deduction for the input tax. This is clearly a matter for OFFICE ACCOUNT only and CLIENT ACCOUNT is not concerned in any way. (See also note (d) below.)
(c) DEBIT the ledger account of the client—OFFICE ACCOUNT—with the tax exclusive amount.
(d) DEBIT the VAT on the Customs and Excise Account. This debit is in respect of the input tax, which the solicitor will be claiming as a deduction

against his output tax. The Customs and Excise Account exists in OFFICE ACCOUNT only and this is another reason why clients' money and CLIENT ACCOUNT could not be used. The solicitor could not credit the Cash Sheet—CLIENT ACCOUNT—and debit the VAT in an Office Ledger Account.

(e) CREDIT Cash Sheet—OFFICE ACCOUNT—with total payment.

Example

Pay counsel's fee £90 plus VAT, Principal Method, on behalf of A. B. Client.

	A. B. Client (CL1)						
		OFFICE ACCOUNT			CLIENT ACCOUNT		
		DR	CR	BALANCE	DR	CR	BALANCE
Cash Counsel		90–					

	Customs & Excise (NL11)			
		DR	CR	BALANCE
Cash		9–		

	Cash						
		OFFICE ACCOUNT			CLIENT ACCOUNT		
		DR	CR	BALANCE	DR	CR	BALANCE
A. B. Client			90				
VAT			9				

(f) When a taxable payment is made using the Principal Method, the client would have to be charged with the VAT at the appropriate time. His ledger account at present fails to show the VAT and thus it is helpful to make some note in the details column (*e.g.* "VAT" is written in). This should be done on the ledger account of the client but only in respect of a taxable payment when the Principal Method is used.

29. *Exercises*

(1) Make the following payments on Adam's behalf. Use the Principal Method.
Pay by cheque £1 plus VAT.
Pay by cheque £2 plus VAT.
Pay Petty Cash £3 plus VAT.
Pay cheque £4 plus VAT.
Pay Petty Cash £5 plus VAT.

(2) Repeat exercise (1) using the Agency Method.
(3) Make the following payments on Bill's behalf:
   Pay cheque £1 plus VAT—Principal Method.
   Pay cheque £2 plus VAT—Agency Method.
   Pay cash £3 plus VAT—Principal Method.
   Pay cash £4 plus VAT—Agency Method.
   Pay cheque £5 plus VAT—Principal Method.
(4) You act for Carol. Receive £400 clients' money.
   Pay (cheque) £50 plus VAT—Principal Method.
   Pay (cheque) £40 plus VAT—Agency Method.
   Pay £30 no VAT.
(5) You act for Dick. Receive £700.
   Pay (cheque) £100 no VAT.
   Pay (cheque) £20 plus VAT—Principal Method.
   Pay (Petty Cash) £8 no VAT.
   Pay (cheque) £60 plus VAT—Agency Method.
   Pay (Petty Cash) £4 plus VAT—Principal Method.
(6) You act for Edward. Receive £600.
   Pay (cheque) £400 plus VAT—Agency Method.
   Pay (Petty Cash) £3 no VAT.
   Pay (cheque) £150 no VAT.
   Pay (cheque) £10 plus VAT—Principal Method.
   Pay (cheque) £50 no VAT.

E. OUTPUT ENTRIES

30. At the time of the tax point for output tax,[1] the solicitor ought to make entries to record the VAT.

31. An entry can be made in the "Bills Delivered Book" but the simplest system is merely to file a copy of the tax invoice (as with profit costs when filing the bill was sufficient).[2]

32. DEBIT the ledger account or card of the client in the Clients' Ledger—OFFICE ACCOUNT.

33. CREDIT the Customs and Excise Account with the TOTAL VAT output tax.

Example
March 5: Deliver a bill to Violet for £160 plus VAT.

		OFFICE ACCOUNT			CLIENT ACCOUNT		
		DR	CR	BALANCE	DR	CR	BALANCE
Mar 5	Costs	160–*					
	VAT	**16–**		176–			

Violet (CL4)

* The credit entry appears on the Costs Account.

[1] See *post*, p. 131.
[2] In some firms it is the practice not to send the clients a tax invoice, except on request. The entries must, however, still be made.

Customs & Excise (NL11)				
		DR	CR	BALANCE
Mar 5	Violet		**16–**	

34. *Exercises*

Show Clients' Ledger only.

(1) Deliver a bill to Fred for £70 costs plus VAT. Receive payment.
(2) Deliver a bill to George for £90 costs plus VAT. Receive payment.
(3) You act for Harold. Pay £40 no VAT. Deliver a bill for £60 costs plus VAT. Receive payment.
(4) You act for Ian. Pay £80 no VAT. Deliver a bill for £120 costs plus VAT £12. Receive payment.

35. The amount of VAT to be debited to the ledger account of a client is the total output tax on the transaction. This is not simply the VAT on the profit costs but the VAT on *all the solicitor's outputs, i.e.*:

(a) The Profit Costs
   plus
(b) Taxable payments made on the Principal Method on the client's behalf.

36. *Example*

You act for A. B. Client.

(a) Pay £4, no VAT, by cheque.
(b) Pay £80 plus VAT by cheque, Principal Method.
(c) Deliver a bill, which includes a charge for costs of £160 plus VAT.
(d) Receive amount due from A. B. Client.

		A. B. Client (CL1)					
		OFFICE ACCOUNT			CLIENT ACCOUNT		
		DR	CR	BALANCE	DR	CR	BALANCE
(a)	Cash	4–		4–			
(b)	Cash VAT	80–		84–			
(c)	Costs	160					
	VAT	24–*		268–			
(d)	Cash. You		268–	—			

   * Taxable outputs are: Costs £160 plus taxable payment £80 = £240 @ 10% = £24.

37. *Exercises*

(1) You act for Jane. On her behalf pay by cheque £10 plus VAT—Principal Method. Deliver a bill for £60 costs plus VAT. Receive the amount due.

(2) You act for Kate. Pay cheque £20 plus VAT—Principal Method. Deliver a bill for £70 costs plus VAT. Receive the amount due.

(3) You act for Lucy. Pay cheque £3 plus VAT—Principal Method. Deliver a bill for £80 costs plus VAT. Receive the amount due.

(4) You act for Mary. Pay cheque £20 no VAT. Pay cheque £30 plus VAT—Principal Method. Deliver a bill for £40 plus VAT. Receive the amount due.

(5) You act for Nancy. Pay cheque £90 plus VAT—Principal Method. Pay cash £10 no VAT. Deliver a bill for £20 plus VAT. Receive the amount due.

(6) You act for Olivia. Pay cheque £1 no VAT. Pay cheque £20 plus VAT—Principal Method. Pay cash £3 plus VAT—Principal Method. Pay cash £4 no VAT. Deliver a bill for £50 plus VAT. Receive the amount due.

F. THE TIMING OF THE TAX POINT—OUTPUT

38. The normal tax point for the solicitor's output is the date of the bill. Thus, along with the bill, the solicitor should send the client a tax invoice,[3] which will include all the taxable outputs in the transaction, *i.e.*:

(a) profit costs
  plus
(b) Principal Method taxable payments.

39. If a solicitor receives a tax invoice in his favour for an item from a supplier (*i.e.* the solicitor is to use the Principal Method) and the client is charged for the item in the bill before the solicitor pays the supplier, the tax point for the output is still the date of the bill. Thus, even though not paid, the item should be included on the tax invoice and the client debited with the VAT.

Example:
June 1: Receive supplier's invoice for £50 plus VAT in respect of A. B. Client.
June 2: Send client a bill including costs £60 plus the £50 item plus VAT.

		A. B. Client (CL1)					
		OFFICE ACCOUNT			CLIENT ACCOUNT		
		DR	CR	BALANCE	DR	CR	BALANCE
Jun 2	Costs	60–					
	VAT	11–		71–			

NOTE that only the input TAX is debited at this time. The payment (tax exclusive) of £50 is debited when actually paid.

Example (contd.)
June 7: Receive the amount due from A. B. Client (*i.e.* £121).
June 8: Pay supplier.
June 9: Transfer to OFFICE ACCOUNT the amount due.

---

[3] In some firms it may prove practical not to send tax invoices to clients except on request.

A. B. Client (CL1)							
		OFFICE ACCOUNT			CLIENT ACCOUNT		
		DR	CR	BALANCE	DR	CR	BALANCE
Jun							
2	Costs	60–					
	VAT	11–		71–			
7	Cash. You.					121–	121–
8	Cash.						
	Supplier	50		121			
	VAT						
9	Cash.						
	Transfer		121–	—	121–		—

Cash							
		OFFICE ACCOUNT			CLIENT ACCOUNT		
		DR	CR	BALANCE	DR	CR	BALANCE
Jun							
7	A. B. Client				121		
8	A. B. Client		50				
	Supplier		5*				
	VAT						
9	A. B. Client						
	Transfer	121				121	

* The debit entry appears in Customs and Excise Account.

40. Very exceptionally a tax point for the output occurs before the bill (and invoice) is sent to the client. This is where there is a receipt of *office money* in respect of a taxable output, and is most likely to occur when a taxable payment is made on behalf of a client using the Principal Method. If the solicitor obtains reimbursement from the client before sending him the bill (and the requisite invoice) the receipt from the client is office money (Rule 9(2) (SAR)) and the date thereof is the tax point.

Example
You hold £500 clients' money on behalf of A. B. Client. You make a payment on his behalf of £40 plus VAT using the Principal Method, *i.e.* payment is made out of office money. You then transfer the requisite amount from the Clients' Bank Account to the Office Bank Account. This receipt by the OFFICE ACCOUNT constitutes the tax point.

In such a case in order to avoid a breach of the Rules or any VAT Regulation the following steps are advised:

(i) Send a client a tax invoice[4] in respect of the particular item and file the carbon.
(ii) Make the double-entry for the tax output, *i.e.*

DEBIT ledger account of client—OFFICE ACCOUNT
CREDIT the Customs and Excise Account

(iii) Record the receipt from the client, *i.e.*

CREDIT ledger account of client—OFFICE ACCOUNT
DEBIT Cash Sheet—OFFICE ACCOUNT.

Example
May 1: Receive £500 clients' money on behalf of A. B. Client.
May 2: Pay supplier £40 plus VAT—Principal Method.
May 3: Send A. B. Client invoice and debit his account with the VAT.

A. B. Client (CL1)							
		OFFICE ACCOUNT			CLIENT ACCOUNT		
		DR	CR	BALANCE	DR	CR	BALANCE
May							
1	Cash. You.					500–	500–
2	Cash.						
	Supplier						
	VAT	40		40			
3	VAT	**4**		44			

Cash							
		OFFICE ACCOUNT			CLIENT ACCOUNT		
		DR	CR	BALANCE	DR	CR	BALANCE
May							
1	A. B. Client				500		
2	A. B. Client		40				
	Supplier						
	VAT		4				

---

[4] This step is necessary if the firm's practice is to send all clients tax invoices automatically and without request.

Customs & Excise (NL11)		DR	CR	BALANCE
		DR	CR	BALANCE
May 2	Cash	4		
3	A. B. Client		**4**	

NOTE that now you are quite safe in receiving in the office bank account full reimbursement *including the VAT.*

Example (contd.)
May 4: Transfer to office account the amount due.

A. B. Client (CL1)							
		OFFICE ACCOUNT			CLIENT ACCOUNT		
		DR	CR	BALANCE	DR	CR	BALANCE
May 1	Cash. You.					400–	400–
2	Cash. Supplier VAT	40–		40–			
3	VAT	4–		44–			
4	Cash. Transfer		**44–**	—	**44–**		356–

41. This is not the only method of dealing with such an item but it is probably the safest.

42. SUMMARY
What to watch for:

    1. You make a Taxable Payment using the Principal Method.
    2. You receive office money in reimbursement (all or part) either direct from the client or by transfer from CLIENT ACCOUNT before billing the client.

What to do:

    1. Record the output tax in the accounts, *i.e.* debit the client, etc.
    2. Record the receipt of office money.

43. *Exercises. Show Clients' Ledger*

    (1) You act for Peter. Pay (cheque) £100 plus VAT (Principal Method). Receive reimbursement from Humphrey.
    (2) You act for Rachel. May 1: Receive £800. May 2: Pay (cheque) £300 plus VAT—Principal Method. May 3: Transfer amount due to OFFICE ACCOUNT.
    (3) You act for Stephen. July 1: Pay (cheque) £80 plus VAT—Principal Method. July 5: Receive £700 from Stephen. July 6: Pay (cheque) £60 plus VAT (Principal Method). July 8: Transfer to OFFICE ACCOUNT.

Chapter 16

MISCELLANEOUS POSTINGS

A. ABATEMENTS

1. (a) Sometimes, after a bill has been sent to a client, the charge for profit costs is reduced. If this is so, a reduction will also be made in the VAT charge.

Example
A. B. Client is charged £200 costs plus VAT (£220). Later, the bill is reduced by £30 plus VAT (£33), *i.e.* balance due £187.

(b) When a reduction is made, send the client a CREDIT NOTE showing:
(i) the reduction exclusive of tax;
(ii) the rate and amount of tax;
(iii) the total of the reduction.
This negatives the VAT invoice previously sent in respect of the amount reduced.[1]

(c) A preliminary entry for the abatement can be made in a number of ways, *e.g.*
(i) by entry in a formal Abatements and Allowances Book or
(ii) by filing a copy of the credit note in an informal Abatements Book.

(d) **Posting to the accounts**
The entries are the reverse of those for charging costs when a bill is delivered. All the entries are in OFFICE ACCOUNT.
(i) The reduction—excluding VAT.

CREDIT the ledger account of the client.
DEBIT the Costs Account.
(ii) VAT.

CREDIT the ledger account of the client.
DEBIT the Customs and Excise Account.

---

[1] If the firm's practice is not to send VAT invoices except when requested, the credit note is only necessary where a tax invoice has previously been sent.

Example

January 2: You act for Barnaby. Deliver a bill for £200 plus VAT.
January 5: Reduce Barnaby's bill by £30 plus VAT.

Barnaby (CL3)								
		OFFICE ACCOUNT			CLIENT ACCOUNT			
		DR	CR	BALANCE	DR	CR	BALANCE	
Jan 2	Costs	200–						
	VAT	20–		220–				
5	Abatement		**30–**					
	VAT		**3–**	187–				

Costs				
		OFFICE ACCOUNT		
		DR	CR	BALANCE
Jan 2	Barnaby		200–	
5	Barnaby	**30–**		

Customs & Excise (NL11)				
		DR	CR	BALANCE
Jan 2	Barnaby		20–	
5	Barnaby	**3–**		

B. BAD DEBTS

2. (a) If an amount owing from a client is written off, in general the whole sum INCLUDING VAT is written off; there is no tax credit.

Example

A. B. Client owes the firm £44 (costs £40, VAT £4), which is to be written off.

(b) CREDIT the ledger account of the client—OFFICE ACCOUNT
(c) DEBIT Bad Debts Account

Example

A. B. Client (CL1)							
		OFFICE ACCOUNT			CLIENT ACCOUNT		
		DR	CR	BALANCE	DR	CR	BALANCE
Dec 31	Balance	44—		44—			
Jan 5	Bad Debts		**44—**				

Bad Debts (NL6)				
		DR	CR	BALANCE
Jan 5	A. B. Client	**44—**		44—

(d) Sometimes there may be a tax credit for the bad debt,[2] in which case the entries are:

CREDIT the ledger account of the client—OFFICE ACCOUNT—with the TOTAL.

DEBIT Bad Debts Account with the TAX EXCLUSIVE amount

DEBIT Customs and Excise Account with the VAT

Example

A. B. Client (CL1)							
		OFFICE ACCOUNT			CLIENT ACCOUNT		
		DR	CR	BALANCE	DR	CR	BALANCE
Dec 31	Balance	44—		44—			
Jan 5	Bad Debts		**40—**				
	VAT		**4—**				

[2] At the time of writing, the tax credit is allowed if the debtor is an individual and is adjudged bankrupt, or a deed of arrangement is made for the benefit of his creditors, or a composition or a scheme proposed by him is approved under Chapter 1 of Part III Insolvency Act 1985 or, after his death, his estate falls to be administered in accordance with an order under Part IV of that Act. If the debtor is a company and goes into liquidation at a time when its assets are insufficient to pay its debts or a person who has been appointed to act as its administrator issues a certificate that, if it went into liquidation, the assets would be insufficient to pay the company's debts the tax credit is also allowed (Value Added Tax Act 1983, s.22).

Bad Debts (NL6)		DR	CR	BALANCE
Jan 5	A. B. Client	**40–**		

Customs & Excise (NL11)		DR	CR	BALANCE
Jan 5	A. B. Client	**4–**		

C. SPLITTING

3. (a) Sometimes a cheque is received comprising partly clients' money and partly office money—a composite cheque. In such a case either:
   (i) split the cheque, *i.e.* pay the clients' money portion into the Clients' Bank Account, and the office money portion into the Office Bank Account; or
   (ii) pay the whole cheque into the Clients' Bank Account and then transfer the office money from the Clients' Bank Account to the Office Bank Account.

 (b) DO NOT PAY THE WHOLE CHEQUE INTO THE OFFICE BANK ACCOUNT AND THEN TRANSFER THE CLIENTS' MONEY TO THE CLIENTS' BANK ACCOUNT.
 (c) *Double-entries if cheque is "split"*
   (i) CREDIT ledger account of client—CLIENT ACCOUNT—with the clients' money
   DEBIT Cash Account—CLIENT ACCOUNT—with the clients' money
   (ii) CREDIT ledger account of the client—OFFICE ACCOUNT—with the office money
   DEBIT Cash Account—OFFICE ACCOUNT—with the office money

Example
Laurence owes you £50.
Receive £60 and split the cheque.

		Laurence (CL2)					
		OFFICE ACCOUNT			CLIENT ACCOUNT		
		DR	CR	BALANCE	DR	CR	BALANCE
	Balance	50–		50–			
	Cash		**50–**	—		**10–**	**10–**

		Cash					
		OFFICE ACCOUNT			CLIENT ACCOUNT		
		DR	CR	BALANCE	DR	CR	BALANCE
	Laurence	**50**			**10**		

NOTE. It is sufficient to enter both the £50 and the £10 on the same line.

(d) *Double-entries if cheque is "not split"*
  (i) CREDIT ledger account of the client—CLIENT ACCOUNT—with total receipt
     DEBIT Cash Account—CLIENT ACCOUNT—with total receipt
  (ii) DEBIT ledger account of the client—CLIENT ACCOUNT—with the office money
     CREDIT Cash Account—CLIENT ACCOUNT—with the office money.
  (iii) CREDIT ledger account of the client—OFFICE ACCOUNT—with the office money
     DEBIT Cash Account—OFFICE ACCOUNT—with the office money

Example
Barnaby owes you £70.
Receive £90. Do not split the cheque.

		Barnaby (CL3)					
		OFFICE ACCOUNT			CLIENT ACCOUNT		
		DR	CR	BALANCE	DR	CR	BALANCE
	Balance	70–		70–			
(1)	Cash. You.					90–	90–
(2)	Cash.						
	Transfer.		**70–**		**70–**		20–

		OFFICE ACCOUNT			CLIENT ACCOUNT		
		DR	CR	BALANCE	DR	CR	BALANCE
(1)	Laurence				90		
(2)	Laurence. Transfer.	**70**				**70**	

(Table heading: Cash)

D. CHEQUES PAYABLE TO A THIRD PERSON

4. If a cheque is received not payable to the solicitor but payable to a third person and the cheque is sent on to that third person there is no need to make any entries at all. However, it is probably unwise to have no record of the receipt and despatch of the cheque. The recording can be done on the file of the papers and correspondence kept for the client, or it can be kept in the accounts themselves. If it is decided to keep the record in the accounts, the double-entry would be:

CREDIT ledger account of client—CLIENT ACCOUNT
DEBIT ledger account of client—CLIENT ACCOUNT
No entry would be made on the Cash Account.

E. INDORSED CHEQUES, ETC.

5. If clients' money is received in cash and immediately paid over in the course of a transaction, or is received by cheque but similarly indorsed over, there is no need to pay such money into a Clients' Bank Account (Rule 9(1) (SAR). However, for the purposes of the book-keeping there is still a receipt of clients' money. NOTWITHSTANDING THEREFORE THAT THE MONEY WAS NOT PAID INTO ANY BANK ACCOUNT THE FULL ENTRIES TO RECORD A RECEIPT AND A PAYMENT OF CLIENTS' MONEY MUST BE MADE, *i.e.*:

(i) CREDIT ledger account of the client—CLIENT ACCOUNT
     DEBIT Cash Account—CLIENT ACCOUNT
(ii) DEBIT ledger account of the client—CLIENT ACCOUNT
     CREDIT Cash Account—CLIENT ACCOUNT

Since, however, no money was ever actually paid into the clients' bank account, some note of this should be made beside the Cash Sheet entries to save trouble when preparing a bank reconciliation statement (*e.g.* in the details column).

Example
You act for A. B. Client receive a cheque for £5,000 which you indorse over.

		OFFICE ACCOUNT			CLIENT ACCOUNT		
		DR	CR	BALANCE	DR	CR	BALANCE
	Cash. Cheque indorsed				**5,000–**	**5,000–**	

(Table heading: A. B. Client (CL1))

	Cash						
		OFFICE ACCOUNT			CLIENT ACCOUNT		
		DR	CR	BALANCE	DR	CR	BALANCE
	A. B. Client Cheque indorsed.				5,000–*	5,000–*	

F. RETURNED CHEQUES

6. (a) If a cheque comprising clients' money is received from a client, banked, but later dishonoured, the entries are:

> DEBIT the ledger account of the client—CLIENT ACCOUNT[3]
> CREDIT Cash Account—CLIENT ACCOUNT

Example
February 1: Receive £40 from A. B. Client.
February 5: Cheque dishonoured.

		A. B. Client (CL1)					
		OFFICE ACCOUNT			CLIENT ACCOUNT		
		DR	CR	BALANCE	DR	CR	BALANCE
Feb							
1	Cash. You.					40–	40–
5	Cash. Cheque dishonoured.			**40–**			—

The credit entry will appear on the Cash Account.

(b) A solicitor may receive a cheque from a client and wish to draw against it before it has been cleared. This is permissible. If, however, the client's cheque is dishonoured a breach of the Rules may now have been committed and, if so, must be rectified (see *ante*, p. 107).

---

[3] This assumes that the cheque received from the client was paid into CLIENT ACCOUNT. If the cheque was paid into OFFICE ACCOUNT the entries would, of course, be in OFFICE ACCOUNT

(c) *Example*

You act for Violet.

March 1: Receive £400.

March 2: Pay £300 clients' money.

March 5: Violet's cheque is dishonoured. You have thus broken the rules and you repair the breach.

		OFFICE ACCOUNT			CLIENT ACCOUNT		
		DR	CR	BALANCE	DR	CR	BALANCE
Mar							
1	Cash. You.					400–	400–
2	Cash.				300–		100–
5	Cash. Cheque dishonoured.				**400–**		300–DR
	Cash. Transfer	300–		300–		300–	—

Violet (CL4)

7. Exercises

Show Clients' Ledger.

(1) You act for Dust. Deliver a bill for £400 plus VAT. Reduce the bill by £20 plus VAT.

(2) Lizzie owes you £47. Receive £60 and split the cheque.

(3) Repeat Exercise 2, but do not split the cheque.

(4) You act for Meff. Send him a bill for £800 plus VAT. Reduce the bill by £50 plus VAT. Receive £900 and split the cheque.

(5) Repeat Exercise 4 but do not split the cheque.

(6) You act for Saunders. (a) Receive a cheque from him for £50 payable to Edgar, who is not a client. You send the cheque to Edgar. (b) Receive a cheque from Saunders for £600 payable to you and indorse it over to Fry. Show Cash Account and Clients' Ledger.

(7) You act for Griffiths. Receive a cheque from him for £8,000 which you indorse over to Hare. Then receive a cheque from Griffiths for £200 payable to you. Later this cheque is dishonoured. Show Cash Account and Clients' Ledger.

(8) You act for Rudge. May 1: Receive £5,000. May 2: Pay £1,000 out of clients' money. May 5: Rudge's cheque is dishonoured. Repair the breach. Show Cash Account and Clients' Ledger.

Chapter 17

REVISION EXERCISES

Show Clients' Ledger only. Your costs are shown exclusive of VAT in each case.

(1) You act for Bill. Receive £400. Pay cheque £50. Pay cash £6. Deliver a bill (costs £70). Transfer the amount due.

(2) You act for Carol. Pay cheque £80 (no VAT). Pay cheque £90 plus VAT—Principal Method. Pay cash £2. Pay cash £10 plus VAT—Principal Method. Deliver a bill (costs £300). Receive the amount due.

(3) You act for David. Pay cash £3 plus VAT—Principal Method. Pay cheque £400 plus VAT—Principal Method. Pay cheque £50 plus VAT—Agency Method. Pay cheque £60. Deliver a bill (costs £700). Receive the amount due.

(4) You act for Ethel. Pay cheque £80 plus VAT—Agency Method. Pay cash £9. Pay cheque £125 plus VAT—Principal Method. Pay cheque £20. Pay cash £3 plus VAT—Principal Method. Deliver a bill (costs £42). Receive the amount due.

(5) You act for George. Receive £70. Pay cheque £8. Pay cheque £9 plus VAT—Agency Method. Pay cheque £10 plus VAT—Principal Method. Deliver a bill (costs £20). Transfer the amount due.

(6) You act for Henry. Receive £80. Pay cheque £20 plus VAT—Principal Method. Pay cash £1. Pay cheque £11. Deliver a bill (costs £30). Transfer the amount due.

(7) You act for Kate. Pay cheque £80. Pay cheque £90 plus VAT—Principal Method. Deliver a bill which includes a charge for costs of £100, plus a taxable payment on the Principal Method not yet paid, of £20, plus VAT. Receive the amount due. Pay the £20 plus VAT by cheque—Principal Method. Transfer the amount due.

(8) You act for Linda. Receive £300. Pay cheque £4 plus VAT—Principal Method. Transfer the amount due. Pay cheque £5 plus VAT—Agency Method. Deliver a bill (costs £60). Transfer the amount due. Pay cheque £70.

(9) Carambas, Solicitors, are instructed by the Phantom Co. Ltd., to appear on their behalf, in a tax matter, before the Special Commissioners. The following events take place.

> April 4 Payment of £11 (including VAT £1) by cheque drawn in respect of the reproduction of documents. This payment is to be treated as an input of Carambas.
>
> April 9 Received the sum of £200 from Phantom Co. Ltd. on account of costs generally.
>
> May 8 Paid fee of £88 (including VAT £8) to expert witness A. N. Accountant. This disbursement is to be treated as an agency disbursement.
>
> May 26 The amount due to Jakes for transcripts (£44 including VAT £4) is paid out of Client Account.
>
> May 31 The bill of costs in respect of the appeal is rendered to Phantom Co. Ltd., showing profit costs of £500 (excluding VAT).
>
> June 21 The balance of monies due from Phantom Co. Ltd. is received and the requisite transfer is made from Client Account to Office Account.

You are required to show the Ledger Account of Phantom Co. Ltd. as it appears in the books of Carambas.

(Part II Qualifying Examination. August 1975).

(10) Inn, Flate & Co., Solicitors, deal with the following events:

Nov. 3   Paid sundry disbursements of £126 in respect of the estate of Cashe, deceased, in which account there was a credit balance on client account of £84.

Nov. 5   Pay a disbursement on behalf of Guy Forkes of £22 (no VAT). Forkes had already paid £100 on account of costs.

Nov. 6   A bill of costs is sent to Forkes showing profit costs £80 plus VAT and the disbursement of £22.

Nov. 8   Received a cheque from Fred (£450) on account of costs generally.

Nov. 16 Paid surveyor on behalf of Fred, the sum of £100 (including VAT), the cheque being drawn on Client Account.

Nov. 17 The bank notified the firm that the cheque from Fred has been returned unpaid by the paying bankers.

Nov. 20 Received completion monies (£31,710) on sale of a house which is being made by the executors of Cashe, deceased.

Nov. 23 A cheque is received drawn in favour of Brown for £1,243. The previous month a fee had been agreed with Brown of £60 plus VAT, which amount had been received by the firm. An abatement of this fee £20 plus VAT is now made. The amount due to Brown is paid by cheque, and the account is then closed.

Nov. 27 Paid by cheque, the sum of £1,200 on behalf of Tree, and received later the same day from Tree, a cheque for £1,000 in partial satisfaction. The balance is to be transferred from the account of the executors of Cashe, deceased, in accordance with their instructions, Tree being a beneficiary under the will.

Nov. 28 Cheque received from Guy Forkes, settling the amount due by him to the firm in full.

Write up the client's ledger cards together with the Cash Sheet, showing all relevant entries. All accounts are to be balanced except the Cash Sheet.
(Part II Qualifying Examination, February 1981—adapted).

Chapter 18

INTEREST ON CLIENTS' MONEY

A. ACCOUNTING TO THE CLIENT FOR INTEREST

1. Specially Designated Deposit

1. If a solicitor receives clients' money which he anticipates holding for longer than a few days, he may place such money in a specially designated deposit bank account. This is a deposit account at a bank and so interest will be earned on money deposited in it. "Specially designated" means that it is reserved exclusively for clients' money belonging to one particular client. Thus, if the solicitor wishes to place clients' money belonging to three different clients in specially designated deposit bank accounts, three such bank accounts will be needed, one for each client.

2. IF CLIENTS' MONEY IS PLACED ON SPECIALLY DESIGNATED DEPOSIT, ANY INTEREST EARNED BELONGS TO THAT PARTICULAR CLIENT AND IS CLIENTS' MONEY.

3. In order to record what moneys are placed on separate designated deposit a separate Cash Sheet is needed. This is reserved for clients' money placed on deposit and will be called "Deposit Cash Sheet." This will have "Office" and "Client" account columns although the "Office Account" columns will never be used.

4. **Placing money on deposit**

   (a) When the clients' money is received from or on behalf of the client it can first be paid into the ordinary current bank account for clients' money; the double-entry is:

   CREDIT ledger account of client—CLIENT ACCOUNT
   DEBIT Cash Sheet—CLIENT ACCOUNT

Example
Receive £8,000 from A. B. Client on May 1.

A. B. Client (CL1)							
		OFFICE ACCOUNT			CLIENT ACCOUNT		
		DR	CR	BALANCE	DR	CR	BALANCE
May 1	Cash					**8,000–**	8,000–

(b) The second step is to transfer the money from the ordinary current bank account for clients' money to the specially designated deposit account. This is done by a bank transfer, thus reducing the amount in the current account.

The double-entry to record this is:
CREDIT Cash Sheet—CLIENT ACCOUNT
DEBIT Deposit Cash Sheet—CLIENT ACCOUNT

Example
Transfer the £8,000 to a specially designated account.

		Cash					
		OFFICE ACCOUNT			CLIENT ACCOUNT		
		DR	CR	BALANCE	DR	CR	BALANCE
May 1	A. B. Client Deposit Cash Specially designated Re A. B. Client				8,000	**8,000**	

		Deposit Cash Re A. B. Client (DC1)					
		OFFICE ACCOUNT			CLIENT ACCOUNT		
		DR	CR	BALANCE	DR	CR	BALANCE
May 1	Cash. Transfer from current account				**8,000**		8,000

(c) THERE IS NO ENTRY ON THE LEDGER ACCOUNT OF THE CLIENT. However, it may be unwise to have no note that the money is on deposit and therefore some note could be made on the ledger account, *e.g.* by writing in the words "On Deposit" in an appropriate place.

If clients' money belonging to more than one client is placed on deposit, the same Deposit Cash Sheet could be used. However, since the two different amounts are in different bank accounts, the solicitor ought to record them separately. Thus the solicitor would have a separate bank account in respect of each client on whose behalf he had placed the money on deposit represented by a separate Deposit Cash Sheet.

5. **Interest**

At the appropriate time the bank will account to the solicitor for the interest earned by the money on deposit. The usual way in which this is done is to credit the appropriate bank account. Thus, if £8,000 belonging to A. B. Client has been placed on deposit, the interest which such money earned should be credited to that deposit account, thus increasing the balance in that bank account.

The double-entry is:
CREDIT the ledger account of the client—CLIENT ACCOUNT
DEBIT Deposit Cash Sheet—CLIENT ACCOUNT

Example
The bank credits A. B. Client's deposit account with £50 interest on June 1.

		OFFICE ACCOUNT			CLIENT ACCOUNT		
A. B. Client (CL1) On deposit							
		DR	CR	BALANCE	DR	CR	BALANCE
May 1	Cash. You.					8,000–	8,000–
Jun 1	Deposit Cash. Interest					**50–**	**8,050–**

The debit entry will appear on the relevant Deposit Cash Sheet (*i.e.* the one for A. B. Client).

6. When the money is withdrawn from the deposit account, either to send to the client or to spend on his behalf, it must first be transferred from the deposit bank account to the current bank account for clients' money by a bank transfer.

The double-entry to record this is:
CREDIT Deposit Cash Sheet—CLIENT ACCOUNT
DEBIT Cash Sheet—CLIENT ACCOUNT

Example
Transfer the £8,050 held for A. B. Client back to current account.

		Cash						
		OFFICE ACCOUNT			CLIENT ACCOUNT			
		DR	CR	BALANCE	DR	CR	BALANCE	
Jun 2	Deposit Cash. Specially designated Re A. B. Client				**8,050**			

		Deposit Cash Re A. B. Client (DC1)						
		OFFICE ACCOUNT			CLIENT ACCOUNT			
		DR	CR	BALANCE	DR	CR	BALANCE	
May 1	Cash. Transfer from current account				8,000		8,000	
Jun 1	Interest				50		8,050	
2	Cash. Transfer to current account					**8,050**	—	

THERE IS NO ENTRY ON THE LEDGER ACCOUNT OF THE CLIENT,
but the note attached to it when the money was first placed on deposit should be
removed. The client's money is now ready for withdrawal in the normal way.

7. Exercises

    (1) You act for Laurence.
        January 2: Receive £5,000.
        January 3: Place in a specially designated account.
        September 1: The bank credits the deposit account with interest of £30.
        September 3: Remove amount in the deposit account to current account.
        September 4: Return the amount due to Laurence.

    (2) You act for Barnaby.
        February 1: Receive £2,000 and place it in a specially designated account.
        August 1: Bank credits the deposit account with interest of £42.
        October 2: Close deposit account by transfer to current account and draw
            cheque on Barnaby's behalf for £2,000 payable to Jacob.
        October 3: Bank credits current (client) account with interest of £18.
        October 4: Send Barnaby the interest due.

(3) You act for Violet.
March 1: Receive £4,500 and place it in a specially designated account.
April 1: Bank credits deposit account with interest of £14.
April 2: You send Violet a bill charging her £20 costs plus VAT.
April 3: Transfer the £4,514 to current account.
April 4: Send Violet the amount due and transfer the costs.

2. *Money not Specially Designated*

8. Even if a solicitor anticipates when receiving clients' money that the money will be held for a considerable time, the solicitor does not have to place such money in a specially designated deposit bank account. The money can be placed in the ordinary current bank account for clients' money.

9. If a solicitor does receive clients' money, does not place it in a specially designated deposit account, and holds such money for a long time the solicitor has to pay the client the interest which the client would have received had such money been specially designated.

10. NOTE
(1) The obligation to pay interest arises whether the holding of the money for a long time was foreseeable or not.
(2) There are two tests:
(a) the amount of clients' money held
(b) for how long it is held.
The Solicitors' Accounts (Deposit Interest) Rules 1988 contain a table, which indicates when interest must be paid.
(3) The solicitor has to pay the interest out of his own money (*i.e.* office money).

11. In order to record the payment of interest in such cases the solicitor needs an account called "Deposit Interest Payable Account." This is a nominal account; it records the *expense* to the business of paying interest to clients (similar to the expense of paying interest to a bank on an overdraft). This account exists in OFFICE ACCOUNT only.

12. If the only transaction involved is sending the interest to the client, draw a cheque on the OFFICE ACCOUNT and record this.
DEBIT Deposit Interest Payable Account
CREDIT Cash Sheet—OFFICE ACCOUNT

Example
Send A. B. Client £60 interest.

Deposit Interest Payable (NL12)			
	DR	CR	BALANCE
Cash. Re. A. B. Client	**60–**		

The credit entry will appear on the Cash Sheet—OFFICE ACCOUNT

THERE IS NO ENTRY ON THE LEDGER ACCOUNT OF THE CLIENT but a note could be made on the account that interest has been sent.

13. If, at the same time as sending the client interest, the solicitor is sending clients' money to him, the solicitor needs to send the client two cheques.

(a) Send a clients' account cheque in respect of the clients' money, *i.e.*

DEBIT ledger account of client—CLIENT ACCOUNT
CREDIT Cash Sheet—CLIENT ACCOUNT

(b) Send an office account cheque for the interest, *i.e.*

DEBIT Deposit Interest Payable Account
CREDIT Cash Sheet—OFFICE ACCOUNT

THERE IS NO ENTRY ON THE LEDGER ACCOUNT OF THE CLIENT to record the interest, but again some note can be made on the ledger account of the client, if desired.

14. Alternatively, the solicitor could send one cheque drawn on CLIENT ACCOUNT for the whole amount, if he first transfers the interest from the Office Bank Account to the Clients' Bank Account. This involves a bank transfer, *i.e.*

(i) Withdrawing the money from the Office Bank Account
(ii) Receiving the money in the Clients' Bank Account.

Step 1. Withdrawing the money from OFFICE ACCOUNT
DEBIT Deposit Interest Payable Account
CREDIT Cash Sheet—OFFICE ACCOUNT

Step 2. Receiving the money in CLIENT ACCOUNT
CREDIT the ledger account of the client—CLIENT ACCOUNT
DEBIT Cash Sheet—CLIENT ACCOUNT

Step 3. Sending the client the total due to him
DEBIT the ledger account of the client—CLIENT ACCOUNT
CREDIT Cash Sheet—CLIENT ACCOUNT

Example

Step 1

Deposit Interest Payable (NL12)				
		DR	CR	BALANCE
	Cash. Re A. B. Client	60–		

Cash						
	OFFICE ACCOUNT			CLIENT ACCOUNT		
	DR	CR	BALANCE	DR	CR	BALANCE
Deposit Interest Payable		60				

Step 2

A. B. Client (CL1)						
	OFFICE ACCOUNT			CLIENT ACCOUNT		
	DR	CR	BALANCE	DR	CR	BALANCE
Balance Cash. Deposit interest					3,000–	3,000–
					60–	**3,060–**

Cash						
	OFFICE ACCOUNT			CLIENT ACCOUNT		
	DR	CR	BALANCE	DR	CR	BALANCE
Deposit Interest Payable A. B. Client		60		**60**		

Step 3

A. B. Client (CL1)						
	OFFICE ACCOUNT			CLIENT ACCOUNT		
	DR	CR	BALANCE	DR	CR	BALANCE
Balance Cash. Deposit interest Cash. You.					3,000–	3,000–
					60–	3,060–
				3,060		—

Cash							
	OFFICE ACCOUNT			CLIENT ACCOUNT			
	DR	CR	BALANCE	DR	CR	BALANCE	
Deposit Interest Payable		60					
A. B. Client				60			
A. B. Client						**3,060**	

This procedure can be used as an alternative to that in 13 above and whenever a solicitor wishes to hold the interest in CLIENT ACCOUNT for the client.

15. *Exercises*

Show Cash Sheet and Clients' Ledger.

(1) You act for Laurence. Receive £5,000. Return to Laurence £5,000 plus interest of £30. (Send two cheques.)

(2) You act for Barnaby. Receive £7,000. Pay £7,000 on Barnaby's behalf to X and send Barnaby interest of £60.

(3) You act for Sue. Receive £5,000. Return to Sue £5,000 plus interest of £30. (Send one cheque.)

(4) You act for Violet. Receive £4,500. Pay on Violet's behalf £4,400. Charge her with £120 costs plus VAT. Allow her interest on the £4,500 of £43. Transfer the costs, etc., due to OFFICE ACCOUNT and send Violet the balance. Show only Violet's account.

B. GENERAL DEPOSIT

16. At any given time, a solicitor will be holding a fair amount of clients' money. Although on an average day the solicitor may be withdrawing clients' money for one client, this will usually be balanced by a receipt on behalf of another client. Consequently, in the normal course of events throughout a year, there will always be a minimum amount held in the Clients' Bank Account, *e.g.* £50,000. Some days the balance will be higher but normally never lower.

17. In such circumstances, instead of keeping all the clients' money in the current bank account, the solicitor can keep some of it in a separate deposit bank account, *e.g.* £40,000 in a general deposit bank account and the rest (*e.g.* £10,000) in the Clients' Current Bank Account.

18. NOTE

(a) A daily watch will need to be kept on the current account to make sure it is never overdrawn. So long as withdrawals are matched by the receipts, this will not occur—a safety margin could be left (*e.g.* £10,000).

(b) THE MONEY ON DEPOSIT IS NOT ALLOCATED TO ANY PARTICULAR CLIENT. This placing of money on deposit has nothing to do with any of the clients. It is purely between the solicitor and his bank.

(c) THE INTEREST EARNED BY SUCH MONEY ON DEPOSIT BELONGS TO THE SOLICITOR, *i.e.* office money. This is allowed by the Solicitors Act, 1974, s.33.

(d) The deposit bank account is a Clients' Bank Account, *i.e.* in the title the word "client" must appear and it is subject to the Solicitors' Accounts Rules 1975.

19. To record when clients' money is placed on general deposit another Deposit Cash Sheet is needed.

20. When clients' money is placed on general deposit, there is a bank transfer from the ordinary current account for clients' money (thus reducing the balance) to the general deposit account for clients' money. To record this:

CREDIT Cash Sheet—CLIENT ACCOUNT
DEBIT Deposit Cash Sheet (General Deposit)—CLIENT ACCOUNT

Example
You hold £10,000 in the current Clients' Bank Account.
Transfer £8,000 to a General Deposit Clients' Bank Account.

Cash							
		OFFICE ACCOUNT			CLIENT ACCOUNT		
		DR	CR	BALANCE	DR	CR	BALANCE
	Balance				10,000		10,000
	Deposit Cash. General deposit					**8,000**	2,000

Deposit Cash General Deposit							
		OFFICE ACCOUNT			CLIENT ACCOUNT		
		DR	CR	BALANCE	DR	CR	BALANCE
	Cash. Transfer from current account				**8,000**		8,000

21. **Interest**

Since any interest received is office money, instructions must be given to the bank to credit such interest to the Office Bank Account and not to the general deposit account for clients' money. When any interest is credited by the bank to the Office Bank Account the double-entry is:

CREDIT Deposit Interest Receivable Account.
DEBIT Cash Sheet—OFFICE ACCOUNT

The Deposit Interest Receivable Account is a nominal account recording a miscellaneous source of income for the solicitor, and is either a Nominal or a Private Ledger Account.

Example
Bank credits £700 interest to Office Bank Account.

Deposit Interest Receivable (PL6)				
		DR	CR	BALANCE
	Cash.		700–	700–

The debit entry will appear on the Cash Sheet—OFFICE ACCOUNT

22. *Exercises*

(1) You hold £20,000 in Clients' Bank Account. Place £15,000 on general deposit. Bank credits £52 interest. Transfer £2,500 from deposit to current account. Bank credits £34 interest. Show all the entries.

(2) You hold £18,000 in current (clients') account. Place £14,000 on general deposit. Receive £8,300 from A (not specially designated). Return to A £8,300 plus £58 interest. Bank credits the Office Bank Account with interest of £108 in respect of money on general deposit. Show the (main) Cash Sheet only.

(3) (a) You receive £4,500 from Adams which you place in a specially designated account.

(b) Your bank pays £70 into your office account in respect of interest on your general client deposit account.

(c) You pay Brown £500 which you have held for him for some considerable time together with £25 interest thereon.

(d) Repay Adams the £4,500 together with £100 interest that it has earned.

Show the clients' ledger and the (main) Cash Sheet.

(4) The following events occur:

May 1: You open a general Clients' Deposit Bank Account and transfer into it £30,000 from the Clients' Current Bank Account. (You may assume that you have sufficient clients' money.)

May 2: You receive £10,000 on behalf of Simon. He is abroad, but has left instructions that it is to be placed on deposit pending his return.

May 3: You receive £20,000 on behalf of Andrew. He cannot be contacted for some time.

September 1: The bank informs you that £35 and £25 interest has been earned on the general Clients' Deposit Account and the account of Simon respectively, and credited as appropriate.

September 2: Simon returns and is sent the sum due to him.

September 3: Andrew returns home and is sent the sum standing to the credit of his account plus £15 interest (one cheque).

Show the (main) Cash Sheet entries. There is no need to show entries in the 'Balance' columns.

(5) Swanning, who intended to go on an extended holiday abroad, deposited the sum of £10,000 with his solicitors on May 1, with instructions that this sum was to be remitted to Taxhaven Ltd. on November 1, to be held on Swanning's account. The solicitors decided to use a designated deposit

account for the money. On October 31, the sum of £10,500 was transferred to the client current account and sent to Taxhaven Ltd. on behalf of Swanning on November 1.

The same firm of solicitors also acted for Martin in the collection of a debt due to him, amounting to the sum of £4,000. On July 1, the debtor gave the solicitors two cheques for the debt, each cheque being for the sum of £2,000; the first cheque was dated July 1, and the second cheque was dated October 1. Both cheques were duly presented and met. The total amount due, after deduction of costs (£40 + VAT), was paid over to Martin on December 31. As neither sum of £2,000 had been placed in a designated deposit account the solicitors accounted to Martin for interest. Interest was calculated at 10 per cent. per annum.

The general deposit account of the firm earned £1,125 in interest for the six months ended December 31.

Record the above transactions in the appropriate client ledger cards (excluding the cash sheets).

(Part II Qualifying Examination. August 1974).

Chapter 19

MISCELLANEOUS ITEMS

Miscellaneous Sundry Disbursements

1. In the course of a transaction on behalf of a client, a solicitor incurs numerous small items of expenditure such as postage stamps, telephone calls and fares. It is obviously unrealistic to keep a note of each item as it is spent in order to charge it specifically to the client. Thus, one would not keep a record of every postage stamp used in a transaction on a particular client's behalf. When it comes to charging the client for acting for him some firms adopt the practice of making a nominal charge for these items; other firms make no charge whatsoever, regarding these items as general overhead expenses which are covered in the charge for profit costs. If, however, a solicitor does decide to make a specific charge for any of these sundry disbursements, *e.g.* fares, separate from the charge for profit costs, VAT must be added on at the standard rate. This is so, notwithstanding that, when the solicitor paid for the item concerned, no VAT was paid, *e.g.* postage stamps, fares.

2. When expenditure is incurred in respect of any of these items the whole of the expenditure is normally debited to the relevant nominal account recording the expense.

Example
September 1: Buy a set of postage stamps £30.
September 2: Pay the quarterly telephone bill of £860.
September 5: Pay £1 in respect of fares.

Postages and Telephones (NL40)				
		DR	CR	BALANCE
Sept 1	P. Cash Stamps	30–		30–
2	Cash. Telephone bill	860–		890–

Fares (NL8)				
		DR	CR	BALANCE
Sept 5	P. Cash. Fares to court	1–		1–

3. If an item of an exceptionally high amount is paid on behalf of an individual client, then instead this may be debited to his ledger account in the normal way.

Example
Pay on behalf of A. B. Client £500 air fare to Cloud-Cuckoo Land.

		A. B. Client (CL1)					
		OFFICE ACCOUNT			CLIENT ACCOUNT		
		DR	CR	BALANCE	DR	CR	BALANCE
Cash. Air fare.		500–		500–			

4. If the solicitor decides to make a specific charge to the client for miscellaneous sundry disbursements in addition to the profit costs charge, the simplest way to deal with this in the accounts is to add the sundry disbursement charge to the profit costs charge and enter the total figure, *i.e.*

DEBIT the ledger account of the client—OFFICE ACCOUNT—with the total of costs plus sundry disbursements.
CREDIT Costs Account and Customs and Excise Account.

Example
Charge A. B. Client £100 profit costs plus £5 in respect of sundry disbursements.

		A. B. Client (CL1)					
		OFFICE ACCOUNT			CLIENT ACCOUNT		
		DR	CR	BALANCE	DR	CR	BALANCE
Costs	100						
Sundries	5	105[1]					
VAT		10–50		115–50			

[1] The credit entry appears on the Costs Sheet.

5. *Exercises*
   Prepare clients' ledger. Your costs are quoted exclusive of VAT.

   (1) You act for Simon. Pay fares £300—this is to be charged to the client. Deliver a bill (costs £400). Receive the amount due.
   (2) You act for Andrew. Pay fares £3. Deliver a bill (costs £100 plus sundry disbursements—including fares—£8). Receive the amount due.

One Party Paying Another's Legal Costs

6. On some occasions one party agrees to pay the legal costs of another party. In litigation matters, the court often orders the losing party to pay all or part of the winning party's costs. In such cases it is essential to distinguish between:

  (i) the party whose bill is being paid; and
  (ii) the party who is paying the bill.

7. The VAT invoice is always addressed by the solicitor to his client, *i.e.* the person to whom he gives the legal advice—the party whose bill is being paid. Thus, if Solicitor A has a Client, B, Solicitor A would address his bill and tax invoice to Client B. This is so, even if the bill is actually being paid by another party, C.

8. Normally the party paying the bill pays the whole of the VAT.

9. The party paying the bill may, however, pay the tax-exclusive amount, but will normally do this only where the client whose costs are being paid can claim an input tax deduction in respect of the VAT, *i.e.*

  (i) the client whose costs are being paid is in business;
  (ii) the services were supplied to his business rather than to him personally;
  (iii) the business is registered for VAT;
  (iv) the business deals in taxable as opposed to exempt supplies.

Where the business client, whose bill is being paid, is partially exempt and partially taxable it may be agreed that a portion of the VAT will be paid by the other party.

Example 1
You act for Laurence. His bill is £100 plus VAT.
The other side, Barnaby, is paying Laurence's bill.
Normally, Barnaby pays £110.

Example 2
You act for Violet in a business matter.
She deals only in taxable supplies.
Her bill amounts to £200 plus VAT. Jacob is paying the bill.
Jacob would pay £200. Violet the £20 VAT.

10. *Exercises*
Prepare clients' ledger.

  (1) You act for James. Pay £50. Deliver a bill (costs £70 plus VAT), the total plus disbursements to be paid by Mick—not a client of yours. Receive payment from Mick.
  (2) You act for Matthew. Pay £10. Deliver a bill (costs £40 plus VAT). Paul—not a client of yours—is ordered to contribute £36 plus VAT towards Matthew's costs. Receive the amount due from both Matthew and Paul.
  (3) You act for John. Pay £30. Deliver a bill (costs £80 plus VAT). Luke, not a client, is to pay John's costs exclusive of VAT. Receive payment from John and Luke.

11. Sometimes this situation can occur where the same solicitor is acting for both parties, *e.g.* when the solicitor is acting for the purchaser of a house, the purchaser is buying the house with the aid of a mortgage, and the solicitor also acts for the mortgagee.

(a) The first step is to charge the client whose bill is being paid with his costs in the normal way.

Example
Charge Laurence with £80 costs plus VAT (eventually to be paid by Barnaby).

		Laurence (CL2)					
		OFFICE ACCOUNT			CLIENT ACCOUNT		
		DR	CR	BALANCE	DR	CR	BALANCE
	Costs	80–					
	VAT	8–		88–			

(b) The second step is to record that these costs are paid or to be paid by the client paying the bill.
The double-entry is:
CREDIT the ledger account of the client who is being paid—OFFICE ACCOUNT
DEBIT the ledger account of the client paying the bill—OFFICE ACCOUNT

Example

		Laurence (CL2)					
		OFFICE ACCOUNT			CLIENT ACCOUNT		
		DR	CR	BALANCE	DR	CR	BALANCE
	Costs	80–					
	VAT	8–		88			
	Barnaby		**88**	—			

		Barnaby					
		OFFICE ACCOUNT			CLIENT ACCOUNT		
		DR	CR	BALANCE	DR	CR	BALANCE
	Laurence	**88–**		88–			

(c) An alternative way of recording this is to transfer clients' money from Barnaby's account to Laurence's account and then make the necessary transfer from CLIENT ACCOUNT to OFFICE ACCOUNT. This, however, cannot be done unless clients' money is held on behalf of Barnaby.

Example
January 2: Receive £90 from Barnaby.
January 3: Charge £60 costs plus VAT to Laurence, payable by Barnaby.
January 4: Make the necessary transfers.

		Laurence (CL2)					
		OFFICE ACCOUNT			CLIENT ACCOUNT		
		DR	CR	BALANCE	DR	CR	BALANCE
Jan 3	Costs	60					
	VAT	6		66–			
4	Barnaby					**66**[1]	66–
	Cash.						
	Transfer		66–[2]	–	66–[2]		–

[1] For this entry the Transfer Sheet was used.
[2] For these entries the Cash Sheet was used.

		Barnaby (CL3)					
		OFFICE ACCOUNT			CLIENT ACCOUNT		
		DR	CR	BALANCE	DR	CR	BALANCE
Jan 2	Cash. You.					90–	90–
4	Laurence				**66–**[3]		24–

[3] For this entry the Transfer Sheet was used.

12. *Exercises*
Prepare clients' ledger

(1) You act for Philip and Bartholomew. Pay £50 on behalf of Philip. Deliver a bill to him for £70 costs plus VAT. The total due is to be paid by Bartholomew. Receive the money due from Bartholomew.

(2) You act for Thomas and Jude. Pay £10 on behalf of Thomas, £20 on behalf of Jude. Deliver a bill to Thomas for £40 costs plus VAT and to Jude for £50 costs plus VAT. Jude is to pay the total due in both cases. Receive the amount due from Jude.

13. A solicitor may have a transaction which is to be executed some distance from his own office and he may therefore instruct a local solicitor to act on his behalf. Such a transaction needs to be looked at from two points of view: (a) that of the instructing solicitor and (b) that of the agent solicitor.

14. *The agent solicitor*

He treats the instructing solicitor as his client and therefore will probably have a ledger account drawn up in the name of that solicitor. Sometimes the agent solicitor when making a charge for profit costs will allow a small commission to the instructing solicitor for introducing the business. In such a case only the net charge for profit costs is entered into the accounts and the commission is totally omitted.

Example

You are instructed by Jones & Co. of Sheffield to act on their behalf in the local county court. You charge them £10 but allow them commission of two per cent.

Jones & Co (CL10)							
		OFFICE ACCOUNT			CLIENT ACCOUNT		
		DR	CR	BALANCE	DR	CR	BALANCE
	Costs	9–80					
	VAT	0–98		10–78			

15. **The instructing solicitor**

(a) Where the instructing solicitor pays the agent solicitor's charges these are entered in a nominal account called Agency Expenses Account. Thus the entries are:

DEBIT Customs and Excise Account with the VAT
DEBIT Agency Expenses Account with the balance
CREDIT Cash Sheet—OFFICE ACCOUNT—with the total.

Example

You pay Godfrey & Co. of Birmingham their charges of £10 less a commission of two per cent. plus VAT for acting for you in the local magistrates courts.

Agency Expenses (NL20)				
		DR	CR	BALANCE
	Cash. Godfrey & Co.	9–80		9–80

Customs & Excise (NL11)			
	DR	CR	BALANCE
Cash. Godfrey & Co.	0–98		0–98

The two credit entries will appear on the Cash Sheet

(b) When the solicitor later charges his own client with profit costs for acting for him he will take into account the work done by the local agent and add on the local agent's fee to his own charge.

(c) Under Rule 10 Solicitors' Practice Rules 1988 a solicitor must acount to a client for any commission received of more than £10. Thus, if the commission is £10 or less the solicitor can normally retain it. If it is more than £10 the solicitor must disclose the amount of the commission to the client and obtain the client's consent before the solicitor can retain it.

Example
At the end of the transaction you decide to charge £30 profit costs in respect of your own work. The total charge of profit costs would therefore be £40 (being £30 in respect of your work and £10 in respect of your agent's work). Note that the full charge of £10 will be made to the client; the two per cent. commission can be retained by you because it is exactly £10.

A. B. Client (CL1)							
		OFFICE ACCOUNT			CLIENT ACCOUNT		
		DR	CR	BALANCE	DR	CR	BALANCE
	Costs	40					
	VAT	4		44–			

(d) Sometimes the agent solicitor incurs a disbursement on behalf of the instructing solicitor and therefore obtains re-imbursement for such disbursement together with payment of his fees. When the instructing solicitor pays the agent solicitor the instructing solicitor should ensure that the account of his client is debited with the disbursements. The simplest set of double-entries to record this is:
DEBIT Customs and Excise Account with the VAT
DEBIT Agency Expenses Account with the agent solicitor's profit costs
DEBIT the ledger account of the client with the disbursements
CREDIT Cash Sheet—OFFICE ACCOUNT—with the total payment.

Example
You pay Godfrey & Co. £13.78 (profit costs £10 less a commission of two per cent. plus VAT and a disbursement of £3).

A. B. Client (CL1)							
		OFFICE ACCOUNT			CLIENT ACCOUNT		
		DR	CR	BALANCE	DR	CR	BALANCE
	Cash Godfrey & Co. Disburse- ment	3–		3–			

Agency Expenses (NL20)				
		DR	CR	BALANCE
	Cash. Godfrey & Co.	9 –80		9 –80

Customs & Excise (NL11)				
		DR	CR	BALANCE
	Cash. Godfrey & Co.	0–98		0–98

Cash							
		OFFICE ACCOUNT			CLIENT ACCOUNT		
		DR	CR	BALANCE	DR	CR	BALANCE
	A. B. Client Disbursement		3				
	Agency Expenses. Godfrey & Co.		9–80				
	VAT		0–98				

Example

July 1: Receive £10,000 from A. B. Client in respect of purchase of a house
which sum includes a premium of £20 due to the Short Life Insurance Co.

July 2: Transfer the premium of £20 from A. B. Client's Ledger Account to the
ledger account of the insurance company.

July 3: Charge the insurance company £3 commission (exempt VAT).

July 4: Transfer to OFFICE ACCOUNT the £3 due;

July 5: Send balance due to insurance company.

A. B. Client (CL1)							
		OFFICE ACCOUNT			CLIENT ACCOUNT		
		DR	CR	BALANCE	DR	CR	BALANCE
July 1	Cash. You.					10,000–	10,000–
2	Short Life Insurance. Transfer Premium				20–		9,980–

Short Life Insurance Co. (CL6)							
		OFFICE ACCOUNT			CLIENT ACCOUNT		
		DR	CR	BALANCE	DR	CR	BALANCE
July 2	A. B. Client Transfer Premium					20–	20–
3	Commission	3–		3–			
4	Cash. Transfer		3	—	3		17
5	Cash. You.				17–		—

Insurance Commission Receivable Account (PL7)				
		DR	CR	BALANCE
July 3	Short Life.		3–	

Cash							
		OFFICE ACCOUNT			CLIENT ACCOUNT		
		DR	CR	BALANCE	DR	CR	BALANCE
July 1	A. B. Client				10,000		
4	Short Life. Transfer	3				3	

20. Note, again, the effect of Rule 10 Solicitors' Practice Rules 1988 (see *ante* page 163). If the commission received by the solicitor is more than £10, the solicitor may have to account to the client for it. If this is so, when the commission is received from the insurance company it is clients' money.

Example. While acting for Paul, you arrange an insurance for him with the Theta Insurance Co. You receive a commission of £300 from the Theta Insurance Co. and decide to account to Paul for it. This is a receipt of clients' money on behalf of Paul, *i.e.*

CREDIT Ledger Account of Paul—CLIENT ACCOUNT
DEBIT Cash Account—CLIENT ACCOUNT

21. *Exercises*
Show clients' ledger.

(1) Receive £34 insurance premium in respect of the Gamma Insurance Co. Charge £5 commission. Send balance to the Company.
(2) Receive £41 from Delta, a client. You then receive instructions that this sum is to be held in respect of a premium due to the Zeta Insurance Co. Send the money to the Insurance Company less commission of £16. Do not show Delta's account.
(3) You act for the Sigma Insurance Co. Charge them £7 commission in respect of an insurance. Receive a premium of £28 to hold on behalf of the Company. Charge a commission of £5 in respect of this amount. Send the balance due to the Company and transfer the amount due to OFFICE ACCOUNT from CLIENT ACCOUNT.
(4) Harry, Peter and Tom, are solicitors, and they deal with the following events:

1980
Jan. 2 Brown (not a client) pays cash (£104) to the firm, who act as agents for the Nonpay Insurance Co. Ltd. Commission currently due to the firm on that agency amounts to £43.
Jan. 7 The firm acts for Black in respect of the sale of Black's house and also acts for the mortgagees of Black, the Savall Building Society. A bill of costs is rendered to the Building Society for acting for it on the redemption; these costs are £20 plus VAT and are to be borne by Black.
Jan. 10 Cheque received drawn in favour of White, for £1,250 (which is endorsed over to the firm). Bill of costs is sent to White in respect of debt collection, showing fee of £40 plus VAT.

Jan. 14 The firm acts for Yellow in a court action, having already paid the counsel's fee of £100 plus VAT (the Principal Method was used). The firm had appointed local agents, and their bill showed profit costs of £120 less agency commission £20 plus VAT and an agency disbursement which consisted of a court fee £12. A bill of costs is sent to Yellow in which costs in respect of work done by Harry, Peter and Tom (*i.e.* exclusive of the agents' work) are shown at £100 plus VAT.

Jan. 17 The net amount due to Nonpay Insurance Co. Ltd. is paid, being the gross premium received (£104) less commission of £15 and prior commission due (£43). Transfer the requisite amount from Client Account to Office Account.

Jan. 18 Received amount due from Yellow, and paid the amount due to the local agents who acted in his court action. Transfer the requisite amount due from Client Account to Office Account.

Write up the clients' ledger accounts together with the Cash Sheet, showing all relevant entries. All accounts are to be balanced except the Cash Sheet.

(Solicitors' Final Examination. Summer 1980).

Chapter 20

CONVEYANCING

A. DEPOSITS

1. It is common practice for a purchaser to pay 10 per cent. of the purchase price on or before the exchange of contracts, as a deposit. Sometimes this deposit is paid to the estate agents who negotiated the sale but often it is paid to one of the solicitors. This will usually be the solicitor acting for the vendor who will have to record the receipt. The entries he makes depends on whether he holds the deposit:

(a) as agent for the vendor
(b) as stakeholder.

2. **Agent for the vendor**
In this case the money belongs to the vendor immediately and so the entries are:
CREDIT the ledger account of the vendor—CLIENT ACCOUNT
DEBIT Cash Sheet—CLIENT ACCOUNT

Example
You act for A. B. Client who is selling his house. On exchange of contracts receive £2,000 as agent for the vendor.

A. B. Client (CL1)							
		OFFICE ACCOUNT			CLIENT ACCOUNT		
		DR	CR	BALANCE	DR	CR	BALANCE
	Cash. Deposit					2,000–	2,000–

3. **Stakeholder**
When the deposit is received as stakeholder, the money is temporarily neither that of the vendor nor that of the purchaser until the relevant matter is completed when it immediately belongs to the vendor. To record this an account is opened in the Clients' Ledger called "Stakeholder Account."
On receipt of the stake, the relevant entries are:
CREDIT Stakeholder Account—CLIENT ACCOUNT
DEBIT Cash Account—CLIENT ACCOUNT
On completion of the transaction a Ledger Transfer must be made from the Stakeholder Account to the account of the vendor, *i.e.*
DEBIT Stakeholder Account—CLIENT ACCOUNT
CREDIT the ledger account of the vendor—CLIENT ACCOUNT

Example

You act for A. B. Client who is selling his house.

May 1: Receive deposit of £2,000 to hold as stakeholder.

June 1: Completion takes place.

		OFFICE ACCOUNT			CLIENT ACCOUNT		
		DR	CR	BALANCE	DR	CR	BALANCE
May 1	Cash. Deposit. Re A. B. Client					2,000–	2,000–
Jun 1	A. B. Client Transfer				**2,000–**[1]		

Stakeholder (CL11)

		OFFICE ACCOUNT			CLIENT ACCOUNT		
		DR	CR	BALANCE	DR	CR	BALANCE
Jan 1	Stakeholder Transfer					**2,000**[1]	2,000–

A. B. Client (CL1)

[1] NOTE: The Transfer Sheet is used for these two entries.

Although as a matter of law any interest earned on deposit held by solicitors as stakeholders belongs to the stakeholder, it is felt that it is right that interest on stakes should accrue to either vendor or purchaser in broadly the same circumstances as those in which a client would be entitled to interest on other money held by a solicitor. Therefore either the contract for the sale and purchase of land should provide expressly for the interest on any stake held by a solicitor or, in default, such interest should normally be treated as if it were covered by Solicitors' Accounts (Deposit Interest) Rules 1988 and the solicitor holding the stake should account to his client under those Rules, *e.g.* if it is the vendor's solicitor who holds the deposit as stakeholder the solicitor should account to the vendor.

B. MORTGAGES

4. When a client is buying a house with the aid of a mortgage, sometimes the same solicitor will act for both the client purchaser and the mortgagee, and sometimes there will be a different solicitor acting for the mortgagee.

5. If the solicitors acting for the purchaser are not also acting for the mortgagee, they will not receive the mortgage advance until they actually arrive at completion. Therefore, they will need to consider how to deal with the payment of the completion moneys to the vendor. The simplest solution to adopt is to provide that the mortgagee's solicitors make their draft for the mortgage advance payable direct to the vendor's solicitors. In this case all the purchaser's solicitors have to do is to draw a draft for the balance of the purchase price, also made payable to the vendor's solicitors.

Example
Your client is buying a house for £20,000 with the aid of a mortgage of £15,000. On the completion, the mortgagee's solicitors will be bringing a draft for £15,000 which can be made payable to the vendor's solicitors. All you need to do is to bring a draft for the balance of £5,000.

6. If the mortgagee's solicitors make their draft payable to the purchaser's solicitors then this could be indorsed over to the vendor's solicitors. The one thing that the purchaser's solicitors will not be able to do is to draw a draft for all the completion moneys on CLIENT ACCOUNT, because their client will only have provided the balance of the purchase price after allowing for the mortgage advance, and thus the solicitors will be holding insufficient clients' money for that particular client.

7. On completion, the deeds, etc., will all be handed over to the mortgagee's solicitors. If, therefore, the conveyance requires stamping and/or the documents require registration at the Land Registry these matters will now have to be attended to by the mortgagee's solicitors on behalf of the purchaser. The stamp duty and the land registry fees are payable, however, by the purchaser. In such a case, the relevant amounts could either be deducted from the mortgage advance and only the net amount handed over by the mortgagee's solicitors or, alternatively, the purchaser's solicitors could hand the mortgagee's solicitors cheques in respect of these items, using clients' money if sufficient funds are available.

8. It is customary for it to be agreed that the purchaser will pay the legal costs of the mortgagee. In such a case it is common for the mortgagee's solicitors to deduct this sum from the mortgage advance.

9. Where one solicitor acts for both the purchaser and mortgagee:
   (a) if the solicitor who acts for the purchaser receives the mortgage advance from the mortgagee before completion takes place, then that solicitor is also acting for the mortgagee. This is as a result of Rule 2 (SAR); the solicitor is now holding clients' money on behalf of the mortgagee;
   (b) the solicitor must have a separate account in his Clients' Ledger for the mortgagee and credit the mortgage advance to that ledger account. The money does not yet belong to the purchaser and so must not yet be credited to the ledger account of the purchaser. The mortgage advance only belongs to the purchaser as from the day of completion. On that day, therefore, the solicitor can make a transfer of the mortgage advance from the account of the mortgagee to the account of the purchaser.

(c) *Example*

Completion moneys due to vendor	£20,000 (paid on January 15)
Mortgage advance	£15,000 (received on January 14)
A. B. Client to provide	£5,000 (received on January 11)

A. B. Client (CL1)

		OFFICE ACCOUNT			CLIENT ACCOUNT		
		DR	CR	BALANCE	DR	CR	BALANCE
Jan 11	Cash. You.					5,000–	5,000–
15	Building Society Transfer					**15,000**–[1]	20,000–
	Cash completion				20,000–		—

Building Society (CL7)

		OFFICE ACCOUNT			CLIENT ACCOUNT		
		DR	CR	BALANCE	DR	CR	BALANCE
Jan 14	Cash. You.					15,000–	15,000–
15	A. B. Client Transfer				**15,000**–[1]		—

[1] NOTE: The Transfer Sheet is used for these two entries.

(d) alternatively, on completion no transfer is made and entries are merely;

DEBIT ledger account of mortgagee—CLIENT ACCOUNT—with mortgage advance

DEBIT ledger account of purchaser—CLIENT ACCOUNT—with the balance

CREDIT Cash Account—CLIENT ACCOUNT—with total payment

A. B. Client (CL1)

		OFFICE ACCOUNT			CLIENT ACCOUNT		
		DR	CR	BALANCE	DR	CR	BALANCE
Jan 11	Cash. You.					5,000–	5,000–
15	Cash. Completion				5,000–		—

Building Society (CL7)							
		OFFICE ACCOUNT			CLIENT ACCOUNT		
		DR	CR	BALANCE	DR	CR	BALANCE
Jan 14	Cash. You					15,000	15,000
15	Cash. Completion				15,000		—

Cash							
		OFFICE ACCOUNT			CLIENT ACCOUNT		
		DR	CR	BALANCE	DR	CR	BALANCE
Jan 11	A. B. Client				5,000		
14	Building Society				15,000		
15	A. B. Client Completion Building Society Completion					5,000 15,000	

(e) *Costs*

The solicitor is basically acting for two clients in three transactions:
  (i) for the purchaser in the purchase of the house;
  (ii) for the purchaser in the grant of a mortgage;
  (iii) for the mortgagee in the receipt of the mortgage;
In theory therefore, the solicitor is entitled to make three charges for profit costs, one for each item. In practice, however, where the same solicitor acts for both purchaser and mortgagee it is customary not to charge twice for the mortgage transactions. Thus the solicitor could either:
  (a) charge the purchaser for acting for the purchaser in connection with the purchase and the mortgage, *i.e.* solicitor waives the charge for acting for the mortgagee[1]; or
  (b) charge the purchaser for acting on the purchase, and charge the mortgagee for acting in connection with the mortgage, *i.e.* solicitor waives the charge for acting for the purchaser on the mortgage.

---

[1] This procedure is questionable. It is arguable that the solicitor did the work for the mortgagee and would probably have difficulty in justifying the charge to the purchaser if challenged.

If the solicitor elects to charge the purchaser with the mortgage costs, he must:
DEBIT the ledger account of the *purchaser*—OFFICE ACCOUNT—with the total profit costs (purchase plus mortgage)

If the solicitor elects to charge the mortgagee with such costs, he must:
DEBIT the ledger account of the *purchaser*—OFFICE ACCOUNT—with the purchase costs, and
DEBIT the ledger account of the *mortgagee*—OFFICE ACCOUNT—with the mortgage costs
NOTE: that this is still so, even if the purchaser is to pay the mortgage costs.[2]

C. CLIENT BUYING AND SELLING HOUSES SIMULTANEOUSLY

10. Frequently it happens that when a client is buying a house he is simultaneously selling another house and the solicitor attempts to arrange completion to take place on the same day. In such a case it is advisable to provide for the sale to take place before the purchase so that the proceeds of sale can be used for the purchase. If the solicitor decides to complete the purchase first, he may be unable to use clients' money for the purchase because he holds insufficient clients' money on behalf of his client.

Example
You act for A. B. Client who is selling one house for £20,000 and buying a second house for £25,000. You receive £5,000 from the client two days before completion. If the sale is completed first, the £20,000 proceeds of sale together with the £5,000 previously received from the client are available in CLIENT ACCOUNT for the use on the purchase. If, however, the purchase is completed first, since only £5,000 clients' money is held on behalf of the client at least £20,000 will have to be drawn from OFFICE ACCOUNT.

		£
(a)	Completion of sale first:	
	1. Received from A. B. Client	5,000
	2. Proceeds of sale	20,000
	3. Available for purchase	25,000
(b)	Completion of purchase first	£
	1. Received from A. B. client	5,000
	2. Borrowed from OFFICE ACCOUNT	20,000
	3. Available for purchase	25,000
	4. Proceeds of sale used to repay OFFICE ACCOUNT	20,000

D. STATEMENTS

11. At some time in most transactions, and in particular in conveyancing, the solicitor will have to account to the client for all moneys paid and received during the transaction and either ask the client to send the balance due to the solicitor or send the balance due to the client.

---

[2] For entries see *ante*, p. 159.

12. It is usual to send the statement to the client at the same time as sending the bill of costs. In conveyancing, when acting for a client who is buying a house, the statement is usually sent to the client just before completion so that the solicitor can collect from the client the necessary amount due in order to finish off the whole transaction. If the only transaction is the sale of the client's house, then the usual time to send the statement (and the bill) is after completion has taken place, when the solicitor is sending the balance due to the client.

13. The statement can be in any form; it is important to realise that it does not have to be laid out in any particular way. The relevant criteria are:

(a) In the statement the solicitor must account for all moneys received and paid on behalf of the client; nothing must be left out.

(b) The statement must conclude with the correct amount due to the client or the correct amount due to the solicitor.

(c) The statement must be laid out neatly and should be relatively easy to follow.

14. A simple system would be to send a statement divided into two sides.

(a) On one side (*e.g.* the left-hand side) list all the items charged to the client in chronological order, *e.g.*

(i) Payments made on behalf of the client.

(ii) Payments to be made on behalf of the client.

(iii) Profit costs charged to the client.

(b) On the other side (*e.g.* the right-hand side) list in chronological order all receipts whether from the client direct or from third persons on the client's behalf.

(c) The difference between the two sides will be the balance due either from the client or to the client.

Illustration

You act for Paul who is buying a house for £50,000. He is borrowing £30,000 from a building society, the loan being secured by a mortgage. You also receive instructions to act for the building society.

February 1: pay search £10. March 11: receive a cheque from Paul for the deposit of 10 per cent. March 14: send your own cheque to the vendor's solicitors for £5,000. You receive a completion statement from the vendor's solicitors showing the purchase price less the deposit, *i.e.* a balance due on completion of £45,000. April 1: send Paul a bill in which your costs are shown at £200 plus VAT; you also charge him £40 for Land Registry fees. You also prepare a bill in respect of your charges for acting for the building society; these costs are £50 plus VAT and are to be paid by Paul. You expect to receive the mortgage advance of £30,000 from the building society on April 13. Completion is due to take place on April 14. Prepare a statement for sending to Paul on April 1.

Paul. Purchase of . . .

Feb 1	Local Search	10	Mar 11	Deposit	5,000
Mar 14	Deposit	5,000	Apr 13	Mortgage Advance	30,000
Apr 1	Costs	200		BALANCE DUE	15,325
	VAT	20			
	L.R. Fees	40			
	Mortgage costs	55			
Apr 14	Completion	45,000			
		50,325			50,325

15. If you are acting for a client who is purchasing one house and selling another, it would be more helpful to the client if the figures in respect of the sale and purchase were shown separately.

Illustration (continued)

You are selling Paul's existing house for £34,000 and on completion you have to redeem a mortgage on it for £20,000. March 11: receive the deposit of £3,400 to hold as stakeholder. April 1: send Paul a bill (Costs £60 plus VAT). Your charges for acting for the building society are £10 plus VAT, which costs are to be paid by Paul.

Paul. Sale of . . . and Purchase of . . .

PURCHASE of . . .

	£		£
Search	10	On account	5,000
Deposit	5,000	Mortgage advance	30,000
Costs	200		
VAT	20		35,000
L.R. Fees	40	Balance	15,325
Mortgage Costs	55		
Completion	45,000		
	50,325		50,325

SALE of . . .

	£		£
Costs	60	Deposit	3,400
VAT	6	Completion	30,600
Mortgage Redemption	20,000		
Mortgage Costs	11		
	20,077		
Balance	13,923		
	34,000		34,000

SUMMARY

	£		£
Purchase	15,325	Sale	13,923
		BALANCE DUE	1,402
	15,325		15,325

16. It must be emphasised that there is no single method of presentation which has to be used. The method used in paragraph 15 above adopts an account form. It would be equally acceptable to use a vertical form of presentation.

Illustration

Paul. Sale of . . . and purchase of . . .

PURCHASE of . . .

	£	£	£
Payments			
Search	10		
Deposit	5,000		
Completion	45,000		
Costs	200		
VAT	20		
L. R. Fees	40		
Mortgage Costs	55		
		50,325	
Receipts			
On account	5,000		
Mortgage advance	30,000		
		35,000	
			15,325

SALE of . . .

	£	£	£
Receipts			
Deposit	3,400		
Completion	30,600		
		34,000	
Payments			
Costs	60		
VAT	6		
Mortgage Redemption	20,000		
Mortgage Costs	11		
		20,077	13,923
Balance Due			1,402

17. *Exercises*

(1) You act for Oliver who is selling Whiteacre for £60,000. It is at present subject to a mortgage of £20,000 which is to be discharged on completion. On June 1 you receive the 10 per cent. deposit from the purchaser's solicitors to hold as stakeholder. On June 10 you receive instructions to act for the mortgagee, Pat, in the discharge of the mortgage, Pat's costs to be paid by Oliver. July 1: Complete the sale and the discharge of the mortgage, the purchaser's solicitors handing over to you a draft for the balance of the purchase price; there are no apportionments. July 4: send Oliver a bill together with the balance due in his favour and also send Pat the amount due to her. Your bill to Oliver comprises the following item: costs for acting for Oliver in relation to the sale of the house £140 plus VAT. You also charge Pat £30 plus VAT for acting for her. Prepare the statement to be sent to Oliver.

(2) You receive instructions to act for Robert who is buying a house for £70,000. He is borrowing £30,000 from a building society, the loan being secured by a mortgage. You are not acting for the building society. On

February 2, make a search for £15. On March 3, you receive the 10 per cent. deposit from Edward and you send your own cheque to the vendor's solicitors for this amount on March 4, when contracts are exchanged. You then receive a completion statement from the vendor's solicitors showing that £63,000 is due on completion. The mortgagee's solicitors tell you that their costs, payable by Robert, amount to £66 including VAT but that they will deduct this from the mortgage advance. On April 1, you send Oliver a bill in which your costs are shown at £340 (purchase £300, mortgage £40) plus VAT. After completion you will be paying Land Registry fees of £80. Prepare a statement for sending to Robert before completion.

(3) You receive instructions to act for Sarah who is selling Greenacre for £80,000 and buying Blueacre for £110,000. There is at present a mortgage of £9,000 on Greenacre in favour of Tom which will have to be discharged on completion and Sarah is borrowing £20,000 from Tom to be secured by a mortgage on Blueacre. September 1: pay search £10. October 2: receive a cheque from Sarah for £11,000. October 6: exchange contracts. Send your cheque for £11,000 to the solicitors for the vendor of Blueacre and receive a cheque from the solicitors for the purchaser of Greenacre for £8,000 in respect of the deposit which you are to hold as stakeholder. You receive a note from the solicitors acting for the vendor of Blueacre that the amount due on completion is £99,000. You receive a note from Tom to send him £9,230 after completion of the sale of Greenacre in order to redeem the mortgage thereon. October 31: pay £8 search. You send Sarah a bill together with a statement. You are charging her £450 for acting on the purchase and £350 for acting on the sale plus VAT. You are also going to have to pay Stamp Duty of £550 after completion. Your charges for acting for Tom in respect of the mortgage on Blueacre are £99 and these costs are to be paid by Sarah.
Prepare the statement to be sent to Sarah before completion.

E. EXERCISES ON CONVEYANCING

18. Prepare entries in the clients' ledger (ignore interest unless the question specifically states to the contrary):

(1) You act for Albert who is selling Blackacre for £20,000. January 2: Receive £2,000 deposit on exchange of contracts to be held as vendor's agent. February 1: Receive balance of sale price £18,000. February 2: Send Albert a bill for £300 costs plus VAT, transfer the amount due to OFFICE ACCOUNT and send the balance due to Albert.

(2) You act for Brian who is buying a house for £10,000. September 1: Pay £1.85 search by cheque. October 1: Brian sends a cheque for the 10 per cent. deposit direct to the estate agents to hold as stakeholders. October 14: Pay £1.50 out of petty cash search. October 15: Send Brian a bill including a charge for £200 costs plus VAT. October 29: Receive from Brian £9,223.35 being the balance of the purchase price plus payment of your bill. November 1: Complete the purchase.

(3) You act for Charles who is buying a house for £18,000. May 1: Pay search £1.85 petty cash. May 16: Receive a cheque from Charles for the deposit of 10 per cent. and send your own cheque to the vendor's solicitors for this amount. June 9: You send a bill to Charles comprising costs of £135.00 and land registry fees of £40.00. On June 19, you receive Charles' cheque for the amount due to complete the matter (*i.e.* the balance of the purchase price

plus payment of your bill). June 24: Complete the purchase. June 25: Pay the land registry fees. Your fees are quoted exclusive of VAT.

(4) You act for William on the purchase of a house. The following events take place:

January 13: Paid search fees £4.

January 19: Received from William the deposit of £3,000.

January 22: Paid survey fee £165 (including VAT £15). The invoice is addressed to William.

January 27: Exchanged contracts and paid deposit to vendor's solicitors as stakeholders.

February 9: Completion statement received from vendor's solicitors showing £27,000 due.

February 12: Paid search £2.

February 13: Sent financial statement to William showing balance of money which will be due from him on completion of the purchase, together with bill of costs (profit costs £220 inclusive of VAT £20).

February 15: William sends cheque for the full amount due.

February 17: Purchase completed.

February 20: Paid stamp duty £72.

(5) You receive instructions to act for Edward who is buying a house for £10,000. He is borrowing £8,000 from a building society, the loan being secured by a mortgage. On January 2, make a search for £6.00 petty cash. On January 3, Edward pays the 10 per cent. deposit direct to the estate agents. On January 10, you make a further search for £4.00 petty cash. You then receive a completion statement from the vendor's solicitors showing that £9,000 is due on completion. The mortgagee's solicitors tell you that their costs, payable by Edward, amount to £55.00 but that they will deduct this from the mortgage advance. On January 20, you send Edward the bill in which costs are shown at £150 (purchase £140, mortgage £10) plus VAT. You ask him to send you a cheque for the amount due in order to complete the whole of the transaction and this is received on January 30. You complete on February 10, when the mortgagee's solicitors hand over a draft for the net mortgage advance direct to the vendor's solicitors. You hand over a draft to the vendor's solicitors for the balance of the purchase price. Prepare Edward's ledger account.

(6) You act for the Fishy Building Society who are lending £8,000 to Edward in order to enable Edward to buy a house. You do not act for Edward. Your costs, payable by Edward, amount to £50 plus VAT and this will be deducted from the mortgage advance. On February 9, you receive the gross mortgage advance from the Building Society. On February 10, you complete the mortgage and hand over the net advance. Prepare the ledger account of your client.

(7) You receive instructions to act for George who is buying a house for £25,000. He is borrowing £15,000 from the Grim Building Society, the loan being secured by a mortgage. You also receive instructions to act for the Building Society. On April 1, you make a search for £7 by cheque. George sends a cheque for the deposit of £2,000 direct to the estate agents. You then receive a completion statement from the vendor's solicitors showing that £23,000 is due on completion. On May 8, you send George a bill in which costs are shown at £400 for the purchase plus VAT (no charge is being made for acting for George in connection with the grant of the mortgage). You also prepare a bill in respect of your charges for acting for the Grim Building Society and your costs are £70.00 plus VAT; these costs are to be paid by George. You ask George to send you a cheque for the amount due

in order to be able to finish off the matter and this is received on May 17. On May 18, you receive the mortgage advance from the Building Society. You complete the transaction on May 19.

(8) You act for Henry who is buying a house for £50,000 with the aid of a mortgage of £10,000 from the Ink Building Society for whom you also act. June 1: Make a search for Henry £3.00 petty cash. June 20: A cheque is received from Henry for the 10 per cent. deposit which is indorsed over to the vendor's solicitors. June 30: Make a search for £4 petty cash on behalf of Henry. July 1: Send Henry a bill charging him £200 for acting on the purchase; you also charge him £100 for stamp duty and £20 for land registry fees. Add VAT where appropriate. You are charging the Building Society £30 plus VAT for acting in connection with the mortgage, such costs to be paid by Henry. July 15: Receive the amounts due from Henry and the Building Society in order to be able to complete the matter. July 16: Complete the purchase. July 17: Pay stamp duty. July 18: Pay land registry fees.

(9) You act for John who is selling his house for £10,000. It is at present subject to a mortgage of £5,000 which is to be discharged on completion. On May 1, you receive the 10 per cent. deposit from the purchaser's solicitors to hold as stakeholder. On May 10, you receive instructions to act for the mortgagee, Kate, in the discharge of the mortgage, Kate's costs to be paid by John. June 1: Complete the sale and the discharge of the mortgage, the purchaser's solicitors handing over to you a draft for £9,000. June 2: Send John a bill together with the balance due in his favour and also send Kate the amount due to her. Your bill comprises the following item: costs for acting for John in relation to the sale of the house £50. You also charge Kate £20 for acting for her. Your costs are quoted exclusive of VAT. Prepare the entries in your Clients' Ledger.

[Time limit for Questions 10–15: 1 hour each]

(10) You act for Mary in the purchase of "Piccadilly Circus" for £20,000 and the sale of "Buckingham Palace" for £15,000. January 2: Make searches for £4 by cheque. February 2: Pay the estate agents £2,000 deposit on the purchase of "Piccadilly Circus." The purchaser of "Buckingham Palace" sends a cheque for a deposit of £1,500 to Noddy & Co. the estate agents who negotiated the sale thereof. February 15: Receive £5,500 on account from Mary. March 1: You complete the sale of "Buckingham Palace" and then complete the purchase of "Piccadilly Circus"—there are no apportionments. March 2: Pay stamp duty of £180 and land registry fees of £70. March 3: Receive a cheque from Noddy & Co. for £1,100, being the deposit on the sale of "Buckingham Palace" less their commission. March 8: Send Mary a bill, which includes an item of £150 for profit costs plus VAT, transfer the amount due to OFFICE ACCOUNT, and send Mary the balance due, if any.

Show the entries in your clients' ledger.

(11) You act for Harvey who is buying Bumper Hall Pen for £14,000. He is borrowing £12,000 from the Facey Building Society on mortgage.

January 2: Receive £1,500 from Harvey.
January 3: Make search £2 petty cash.
February 3: Receive tax invoice addressed to you from S. & Co. surveyors for £50 + VAT in respect of the survey. Pay S. & Co.
February 4: Exchange contracts and send deposit to V. & Co. vendor's solicitors, to hold as stakeholders.
March 5: Receive completion statement from V. & Co. showing £12,600 due on completion.

March 6: Send Harvey a bill which includes
  (i) costs on purchase £150 plus VAT.
  (ii) rail ticket £25.

Harvey has instructed you to attend completion personally. This is some distance away and, contrary to your normal practice, you are charging Harvey specifically with the rail fare.

The Building Society costs, payable by Harvey, are £50 plus VAT.

March 16: Receive amount required to finish the matter from Harvey.
March 17: Receive mortgage advance from the Facey Building Society.
March 18: Buy rail ticket £25.
March 20: Complete purchase.
March 23: Pay land registry fees £40.

> Show the entries in your clients' ledger and the statement sent to Harvey on March 6.

(12) You are instructed to act for Mrs. Dick who is selling "The Habendum" for £40,000 and buying "The Testatum" for £58,000. There is at present a mortgage of £3,000 on "The Habendum" in favour of the Gibson Building Society which will have to be discharged on completion. In order to finance the purchase of "The Testatum" Mrs. Dick is borrowing £15,000 from the Tyler Building Society.

The deposit in respect of the sale is paid direct by the purchaser to the estate agents who negotiated the sale and Mrs. Dick pays the deposit in respect of "The Testatum" direct to the estate agents. You calculate that the amount due from the purchasers of "The Habendum" on completion is to be £36,000. You receive a note from the solicitors acting for the vendor of "The Testatum" that the amount due on completion is £52,200. You receive a note from the Gibson Building Society to send them exactly £3,000 after completion of the sale of "The Habendum" in order to redeem the mortgage thereon. You receive a note from the Tyler Building Society that their legal costs will amount to £115 which will be deducted from the mortgage advance and in addition you are instructed that the land registry fees payable are also to be deducted from the mortgage advance.

On March 1 you make a search and pay £10 out of petty cash.

On May 1 Mrs. Dick pays £5,000 on account. You inform the Tyler Building Society that the land registry fees payable and deductible from the mortgage advance are £440. On May 5 you complete the purchase and the sale. You also send the amount due to the Gibson Building Society.

On May 8 you send Mrs. Dick a bill of costs together with a statement. You are charging her £400 for acting on the purchase and £200 for acting on the sale plus VAT. The costs for acting in the mortgage redemption charged to the Gibson Building Society, but payable by Mrs. Dick, are £20 plus VAT.

Transfer the amount due to OFFICE ACCOUNT.

Prepare the entries in your clients' ledger and the statement sent on May 8 to Mrs. Dick.

(13) George & Co. acted for Hotspur (for whom they had not previously acted) on the sale of "Blackwater" and the purchase of "Greenmead." Below is a diary of events:

August 27 1968: Notified of proposed purchase at £65,000.
August 31, 1968: Notified of proposed sale at £40,000.
Paid Local Search fees £3. H.M.L.C.R search fees £1.

September 3, 1968: Instructions received from Whinshire Building Society to act in connection with advance to Hotspur of £25,000 on security of "Greenmead" and life policy for £2,500. The initial fire insurance premium of £10 and life policy premium of £150 are to be deducted from the advance.

September 17, 1968: Exchanged contracts for sale of "Blackwater" and received 10 per cent. deposit as agent for vendor. Also exchanged contracts for purchase of "Greenmead" and paid 10 per cent. deposit to Mowbray & Co., the vendor's solicitors as stakeholders. The balance required for the deposit being advanced by George & Co.

September 23, 1968: Mowbray & Co. sent completion statement showing balance of purchase money.

September 30, 1968: Sent financial statement to Hotspur, together with bill of costs showing costs on sale £60, costs on purchase £74, plus VAT. The mortgagee's costs are £16 plus VAT and it has been agreed that these will be borne by Hotspur.

October 12: Hotspur sent a cheque for amount required.

October 16: Paid H.M.L.C.R. fees £1 out of petty cash.

October 17, 1968: Received net advance cheque from Building Society.

October 18, 1968: Completed sale of "Blackwater." Completed purchase of "Greenmead."

October 19, 1968: Paid stamp duty on conveyance £325 and Land Registry fees £20.

October 30, 1968: Transferred amount due to OFFICE ACCOUNT and closed files.

1. Prepare the financial statement sent to Hotspur on October 1, 1968.
2. Write up clients' ledger accounts showing all the necessary entries to deal with the above events.

(Part II Qualifying Examination, February 1969—adapted)

(14) You are acting for Norman who has agreed to buy a freehold house "Tree Tops" for £25,000. On November 30, you pay by cheque a search fee of £4. The deposit of £2,500 is paid by you on January 2, to the Vendor's solicitors to act as stakeholders. Norman immediately negotiates a sub-sale to Oliver at £35,000 and agrees to waive the payment of a deposit. Norman then agrees to buy "Windy Ridge" for £50,000 and he pays a deposit of 10 per cent. on January 10, to the estate agents. "Windy Ridge" is leasehold held under a 99-year lease from June 1, 1974, at a ground rent of £12 per annum payable in advance on January 1, annually. Norman arranges a mortgage advance of £30,000 from the Labrynth Assurance Office Limited to assist in the purchase of "Windy Ridge." On January 11, you pay by cheque a search fee of £5.

Your costs re "Tree Tops" amount to £160 plus VAT. Your costs re "Windy Ridge" amount to £180 plus VAT. The following disbursement is also relevant: Land Registry fees £500. The mortgagee's solicitors charges are £30 plus VAT. Completion is to take place on February 28, next.

Prepare:

(1) A statement showing what money is required from Norman before completion.
(2) Norman's ledger account—showing the entries which will be made prior to and after completion.

(Part II Qualifying Examination. February 1967—adapted)

(15) Pearl, has recently retired and disposed of his business interests, and he now decides to sell his house "Millstone" for £150,000, and purchase a cottage "Avarest" for £75,000 together with an apartment in Spain for £40,000. There is a mortgage on "Millstone" of £25,000, the mortgagees being the Coral Building Society. Both Pearl and the Coral Building Society instruct the same firm of solicitors, Sapphires, to act on their behalf with regard to the purchase of "Avarest" and the sale of "Millstone" and the mortgage thereon.

The following events and transactions take place, and you are required to show the ledger accounts of Pearl and the Coral Building Society, making all the necessary entries to deal with the events and transactions, and to prepare a suitable financial statement showing any balance of money due to Pearl after completion. Pearl's transactions are recorded in one ledger account.

Ignore all forms of taxation, except stamp duty and VAT.

In making the necessary entries, it is important that the account in which the corresponding entry would be made, is clearly identified by the appropriate entry in the details column.

1987

Apr. 3: Received cheque from Pearl for £500 on account of costs generally.

Apr. 6: Local land charges search fee re "Avarest" (£14) is paid from petty cash.

Apr. 10: Paid survey fee (£200 plus VAT) in respect of "Avarest," the invoice being addressed to Sapphires.

Apr. 15: Pearl is unable to find the deposit on "Avarest" from his own resources as his funds have been invested elsewhere, and after negotiation, and a suitable undertaking has been given by the firm, a cheque for £7,500 is received by the latter from the Brite Emerald Finance Company Ltd. to be used as a bridging loan.

Apr. 17: Contracts are exchanged for the sale of "Millstone," the deposit of £15,000 being paid to Sapphires who are to act as stakeholders. On the same day, contracts are exchanged for the purchase of "Avarest," the deposit of £7,500 being paid to the solicitors acting for the vendor of the house who are to act as stakeholders.

May 1: Sent completion statement to purchaser's solicitors in respect of "Millstone" showing the balance due in respect of the purchase monies (£135,000).

May 5: Received completion statement in respect of "Avarest," showing balance of purchase monies due (£67,500).

May 8: Received invoice from estate agent addressed to Pearl, showing commission due in respect of the sale of "Millstone" £1,500 plus VAT.

May 8: Sent financial statement to Pearl, together with bill of costs. The financial statement shows, *inter alia*, the following details:

Estage Agent's commission	£1,500 plus VAT
Interest on bridging loan	£94
Stamp Duty	£750
Land Charges Search fee	£5
Land Registry fees	£125
Redemption of mortgage on "Millstone" (including interest to date of completion)	£25,724

The bill of costs shows profit costs of £700 exclusive of VAT (Purchase of "Avarest" £300. Sale of "Millstone" £400).

The profit costs for acting for the Coral Building Society (to be borne by Pearl) in the redemption of the mortgage, amount to £20 exclusive of VAT.

May 13: Paid £5 from petty cash in respect of land charges search.

May 15: Completed sale of "Millstone" and purchase of "Avarest."

Repaid loan of £7,500 together with accrued interest of £94, to the Brite Emerald Finance Company Ltd.

Transferred redemption monies to building society's ledger account, and sent cheque in respect thereof the same day.

Paid stamp duty and Land Registry fees.

May 18: Paid estate agent's commission plus VAT.

Sapphires, acting upon further instructions from Pearl, send a cheque for £3,000 to Pearl's grandson.

May 20: Transferred costs and disbursements from client account to office account.

June 15: Sent bank draft to Spanish law firm for £41,623, in respect of the purchase price of the Spanish property together with their costs.

June 16: Paid the balance of monies now held on his behalf, to Pearl, including interest allowed by the firm of £449 (including an amount in respect of interest on the deposit held by the firm as stakeholders), thereby closing the client's ledger account.

(Solicitors' Final Examination. Summer 1987)

Chapter 21

TRUSTS

1. Frequently, a solicitor is asked to act as a trustee to a trust and in such a case will, from time to time, receive money belonging to that trust. It should be noted that where the solicitor is not a trustee for a trust himself but is acting for the trustees (*i.e.* they are his clients) then any money received on behalf of that trust, and the trustees, is clients' money. In such a case the normal rules apply, *i.e.* the money must be paid into the ordinary clients' bank account and a ledger account opened in the Clients' Ledger in the name of the trustee. Where, however, the solicitor is a trustee himself certain special considerations apply.

2. Any person who is a trustee must keep proper, faithful and accurate accounts for that trust and such accounts must be kept separately from other matters. Failure to comply with this requirement will render a trustee liable to an action by a beneficiary for breach of trust. Further, a solicitor who is a "solicitor-trustee" must comply with the Solicitors' Trust Accounts Rules 1975, otherwise he will be liable to disciplinary proceedings. Consequently, whether a solicitor is a solicitor-trustee (*e.g.* a sole trustee) or an ordinary trustee (*e.g.* a trustee jointly with a layman who is not an employee in the solicitor's firm) he will need to keep separate records and books of account for each trust of which he is a trustee. Such accounts are, however, outside the scope of this book. In addition the solicitor ought to have a separate bank account for each trust so as to avoid any problems of mixing moneys belonging to different trusts.

3. If the solicitor receives trust money he may pay such money into either:

(a) the firm's clients' bank account; or
(b) the bank account of the individual trust.

4. If the money is paid into the firm's clients' bank account such sum is now governed by the Solicitors' Accounts Rules 1975. Thus, any withdrawal can only be made under rule 7(*b*) (SAR) and the receipt must be properly recorded under Rule 11, *i.e.*
  CREDIT an account in the Clients' Ledger—CLIENT ACCOUNT—in the name of the trust.
  DEBIT Cash Sheet—CLIENT ACCOUNT.

5. If the money is paid into the bank account for the particular trust the entries are made in the books of account kept for that particular trust—NO ENTRIES ARE MADE IN THE FIRM'S BOOKS. If the solicitor is a solicitor-trustee the money is now governed by the Solicitors' Trust Account Rules 1975.

6. **Withdrawals**

(a) If payment is made out of money held in the firm's CLIENT ACCOUNT under Rule 7(*b*) (SAR), this payment must be properly recorded, *i.e.*
  DEBIT the ledger account in the name of the trust in the Clients' Ledger—
  CLIENT ACCOUNT
  CREDIT Cash Sheet—CLIENT ACCOUNT

    (b) If the payment is made out of money held in the Trust Bank Account, the withdrawal is recorded in the books of the trust, and NO ENTRY IS MADE IN THE FIRM'S BOOKS.

7. If a solicitor is a trustee of a trust (whether solicitor-trustee or ordinary trustee) he can pay trust money into his ordinary current account for clients' money. *However, if some of the clients' money has been placed on general deposit he should not do this.* It could involve the solicitor in an accidental breach of trust, because it could be alleged that the trust money assisted him to earn the interest, and in such a case a proportionate part of the interest would belong to the trust. Thus, if a solicitor has clients' money on general deposit, and he receives some trust money, either this should be placed in the bank account of the particular trust or yet another bank account in the firm's name—a Clients' Bank Account—should be opened, reserved exclusively for trust money.

Chapter 22

REVISION EXERCISES

A. THE GENERAL RUNNING OF THE BUSINESS

[Time limit for all these questions: 1 hour except where indicated otherwise.]

1. Mr. White is a solicitor. Prepare his final accounts for the year ending
December 31, (including a trial balance) from the following information:

Capital £32,864. Drawings £8,290. Debtors £9,529. Creditors £8,012. Rent
and Rates £980. Light and Heat £359. Salaries and Wages £37,952. Bad
Debts £322. Insurances £142. General Expenses £1,039. Bank Balance
(office account) £2,237. Library £7,500. Depreciation on Library £2,700.
Deposit Interest Paid £1,058. Freehold Premises £22,000. Fixtures and Fittings £5,000. Depreciation on Fixtures and Fittings £2,300. Deposit Interest
Received £1,000. Work in Hand at the beginning of the year was £7,244.
Bills sent out during the year amounted to £56,776. Work in Hand at the
end of the year is estimated at £8,204. Depreciation is to be charged on the
Library at 20 per cent. of cost per annum and on the Fixtures and Fittings
at 10 per cent. of cost. The rates are paid in advance £40. The electricity bill
is now due £82. A provision for estimated bad debts is to be made of £595.
Included in the Insurances account is an item of £63. This was a mistake
and should have been entered on the Deposit Interest Paid account.

2. Prepare the final accounts of King Jones & Co. from the following figures:

Capital: A £25,000, B £5,000. Drawings: A £11,000; B £5,500. Costs
£44,500. Insurance Commissions received £300. Interest received £4,200.
Interest paid £1,400. Salaries £10,000. Rent £8,500. Stationery £4,200.
Light and Heat £2,800. Premises £11,400. Furniture and Fittings £7,000.
Depreciation on Furniture and Fittings £1,400. Library £12,000. Creditors
£600. Amounts owing by clients £2,000. Cash in Office Account £5,200.
Cash in Client Account—(Current) £40,000. Clients' money on deposit
£10,000. Amounts owing to clients £50,000.

Work in hand at the end of this year £4,000. Rent paid in advance £300.
Stationery stock £400. Depreciation on Furniture 10 per cent. of cost price.
Library is written down by 25 per cent. Light and Heat bill due and unpaid
£100.

A and B are each to be entitled to interest on capital of 10 per cent. Any
resulting net profit is to be shared in the ratio A : 3, B : 2.

3. Prepare the Final accounts of A, B, C and D & Co. for the year ending
December 31, from the following figures:

Salaries £107,288. Postages and Telephones £7,202. Stationery and Print-
ing £1,950. Fares £5,200. Rent and Rates £31,850. Light and Heat £12,674.
Deposit Interest Paid £600. Bad Debts £1,331. Sundry Expenses £4,768.
Costs £185,280. Deposit Interest Received £8,913. Investment Income

£563. Leasehold Premises £8,000. Furniture and Fittings £6,000. Machinery and Equipment £4,000. Depreciation on Premises £800, on Furniture £600, on Machinery £400. Debtors £19,035. Creditors £5,200. Cash in Hand £42. Bank Overdraft £900. Investments £14,800.

Depreciation is to be calculated on all the fixed assets (except investments) at 10 per cent. of cost. Work in hand is estimated at £17,628. Rent and Rates have been paid in advance £4,550, and there is a bill due and unpaid in respect of Telephones of £900. A provision is made for estimated Bad Debts of £121.

The balances on the various capital accounts are A: £20,000; B: £10,000; C: £8,000; D: £5,000. There is a loan from X due to be repaid in eight years time of £7,000. Each partner has a debit balance on his current account as follows: A: £5,107; B: £9,009; C: £7,800; D: £6,000. Each partner is entitled to interest on his capital account of 8 per cent. B, C and D are each to be entitled to a salary of £5,000. Any resulting profit is to be shared in the proportion A : 3, B : 3, C : 3, D : 1.

4. Prepare a Profit and Loss Account and Balance Sheet for the year ending December 31, from the following figures:

Costs £33,419. Salaries £27,000. Postage and Telephones £1,820. Commissions Received £1,320. Stationery £1,136. Agency Expenses Paid £210. Fares £1,090. Rates £2,950. Rent Received £7,200. Light and Heat £1,300. Bank Charges £270. Insurance £1,522. Furniture and Fittings £3,100. Audit Fees £450. Deposit Interest Paid £320. Deposit Interest Received £740. Library £1,800. Bad Debts £650. Professional Subscriptions £330. Courses £1,060. Motor Cars £2,600. Debtors £1,400. Overdraft £6,950; Creditors £5,300. Capital Accounts: A £9,000, B £7,000. Drawings: A £5,981, B £5,920. Premises £10,600. Depreciation (on Library) £100 (on Furniture and Fittings) £480.

There is a bill due and unpaid of £100 in respect of Stationery and the Rates have been paid in advance by £150. A provision is made for estimated Bad Debts of £60 and the Work in Hand is estimated at £3,200. Depreciation on Furniture and Fittings is calculated at 5 per cent. of cost, on the Library at 5 per cent. of cost, and on the Motor Cars at 25 per cent. of cost. A and B are each to be entitled to a salary of £3,000 and any resulting profit or loss is to be shared between them equally.

5. On January 1, 1977 a Solicitor buys premises valued at £32,000. Rates are £600 per annum payable half-yearly in advance on April 1 and October 1. The vendor has paid the rates up to December 31, 1976 and therefore on January 1, 1977 the Solicitor pays the apportioned rates up to April 1, 1977.

On September 1, 1977 the Solicitor sells his premises for £38,000, the purchaser refunding to the Solicitor the rates paid for the month of September.

On the same date the Solicitor purchases new premises valued at £35,000 paying £75 to the vendor for the apportioned rates for September. The second instalment of rates is paid when it falls due on October 1, 1977.

On December 31, 1976 a provision of £800 was made for bad debts. During 1977 the following bad debts are written off:

January 31 Mr. A. a debtor goes bankrupt owing £250.
May 31 Mr. B. a debtor leaves the country owing £200.

On December 31, the total debtors are £11,000. The Solicitor decides to write off the following debts incurred in 1977:

Mr. C £750

Mr. D. £250

and to make his provision for bad debts 15 per cent. of his remaining debtors.

On December 31, he decides to depreciate his motor cars by 10 per cent. From the above information, show the Solicitors Final Accounts. The balances on the remaining accounts as at December 31, are as follows:

Costs	£32,311
Fixtures & Fittings	9,150
Creditors	11,000
Drawings	9,922
Cash	7,000
General Expenses	12,990
Light and Heat	999
Wages	8,420
Cars	3,000
Capital	48,745

N.B. Work in hand at the end of the year was valued at £9,340.

6. On January 1, A. Solicitor received a statement from his bank which disclosed a debit balance of £4,956, bank charges of £400, a standing order for rent paid on December 31 of £1,700, unpresented cheques of £974, and late credits of £1,240. The balances in the books of A. Solicitor as at December 31, were: Capital £60,000. Drawings £4,000. Bad Debts £100. Investment Income Account £20. Agency Expenses Paid £300. Deposit Interest Paid £4,000. Deposit Interest Received £2,300. Light and Heat £4,730. Rent and Rates £6,400. Salaries £8,750. Fixtures and Fittings £12,000. Costs £15,000. Leasehold Premises £35,000. Library £3,000. Creditors £2,000. Debtors £3,600. Bank Overdraft £2,590. Cash in Hand £30. The following adjustments need to be made: Work in Hand £4,000. Bill due in respect of Light and Heat £230. Rent and Rates paid in advance £1,600. Bad Debts Provision £200. Depreciation on Lease 16 per cent. per annum and Depreciation on Library 20 per cent. per annum.

From the above figures prepare a Bank Reconciliation Statement and the final accounts of A. Solicitor for the six months ending December 31, including a trial balance.

7. A, B and C were in partnership. Their financial year ended on April 5. On October 5, 1981 A died. The final accounts were prepared from April 6, until A's death and the balance sheet of the firm as at October 5, was as follows:

CAPITAL EMPLOYED

Capital Accounts

	A	17,000	
	B	12,000	
	C	8,200	37,200

Current Accounts

	A	100	
	B	50	
	C	20	170
			37,370

EMPLOYMENT OF CAPITAL

Fixed Assets			
Leaseholds		28,000	
Fixtures	3,000		
less Depreciation	700	2,300	30,300
Current Assets			
Work in hand		7,100	
Debtors	3,300		
less Provision	300	3,000	
Cash		1,200	
		11,300	
less *Current Liabilities*			
Creditors		4,230	
Net Current Assets			7,070
			37,370

It was agreed that the firm would immediately pay to A's estate the balance on his current account and £1,000 out of his capital account. The balance on A's capital account was to be left on loan and to be repaid over 2 years by equal half-yearly payments, the first of which was to be payable on April 5, 1982; this was duly paid. Interest was to be payable on the balance outstanding on A's capital account at 14 per cent. per annum half-yearly, the first instalment being payable on April 5, 1982; this also was duly paid. An annuity of £6,000 a year was to be payable half-yearly to the widow of A and the first instalment was duly paid to her on April 5, 1982.

During the year fixtures originally purchased for £500 and depreciated by £280 were sold for £200 and new fixtures were purchased for £1,000.

As at April 5, 1982 the balances on the remaining accounts were as follows:

General expenses £66,860. Bad debts £2,100. Current accounts (debit): B £7,500, C £5,000. Creditors £6,800. Cash £120. Debtors £4,200. It is discovered that bills sent out for the period from October 6 to April 5 amounted to £89,100. Work in hand as at April 5 is estimated at £8,200. It is decided to depreciate the Leaseholds by £1,000 and to depreciate the fixtures by a further £700. The new provision for bad debts is to be £400. Any resulting profit is to be shared between B and C in the ratio 3 : 2.

From the above information prepare the final accounts of B and C up to April 5, 1982

8. A and B are in partnership as solicitors. The balances on their Capital Accounts are A £18,000; B £18,000. Under the partnership agreement each is entitled to interest on capital at the rate of 10 per cent. per annum and any resulting profit or loss is shared between them equally.

As at April 1, they decide to admit C as a partner and as from that date interest on Capital Account is to continue to be payable at 10 per cent per annum and any resulting profit or loss is to be shared in the ratio:– A : 2; B : 2; C : 1. C introduces £4,000 capital by way of cash as at the date of his admission and it is decided to revalue the fixed assets as follows: Furniture and Fittings appearing in the Balance Sheet at £6,500 are revalued at £5,000; Premises which appeared in the Balance Sheet at £9,500 are revalued at £15,000.

As at December 31, the balances on the remaining accounts are as follows: Costs for the year ending December 31 £465,000; Expenses £439,000; Debtors £4,000; Creditors £2,000; Overdraft £6,400; Current Accounts A £2,000 (credit); B £1,600 (credit); Drawings: A £26,000; B £26,000; C £6,000; Work in Progress as at December 31, is estimated at £35,000; there are bills outstanding of £900 and pre-payments made of £300.

From the above information prepare a Profit and Loss Account for the year ended December 31, together with a Balance Sheet as at that date.

9. Tom's Cash Sheet shows the following entries for the month of July:

Cash Sheet				
		DR	CR	BALANCE
July				
1	Balance		372	372 CR
2	LM		680	1,052 CR
3	AB	1,150		98
4	OP		540	442 CR
12	CD	166		276 CR
14	QR		1,970	2,246 CR
20	EF	1,282		964 CR
20	GH	268		696 CR
22	ST		82	778 CR
24	UW		468	1,246 CR
26	YZ		1,442	2,688 CR
28	JK	42		2,646 CR

The Bank Statement for the same period shows
Midwest Bank Ltd.

			PAY	REC	BCE
July	1	Balance			− 168
	4	Credits		1,036	868
	6	526	280		588
	8	Credits		1,150	1,738
	12	528	680		1,058
	14	527	960		98
	18	Credits		166	264
	19	Standing Order	120		144
	20	Credits		1,550	1,694
	22	Charges	68		1,626
	24	The Law Society		1,234	2,860
	26	530	1,970		890
	28	531	82		808
	29	529	540		268

Prepare a bank reconciliation statement and make any necessary Cash Book entries.

[Time limit: 20 minutes]

B. THE HANDLING OF TRANSACTIONS ON BEHALF OF CLIENTS

Unless the question states to the contrary please ignore any interest on deposits.

10. You are forming a new company called N.U. Ltd. Pay Capital Duty to I.R.C. £300. Pay Companies' Registration Fee £50. You send the client company a bill in which you charge it £200 plus VAT in respect of profit costs. Your bill also includes a disbursement, as yet unpaid, of £40 in respect of the Law Stationer's fees (zero-rated). You receive the amount due from your client company. You pay the Law Stationers £40. Prepare the clients' ledger.

[Time limit: 20 minutes.]

11. Prepare the ledger account of Albert Hill. Pay £7 for a Police Report, no VAT. Pay £30 for a medical report. Receive £1,500 from the defendant in full settlement. Deliver a bill to Albert for £75 plus disbursements, plus VAT. Send Albert the balance due to him.

[Time limit: 15 minutes.]

12. You acted for Bill in connection with an action against Charles for £2,000. You won and were awarded costs. These were as follows: Profit costs £50, Counsel's fee £30, Court fee £20, Conduct money paid in cash to witnesses £5. The amount of the bill payable by Charles is taxed at £40 costs, £25 counsel's fee, £18 court fees, and £5 conduct money. You receive the amount of the claim plus costs from Charles' solicitors and send the balance due to Bill. Prepare Bill's ledger account. (Your costs and counsel's fee are subject to VAT and are quoted exclusive of tax.)

[Time limit: 25 minutes.]

13. You act for Romeo, who is divorcing his wife Juliet. May 1: Receive £40, generally, on account of costs and disbursements. May 4: Pay enquiry agent £30—no VAT. May 10: Pay court fees of £20. May 15: You instruct Fred and Co., Local Agents, to attend the hearing on your behalf. June 1: You hear from Fred and Co. that your client was granted a decree and Juliet was ordered to pay Romeo's costs. You send Fred and Co. a cheque in payment of their fees which were £15 less a commission of 8 per cent. plus VAT. June 10: You pay a witness fee of £20 plus VAT (use the Agency Method) and you pay counsel's fees of £50 plus VAT (use the Principal Method). July 1: You send your client a bill in which the total charge for profit costs is £75 representing £60 for work done by you and £15 done by your local agents (this includes the taxed costs of £55). July 11: The proportion of your costs to be paid by Juliet is taxed at £55 and counsel's fees of £40 are also allowed together with court fees of £20. July 20: You receive from Juliet's solicitors a cheque in respect of the taxed costs. July 26: Transfer to OFFICE ACCOUNT any balance on CLIENT ACCOUNT. August 1: You receive the balance due from Romeo. Prepare Romeo's ledger account. All your charges etc. are quoted exclusive of VAT.

[Time limit: 30 minutes.]

14. You act for Desmond, who is defending an action brought by Percy. The following events occur: January 2: Receive £400 on account from your client. It is not specially designated. January 3: Pay court fees £10 in cash. February 3: Pay enquiry agent £30 plus VAT, his invoice is addressed to

you. February 4: Pay expert witness £20 plus VAT, his invoice is addressed to Desmond. February 5: Pay a second witness £9, no tax. March 6: You lose the case. The other side is awarded £1,000 plus costs. April 7: The other side's costs and disbursements are taxed at £400 plus £27.20 VAT. April 18: You send Desmond your bill. This includes an item for profit costs of £200 and counsel's fee of £60 (excluding VAT). You send a statement with your bill showing the amount required from your client to finish this transaction. You inform him that because you have held some money on his behalf on CLIENT ACCOUNT for some time that you are paying him £31 interest. However, instead of sending him the money you will set this off against the amount owing. April 29: You receive the amount due from Desmond. May 1: Pay the other side's solicitors £1,427.20. May 2: Pay by cheque, counsel's fee £60 plus VAT, use the Principal Method. May 3: Do any more entries necessary to complete this matter. Prepare clients' ledger.

15. You act for George, a widower who has just died. You are one of the executors of the will and the other executor is George's accountant. George's bank has now closed George's account but agrees to advance any necessary money to pay I.H.T. which you are to repay in due course. May 30: You pay X & Co. £200 plus VAT for valuation—use the Principal Method. June 1: Pay £7 in respect of newspaper advertisements inclusive of VAT— use the Agency Method. June 2: Receive I.H.T. advance from the bank— £1,200. June 3: Pay probate fees £10 by cheque and Inheritance Tax of £1,200. July 20: Receive £3,400 from George's Building Society Account. July 21: Receive £800 from George's bank being the balance on George's account as at the date of death. July 22: Receive assurance policy moneys on George's life of £4,200. July 24: Pay Income Tax arrears of £600 and repay the £1,200 bank loan. August 2: Pay legacies of £1,000 each to George's sister Ethel and brother Frank. August 31: You deliver a bill for £300 profit costs plus £30 general disbursements plus VAT. The balance of George's estate is to be divided equally between his daughter and son and you send the balance due to each of them. Prepare clients' ledger.

16. Prepare the firm's Cash Account from the following information:

April 11: Receive £40 insurance premium on behalf of the Tempest & Flood Insurance Co.
April 15: Send to the Tempest & Flood Insurance Co. £38 being the premium due to them less commission charged of £2. Transfer the £2 to the OFFICE ACCOUNT.
May 8: You act as a local agent for Dodds & Co. of Penzance. Pay enquiry agent a fee of £20 plus VAT (use the Principal Method).
May 9: You send a bill to Dodds & Co. which includes an item of £40 for profit costs (this figure is quoted exclusive of VAT).
May 15: Receive the amount due from Dodds & Co.
May 16: You receive £5,000 to hold on behalf of Margaret.
May 18: You send Margaret a bill in which you charge her £140 plus VAT and you send the balance due to her. Transfer the amount due to OFFICE ACCOUNT.
May 20: As a result of a telephone conversation with Margaret you agree to reduce your fees from £140 to £130 exclusive of VAT.
Do not show the balances.

[Time limit: 30 minutes.]

17. Prepare the firm's Cash Account from the following information:
September 5: Receive a cheque from Tom for £800 on account.

September 6: Draw a clients' account cheque on Tom's behalf for £63.

September 7: Receive a cheque for £4,270 to be held on behalf of the Jones Family Trust. You are one of the trustees and decide to pay the cheque into the firm's client bank account.

September 8: Receive a cheque from Simon for £57. He owes you £100 in respect of costs and disbursements.

September 9: Receive a cheque from Michael, a partner in the firm, for £12,340 being the amount required from him to complete the purchase of a house. You are acting for him in the purchase.

September 12: Receive notification from the bank that the cheque received from Tom on September 5 has been dishonoured.

September 13: Draw a cheque on behalf of the Jones Family Trust for £2,500 and transfer to the trust's bank account the balance of £1,770.

September 14: Receive a cheque from Nancy for £8,000 which is immediately indorsed over on her behalf.

Do not show the balances.

[Time limit: 30 minutes]

18. Prepare the firm's Cash Account from the following information:

May 1: You are the trustee of the Albert Deceased Will Trust. You receive a cheque for £10,000 in respect of the trust which you pay into the trust's bank account.

May 2: You withdraw £2,000 from the trust's bank account on behalf of the Albert Deceased Will Trust in respect of purchase of shares.

May 3: You act on behalf of Bill, on whose behalf you are holding £3,000; you have placed this in a specially designated deposit bank account. You receive a note from your bank that interest of £40 in respect of this item has been credited to your office bank account.

May 4: Transfer from your general clients' deposit bank account £500 to your clients' current account.

May 5: You act for Christine. You have held £6,000 on behalf of this client for some time; it has not been specially designated. Return this sum to her together with interest of £42. Send one cheque only.

May 8: Receive £200 from Peter generally on account of costs.

May 9: Receive £14,000 from Robert which is placed in a specially designated bank account.

May 15: Return to Stephen £8,000 clients' money held on his behalf. Since this sum has been held for some time and has not been specially designated it is decided to send him interest of £50. Send him two cheques.

May 16: You act for Ethel. Receive £200 on account from her.

May 17: Pay on Ethel's behalf stationers' fees £30 plus VAT (use the Principal Method).

May 18: Transfer from CLIENT ACCOUNT to OFFICE ACCOUNT the amount due to OFFICE ACCOUNT in respect of Ethel.

May 19: You act for Frances in connection with drafting her will. She calls into the office to sign the will and you agree your fee for this matter at £20. Frances immediately hands you the cash.

May 20: Pay £320 on Peter's behalf.

May 22: Receive £40 cash from Peter in respect of the amount owing.

May 30: Receive notification from the bank that £85 has been credited to your CLIENT ACCOUNT in respect of interest earned by clients' money on general deposit.

Do not show the balances.

19. The clients' ledger shows the following balances at the close of the entries for yesterday:

	Office A/C £ p	Client A/C £ p
Zebedee	52.35	11.05
William	17.50	
Thomas		50.00
Susan	52.50	
Quentin		40.50
Pauline	62.85	
Oliver Trust	10.50	800.00
Nancy	4.40	45.00
S. Building Society		4,400.00

The following events occurred during the course of today's business:

(a) A cheque for £710 was received from Lucy & King, being the deposit on 2, Railway Terrace, which is being sold by Quentin for whom the firm acts. The money is to be held by the firm as stakeholder.

(b) A cheque for £75 payable to the firm was received from Marshire County Council for one month's salary as clerk to the Marshbridge Magistrates' Court, a part-time post filled by one of the firm's partners, Ian.

(c) A cheque for £18 was received from Ian and Jane Ltd. on general account of costs in connection with a matter being conducted on their behalf. One of the partners in the firm is the majority shareholder in Ian and Jane Ltd.

(d) A cheque for £20.75 was drawn for Land Registry fees in connection with the purchase of 10, Station Road for Zebedee.

(e) A cheque for £800 was drawn in favour of Violet, the beneficiary under the trust fund held by Trustees of Oliver, who consist of all the partners in the firm.

(f) Susan called in and paid £30 in cash on account of an agreed fee for work done.

(g) A cheque for £612.85 was received from Pauline *re* Fish Hall, being the amount shown on the completion statement sent to her which included costs and disbursements of £62.85. Later in the day, completion took place and a draft for £4,950 drawn on the firm's bank was handed over to Messrs. Graham & Hilary, the vendor's solicitors. This sum included £4,400 held for the S. Building Society, in connection with an advance to Pauline.

(h) The following cheques were drawn at the end of the day and sent out in the post:
  (i) Rotton Insurance Co. Ltd. £47.50 on behalf of Nancy; premium on an insurance policy issued to Nancy.
  (ii) Marshire R.D.C. £127.30: for rates, being £82.80 for the firm's premises and £44.50 for a partner's (Ian's) house.
Draw up the firm's Cash Account to record the above items.

20. You act for Pauline and Robert who are the executors of the will of Simon deceased. Simon's will has left a pecuniary legacy of £5,000 to a friend, Timothy, and all the rest of his estate to his sole surviving son William. Pauline and Robert tell you that Simon's assets comprise £200 in a bank account, some investments, and a house.

January 2: The executors open a bank account with an overdraft facility of up to £5,000.

February 1: You ascertain that the Inheritance Tax amounts to £4,000; the deceased's bank credits this sum to your Client Account and debits the executors' bank account.

February 3: You draw a cheque in favour of the Inland Revenue for the Inheritance Tax and another cheque for £38 in respect of the probate fees.

February 12: Grant of probate received and registered with the bank who transfer all moneys due to the deceased by them to the executor's loan account.

February 20: You receive instructions to sell the deceased's house at an agreed fee of £100.

March 22: Exchange contracts on the sale of the house for £48,000 and receive a 10 per cent. deposit to hold as agent for the vendor.

March 25: Investments held on the behalf of the deceased are sold for £700 and you receive the proceeds.

March 26: Pay funeral expenses of £125 and the debts of Simon deceased amounting to £3,100.

April 22: The sale of the house is completed and the balance of the proceeds of sale are received; there were no apportionments. You send a cheque to Pauline and Robert for £3,800 to repay the overdraft on their executors' bank account.

May 3: You deliver a bill in respect of your costs for acting on the probate in the sum of £400 plus VAT. You pay the pecuniary legacy of £5,000 and send a cheque to William for the balance due to him.

Prepare the ledger account of the executors of Simon deceased.

21. You acted for Mr. Hare on the sale of his house, "The Count House" for £15,800 and on the purchase of his new house "Tangerine Cottage" at £30,000. You also received instructions from the Plenty Building Society in connection with an advance of £25,000 which it is to make on the new house. "The Count House" was mortgaged for £11,000 to the Smiles Building Society for whom you do not act. It is your practice to transfer money due to OFFICE ACCOUNT from CLIENT ACCOUNT on the first of each month.

June 2: Contracts exchanged on both properties. Deposit of £1,580 received for "The Count House" to be held as stakeholders. Deposit of £3,000 sent to the vendor's solicitors for "Tangerine Cottage."

June 28: You receive mortgage advance from the Plenty Building Society. Completion Statement received for "Tangerine Cottage" showing £27,000 due on completion.

June 29: Purchase of "Tangerine Cottage" completed.

June 30: Sale of "The Count House" completed at mortgagees solicitors, when a bank draft in their favour for £10,187 was handed over by the purchaser's solicitors; you yourself received a draft for £4,033, the balance due on the sale.

July 18: Pay land registry fees of £80.

July 28: Bill of costs drawn. The profit costs on purchase amounted to £300 (excluding VAT) and general disbursements of £20 were charged. The profit costs on sale amounted to £200 (excluding VAT). Mortgage costs, charged to Plenty Building Society and payable by Mr. Hare, are £33.

Prepare the Ledger Account of Mr. Hare in the books of the practice, and the statement sent to Mr. Hare on July 28.

22. You act for Simpson who is selling "Bolt House" for £40,000. It is at present mortgaged to the Whiting Building Society for £35,000. He is buying "Dyer Hall" for £50,000 and will get a new mortgage of £40,000 from the Mercer Building Society. You act for the Mercer Building Society but not the Whiting Building Society. March 1: Simpson sends you a cheque for the deposit on "Dyer Hall" payable to you. March 2: You send the deposit to the vendor's solicitors. March 3: Pay search fees £2 by cheque. April 1: Receive a cheque for the deposit on the sale which you are to hold as stake-

holder. May 25: Pay search fee of £3, petty cash. June 1: Receive the mortgage advance from the Mercer Building Society and receive £300 from Simpson. June 3: Complete the sale of "Bolt House" and redeem the mortgage thereon. You complete the purchase and mortgage of "Dyer Hall." June 6: Deliver a bill to Simpson for £400 costs (purchase £250, sale £150) and a bill to the Mercer Building Society for £50, both exclusive of tax, the latter bill to be paid by Simpson. Prepare the entries in your Clients' Ledger, and the statement sent to Simpson on June 6.

23. You act for Jack who is buying 1, Half Moon Street for £30,000 and selling "The Manor House," Woolton for £20,000. "The Manor House" is subject to a mortgage for £13,000 from the Ernest Building Society and Jack will be borrowing £18,000 on the security of Half Moon Street from the Ernest Building Society. You also act for the Building Society. March 1: Jack pays a deposit of £3,000 in respect of Half Moon Street direct to the estate agents and you receive a deposit of 10 per cent. in respect of "The Manor House" to hold as stakeholder. March 3: Make a search £10 cheque. April 1: You send Jack a bill in which you charge him £100 for acting on the sale, £140 for acting on the purchase plus VAT. You are charging the Ernest Building Society £60 plus VAT for acting on their part. April 11: Receive £18,000 from the Ernest Building Society and receive from Jack the amount due from him in order to complete the matters. April 12: Complete the sale of "The Manor House" and then complete the purchase of Half Moon Street. Send to the Ernest Building Society the £13,000 due to them. Prepare the entries in your Clients' Ledger, and the statement sent to Jack on April 1. The mortgage costs are payable by Jack.

24. You act for Ellie. She is selling "Heartbreak House" for £25,000. It is at present subject to a mortgage of £10,000 in favour of the Hector Building Society. She is buying "Horseback Hall" for £30,000 with the aid of a new mortgage from the Society of £13,000. You are not acting for the Society.
    April 10, you make a search in respect of "Horseback Hall" and pay £10 by cheque. The deposit of 10 per cent. on "Heartbreak House" is paid direct to the estate agents by the purchaser and Ellie pays the deposit on "Horseback Hall" direct to the estate agents. You arrange a bridging loan from Ellie's Bank of £10,000 because the Building Society wish you to redeem the mortgage on "Heartbreak House" before they lend the £13,000 in respect of "Horseback Hall." Their solicitors' charges are £270 including VAT.
    On May 25: You send Ellie a bill in which you charge her £300 costs in respect of the sale, £400 in respect of the purchase and £130 for disbursements, plus VAT where appropriate. She sends you the amount due on June 1. On the morning of June 2, you obtain a draft from Ellie's bank in your favour for £10,000. You bank it and draw against it a draft in favour of the Hector Building Society for £10,000. You use this to redeem the mortgage of "Heartbreak House" that afternoon.
    On June 3, the following events take place:
    11.30 a.m. You complete the sale of "Heartbreak House" at your offices.
    12.30 p.m. You complete the purchase of "Horseback Hall" at the offices of the vendor's solicitors at which the solicitors for the Hector Building Society attend.
    2.00 p.m. You pay into your client bank account the net balance left after the completions.
    2.30 p.m. You repay the bridging loan to Ellie's bank by paying in a cheque drawn on your Client Account.
    On June 4, you send the land registry fees on "Horseback Hall" of £120 to the mortgagee's solicitors, which you forgot to hand them on June 3.

Prepare Ellie's ledger account. You may assume that the deposit on "Heartbreak House" is sent direct to Ellie after completion by the estate agents. Also prepare the statement sent to Ellie on May 25.

C. REVISION TESTS

[Time limit for each test: 2 hours.]

Test One

1. The following balances appeared on the relevant clients' ledger accounts of Milky Way & Co., Solicitors, as at March 7:

Saturn	Office Account	£75	Client Account		£1,294
Neptune	"	£15	"	"	£ nil

The firm is informed that Saturn died on February 26, and the executors appointed in the will instruct the firm to act in the administration of the estate generally. The estate consists of a house "Eudsetar" valued at £70,000 and personalty valued at £47,500. There are sundry debts due by the estate (£1,500) together with a loan from an insurance company (secured on a life insurance policy) amounting to £5,000. The residue of the estate has been left to Neptune, a nephew who is in the process of purchasing a cottage "The Wild Leap," a matter which is being dealt with by the firm.

During the administration, the following events take place:

Mar. 9: House insurance premium (£95) on "Eudsetar," now due, and the firm debits the executors' account, the amount being transferred to the account of the insurance company, for whom the firm acts.

Mar. 14: The deceased's bank agrees to advance £16,700 to the executors in respect of Inheritance tax and interest payable by the estate. Consequently, a cheque is drawn by the executors, payable to the Inland Revenue, and handed over to Milky Way & Co. Probate fees of £70 are paid by cheque.

Mar. 19: The grant is received and registered with the bank, which then transfers £1,234 from the deceased's current account to the executors' loan account.

Mar. 26: The amount invested by the deceased with the Constellation Building Society is, after registration of the grant, withdrawn and a sufficient sum to close the executors' loan account with the bank is transferred thereto, the remainder amounting to £590 being paid into client account.

Mar. 27: With the executors' concurrence, the net amount outstanding in Saturn deceased's account at March 7 is transferred to the executors' account. The firm draws a cheque in respect of statutory advertisements (£22), and pays £12 out of petty cash in respect of the local advertisement, both inclusive of VAT.

Mar. 29: Received cheque from the Pluto Insurance Co. Ltd., for the sum of £6,342, being the net sum receivable from the company after the deduction of £5,158 in respect of the loan together with accrued interest.

Mar. 30: Debts amounting to £1,500, together with funeral expenses of £1,000, are paid out of client account.

The executors having agreed to an interim distribution of £4,000 to Neptune, which is effected by transfer to Neptune's client account, the firm sends a cheque (£4,000) to the solicitors acting for the vendor of the cottage "The Wild Leap," for them to hold as stakeholders, contracts being exchanged the same day.

Apr. 3: Paid by petty cash, fee for office copy entries re "Eudsetar" £5.

Apr. 5: Exchanged contracts for the sale of "Eudsetar," the deposit of £7,000 having been received by the firm for them to hold as stakeholders.

Apr. 12: Sundry fees (£3) paid from office account *re* the transmission of shares to Virgo, a beneficiary in the estate of Saturn, deceased.

Apr. 26: Received completion statement in respect of "The Wild Leap," showing £36,000 due, being the balance of purchase monies. Sent financial statement to Neptune same day, showing profit costs of £300 excluding VAT (as per bill of costs attached thereto), Land Registry fees £70, Stamp Duty £400 and search fees £16 of which £15 had been expended prior to March 7. Paid £1 from petty cash, in respect of bankruptcy search.

Apr. 30: Completed purchase of "The Wild Leap," the balance of purchase monies being received by the firm from the Bank of Aries as a loan, an undertaking having been given that the sum would be repaid to them from the proceeds of sale of "Eudsetar." The executors had previously agreed to this arrangement.

May 2: Completed sale of "Eudsetar," receiving a bank draft (£63,000) in respect of the balance of purchase monies.

Paid stamp duty and Land Registry fees re "The Wild Leap."

May 9: The firm agrees the bills of cost for the sale of the house and the administration of the estate with the executors. Profit costs with regard to the sale amount to £440 (excluding VAT), and with regard to the administration £700 (excluding VAT), together with disbursements in both cases. With the executor's agreement, a sum amounting to £36,146 is transferred from the account of the executors to the account of Neptune, and a cheque for this amount is sent to the Bank of Aries in accordance with the firm's undertaking.

May 16: All monies due to the firm from the estate are transferred to office account.

May 17: The balance of monies, held by the firm on behalf of the executors is transferred to the account of Neptune at the request of the executors, such sum being inclusive of interest allowed by the firm of £567.

All monies due to the firm from Neptune are transferred to office account, the balance due to Neptune being held pending further instructions.

You are required to show the ledger accounts of:
(i) Neptune;
(ii) the executors of Saturn, deceased;
recording all the above transactions.

In making the necessary entries, it is important that the account in which the corresponding entry would be made, is clearly identified by the appropriate entry in the details column.

(Solicitors' Final Examination. Summer 1984)

2. The following information is extracted from the books of Brown, a practising solicitor, in respect of the year ended May 31, 1987:

Balances on ledger accounts:	£
Capital Account	63,125
Bank Loan	15,000
Drawings	33,600
Due to Clients	181,440
Fixtures, Furniture and Office Equipment at cost	22,500
Accumulated depreciation on Fixtures, Furniture and Office Equipment to 31st May 1986	11,000
Motor Cars at cost	27,000
Accumulated depreciation on Motor Cars to 31st May 1986	11,750
Cash at Bank (Clients Account)	
Current Account	31,440
Deposit Account	150,000
Lease at cost	30,000
Creditors	7,143
General Expenses	90,970
Due from Clients	26,781
Cash at Bank (Office Account)	2,519
Petty Cash Balance	50
Interest Received	7,896
Profit Costs	129,818
Work in Progress at 31st May 1986	14,322
Bad Debts	320
Miscellaneous Income	2,330

The amount shown above for Motor Cars (£27,000), includes the cost of a car (£7,000) which had been purchased by Brown in March 1986. This car was sold in April 1987 for the sum of £5,000, and the proceeds of the sale were inadvertently credited to Capital Account. It is the practice of the firm to charge a full year's depreciation on fixed assets in the year of acquisition, but not to charge depreciation in the year of disposal. No accounting entries have yet been made in respect of the sale of the car, other than the posting of the aforementioned proceeds of sale.

Additional bad debts amounting to £450 are to be writen off. An adjustment is to be made in respect of a cheque for £230 which had been issued on May 30, 1987 without any entry having been made in the relevant accounts. The cheque was presented to the bank on June 9, 1987. The cheque had been drawn in favour of a creditor, and was included in the amount of £7,143 shown above for Creditors.

The following additional information is pertinent:
(a) Work in Progress at May 31, 1987, is valued at £16,217.
(b) During the year, Brown purchased some reproduction antique furniture for use in the office. Due to an error made by the supplier, the amount paid by the firm in respect thereof, included the sum of £500 in payment for furniture for Brown's private use. No adjustment has yet been made in respect of this error.
(c) Miscellaneous Income includes the sum of £100, representing Rent Receivable in respect of June 1987.
(d) Depreciation is to be charged (straight line basis) at the following rates:

Fixtures, Furniture and Office Equipment   10 per cent per annum
Motor Cars   25 per cent per annum

(e) In addition to the above adjustments, there are bills outstanding at May 31, 1987, in respect of General Expenses which have not yet been accounted for, and these amount to £496.

From the foregoing information, you are asked to prepare a Profit and Loss Account for the year ended May 31, 1987, together with a Balance Sheet as at that date. (Use the vertical form of presentation.)

Taxation (including VAT) is to be ignored, for the purpose of the preparation of these Accounts.

(Solicitors' Final Examination. Summer 1987)

Test Two

1. Hedge, Fence & Co., Solicitors, deal with the following events:

1977

(1) Oct. 2: Received cheque for £84 on behalf of the Bull Dogge Co. Ltd., for whom the firm acts in debt recovery matters. Bull Dogge Co. Ltd. currently owes the firm £16 for profit costs, a bill already having been delivered.

(2) Oct. 4: Paid sundry disbursements of £146 in respect of the Estate of John, deceased, in which account there was a credit balance on clients account of £83.

(3) Oct. 6: Paid by cheque the sum of £963 on behalf of George, who agrees to repay the amount, together with costs of £33, (including VAT) on October 24th next.

(4) Oct. 10: Cheque received drawn in favour of Black, a client, for £500. The cheque is endorsed over to the firm by Black in satisfaction of a debt due by him to White, another client of the firm.

(5) Oct. 12: The firm act for Pink, a client, in an action to collect £800 for services rendered to Green, who lives some distance from the locality of the practice. Hedge, Fence & Co., appointed an agent, and the action was settled on payment of £800 by Green, each side bearing its own costs. The agent's bill, and a cheque of £800 from Green, are received.

The agent's bill contained:

	£
Profit costs	66
Less: Agency commission	6
	60
VAT	6
Add: Agency disbursements	10
	76

The same day, a bill of costs is sent to Pink, showing profit costs of £80 (including agent's profit costs) plus VAT and the disbursements of £10.

(6) Oct. 14: Received £400 from the National Savings Bank in respect of the estate of John, deceased.

(7) Oct. 15: Received a cheque for £15,678 being the net proceeds of the sale of shares effected by the firm on behalf of Peter, who is at present on a business trip to the Bahamas. Peter has intimated that

the proceeds are to be held by the firm, pending his return in two months time.

(8) Oct. 18: A cheque for the net balance (£702) due to Pink is sent, and a cheque is sent for the amount due (£76) to the agent.

(9) Oct. 19: Received a cheque for £2,000 from Clarence (who is not a client) being the deposit on the sale of a house by Richard, the firm to hold as stakeholders. Paid petty cash disbursements of £24 same day, in respect of Harold's pending court action.

(10) Oct. 24: Received cheque from George (£996) in settlement of the amount advanced on his behalf together with costs.

(11) Oct. 24: Harold pays £250 on account of his costs, generally.

(12) Oct. 25: Having rendered a further bill of costs for £11 to the Bull Dogge Co. Ltd., a cheque for the net amount due, £57, is remitted to the client.

(13) Oct. 31: Bank notifies firm that the paying bankers have returned, unpaid, the cheque received from Harold for £250.

Write up the clients' ledger accounts together with the cash sheet, showing all the relevant entries.

The cash sheet is not required to be balanced.

(Part II Qualifying Examination. February 1978—adapted)

2. Shrimp has been in practice as a solicitor for many years, and he decides to admit Whelk, his senior assistant, into the firm as a partner. Those parts of the partnership agreement which are relevant to the preparation of the annual accounts, are as follows:

(a) The name of the firm is to be Shrimp and Whelk.
(b) Whelk is to be admitted into the firm as a partner, with effect from January 1, 1986.
(c) Profits and losses are to be shared between the partners, as to Shrimp three fifths and Whelk two fifths, after allowing a salary of £12,000 per annum for Whelk, and providing for interest on capital.
(d) Interest is to be allowed on capital at the rate of 10 per cent. per annum.
(e) The following business asset owned by Shrimp, is to be revalued as at December 31, 1985, the new valuation to be entered into the books being:

Freehold Premises   £80,000

(f) Whelk is to contribute the sum of £30,000 as his share of the capital of the firm.

The firm's accountant produces the following list of balances, which he has extracted from the firm's books, for the year ended June 30, 1986:

		£
Capital Accounts:		
Shrimp (at 1 July 1985)		40,000
Whelk (at 1 January 1986)		30,000
Cash at Bank—Clients' Account		
	Deposit Account	300,000
	Current Account	47,586
	Office Account	8,965
Petty Cash Balance		45
Clients' Ledger Balances:		
Office Account		33,242
Clients' Account		347,586

Drawings:	
Shrimp	42,000
Whelk	9,500
Profit Costs	284,596
Work in progress at 30 June 1985	22,993
Interest Receivable	14,986
Sundry Creditors	8,942
Administrative and General Expenses	204,649
Freehold Premises	60,000
Furniture and Library at cost	8,400
Motor Cars at cost	18,750
Provision for Depreciation Accounts at 1 July 1985:	
Furniture and Library	2,520
Motor Cars	7,500
Bank Loan	20,000

During the year, Shrimp has been appointed legal adviser to a trade association and his remuneration due in respect of the appointment, at June 30, 1986, amounts to £4,000. It has been agreed between the partners, that one half of the remuneration should be treated as partnership income and should be taken into account in determining the profits and losses for the year ended June 30, 1986, notwithstanding the fact that the amount was not received until July 1986. The other half of the remuneration is to be treated as the personal income of Shrimp.

Subsequent to the extraction of the above balances, it has been discovered that a cheque received (£80) from a client, has been returned by the paying bankers marked "refer to drawer." The cheque had been banked and recorded in the office books, on June 27, 1986. It has been decided that the amount should be written off as a bad debt, as at June 30, 1986.

The following additional information is pertinent:

(a) Depreciation is to be charged at the following rates (straight line basis):

Furniture and Library	10 per cent per annum
Motor Cars	20 per cent per annum

(b) The new valuation for the fixed asset as at January 1, 1986, has not yet been recorded in the partnership books.

(c) There are bills outstanding at June 30, 1986 in respect of Administrative and General Expenses, which have not yet been accounted for, and these amount to £3,863.

(d) The firm had paid a personal bill (£100) on behalf of Shrimp, and the amount has inadvertently been included in Administrative and General Expenses. No adjustment has yet been made in respect of this amount.

(e) Work in Progress at June 30, 1986, is valued at £12,293.

(f) Profits are to be allocated between partners on a time basis. (All calculations to be made in months.)

From the foregoing information, prepare a Profit and Loss and Appropriation Account for the year ended June 30, 1986, together with a Balance Sheet as at that date. (Use the vertical form of presentation.)

Movements on partners' current accounts must be shown in detail.

Taxation (including VAT) is to be ignored, for the purpose of the preparation of these Accounts.

(Solicitors' Final Examination. Summer 1986).

Test Three

1. Black, Bobb & Co., are solicitors, and they deal with the following events:

    1976

    (1) Nov. 3: Paid by cash (i) search fees £2 in respect of the purchase of "The Padd" by Smith, (ii) agency disbursements £11 (including VAT) on behalf of solicitors representing Brown, by whom they have been requested to act as agents.

    (2) Nov. 9: Paid survey fee £165 (including VAT £12) in respect of "The Padd."

    (3) Nov. 11: Instructions received from Highrate Building Society to act for them in granting an advance of £7,000 to Smith on security of "The Padd."

    (4) Nov. 15: Cheque for £2,400 received from solicitors for Bungo who had been disputing a debt owed to Brown.

    (5) Nov. 16: Received from Nonsuch Bank cheque for £2,500 as bridging loan on behalf of Smith.

    (6) Nov. 18: Cheque for £2,246 sent to solicitors for Brown, together with bill of costs showing:

	£
Professional charge	144
Less: Agency commission allowed	14
	130
Add: VAT	13
	143
Add: Agency disbursements (including VAT)	11
	154

    (7) Nov. 20: Exchanged contracts for the purchase of "The Padd" and paid 10 per cent. deposit (£2,500) to the vendor's solicitors who are to act as stakeholders. On the same day contracts were exchanged for the sale of Smith's house "Coslot" and a deposit of 10 per cent. (£1,600) was received, Black, Bobb & Co. acting as stakeholders.

    (8) Dec. 5: Received completion statement from vendor's solicitors in respect of "The Padd" showing £22,500 due, being the balance of purchase money.

    (9) Dec. 5: Completion statement sent to purchaser's solicitor in respect of "Coslot" showing balance of £14,400 due in respect of the balance of purchase money.

    (10) Dec. 6: Received cheque for £7,000 from the Highrate Building Society. The profit costs to be charged in respect of the advance are £44 (including VAT).

    (11) Dec. 8: Sent financial statement to Smith showing balance of money which will be due from him on completion of the sale and purchase, together with bill of costs for £1,106 (being search fees, survey fee, stamp duty £250, Land Registry fees £51, profit costs on sale £90 plus VAT, profit costs on purchase £140 plus VAT, and estate agents commission £385 inclusive of VAT).

    (12) Dec. 11: Cheque received from Smith being the balance of purchase money and payment of costs.

    (13) Dec. 14: Completed purchase and sale of properties.

Net advance transferred from the Highrate Building Society account to Smith's account.

Loan of £2,500 repaid to Nonsuch Bank, interest thereon being charged by the bank to Smith's current account with the bank.

Transferred £1,600 from Stakeholder Account to Smith's account. Paid stamp duties and Land Registry fees.

(14) Dec. 15: Paid estate agents commission £385.

(15) Dec. 31: Transferred costs and disbursements from client account to office account.

Ignore interest on the deposit.

Write up the ledger account of Smith and the agency account for the solicitors representing Brown, showing all the entries necessary to deal with the above events, and prepare a Financial Statement suitable for presentation to Smith on December 8, 1976, showing how the balance of money due on completion is calculated.

(Part II Qualifying Examination. February 1977—adapted)

2. Pen and Ink are in partnership, as solicitors, sharing profits and losses in the ratio 3 : 2. Each partner is entitled, under the partnership agreement, to interest on capital at the rate of 10 per cent. per annum, and Ink is entitled, in addition, to a partnership salary of £12,000 per annum.

On January 1, 1982, Paper is admitted into the partnership, contributing £10,000 as his share of the capital in the firm. The new partnership agreement provides that, as from January 1, 1982, profits and losses will be shared between Pen, Ink and Paper, in the ratio of 2 : 2 : 1 respectively. Furthermore, partnership salaries of £20,000, £15,000 and £10,000, will be allowed to Pen, Ink and Paper respectively. No interest is to be allowed on capital, and no interest is to be charged on partners' drawings.

Partners' drawings have been debited to their respective current accounts, as soon as they have occurred.

An abridged trial balance, prepared from the partnership books, shows the following position as at June 30, 1982:

	£	£
NET PROFIT for the year, before charging interest on capital, and other appropriations		50,000
Partners' Current Accounts:		
Pen	19,700	
Ink	18,400	
Paper	6,000	
Partners' Capital Accounts:		
Pen		40,000
Ink		20,000
Paper		10,000
Sundry Assets	80,500	
Sundry Liabilities		4,600
	124,600	124,600
Amounts due to Clients		87,322
Cash at Bank—Clients	87,322	
	£211,922	£211,922

From the above information, prepare the Profit and Loss Appropriation Account for the year ended June 30, 1982, together with a Balance Sheet as at that date. The allocation of profits between the partners is to be determined on a time basis. (Calculations to be made in months.) Details of movements on partners' current accounts, must be shown.

(Solicitors' Final Examination. Summer 1982)

3. The Cash Account of Smith, shows a debit balance of £642 as at April 30, 1982, but when the bank statement for that month is received it shows that Smith has an overdraft of £247. Smith cannot understand how the difference between the two balances has arisen, as they have both been ascertained as at April 30, 1982, and he banks all receipts and makes all payments by cheque. Smith now has to meet a payment of £228, and he requests that you investigate the position. Prepare a bank reconciliation statement for Smith, and effect any other accounting entries in the Cash Account you deem necessary, so that the books accurately reflect the transactions and accord with normal accounting practise.

Smith's Cash Account shows the following entries for the month of April, 1982:

Cash Account		DR £	CR £	BALANCE £
April				
1	Balance	747		747
2	PQR Ltd.		456	291
6	FG		679	388 Cr
7	M. Ltd.	463		75
8	PU & Co.	197		272
10	DBN Ltd.		156	116
14	STD Ltd.	965		1,081
15	KOJ		431	650
16	S. Ltd.	87		737
20	FGR		420	317
21	TP Ltd.	452		769
23	ABC	780		1,549
	JQN		95	1,454
28	CGE		323	1,131
29	KLM	345		1,476
	Smith		600	876
30	TDB	876		1,752
	Wages etc.		837	915
	JHO		273	642

The bank statement shows the following entries:

Ossific Bank Limited

Account: Smith

		Withdrawals £	Deposits £	Balance £
1982				
Apr				
1	Balance			1,296 CR
1	Credits		295	1,591 CR
2	223	305		1,286 CR
6	225	456		860 CR
7	224	539		291 CR
7	Credits		463	754 CR
8	Giro direct transfer		323	1,077 CR
8	Credits		197	1,274 CR
13	226	679		595 CR
15	Credits		965	1,560 CR
15	227	156		1,404 CR
19	Credits		87	1,491 CR
19	228	431		1,060 CR
23	Credits		1,232	2,292 CR
23	229	420		1,872 CR
28	Cheque returned	87		1,785 CR
28	Standing bankers order	300		1,485 CR
29	230	295		1,190 CR
30	233	837		353 CR
30	232	600		247 DR

The cheque issued to JQN on April 23, 1982, for £295, was entered into the Cash Sheet as £95 in error.

(Solicitors' Final Examination. Summer 1982—adapted)

Test Four

1. The following balances appeared in the relevant clients' ledger accounts of Tremor, Quake & Co., Solicitors, as at December 1, 1987:

Chasm	Office Account	£482	Client Account	£989
Fissure	Office Account	£104	Client Account	£nil

Chasm dies on December 3, 1987, and his executors instruct the firm to act in the administration of the estate generally. The estate consists of personalty valued at £62,750 and a house, "Goodinvest," which is valued at £120,000. There is a mortgage on the house (£20,000) and there are other sundry debts amounting to £2,424. Subject to legacies of £5,000 to Chasm's secretary and £1,000 to a local charity, the residue is left to Fissure who is presently purchasing a house "Epicentre," a matter which is being dealt with by the firm.

During the administration of the estate, the following events take place:

1987.

Dec. 10: House insurance premium (£245) on "Goodinvest," now due, and the firm debits the executors' account, the amount being transferred to the account of the insurance company, for whom the firm acts.

Dec. 11: The deceased's bank agrees to advance £22,923 to the executors in respect of inheritance tax payable by the estate. A loan account is opened by the bank for the executors and a cheque for £22,923 is drawn up by the executors, payable to the Inland Revenue, and handed over to Tremor, Quake and Co.
Probate fees of £100 are paid by cheque.

1988.

Jan. 4: The grant is received and registered with the bank, who transfer the sum of £12,420 from the deceased's deposit account to the executors' loan account.

Jan. 5: Cheque drawn for £40 plus VAT in respect of statutory advertisements. The cost of the local advertisement (£20 plus VAT) is paid from petty cash. In both cases the disbursement is to be treated as an input of Tremor, Quake & Co.

Jan. 7: The amount invested by the deceased with the Big Bang Building Society is, after registration of the grant, withdrawn by the executors and a sufficient sum to close the executors' loan account with the bank is transferred thereto, the remaining amount of £4,876 being paid into the firm's client account.

Jan. 11: With the executors' concurrence, the net amount outstanding in Chasm deceased's account at December 1, 1987, is transferred to the executors' account.

Jan. 12: Proceeds of life assurance policy amounting to £23,400 received by the firm and placed in a designated deposit account.

Jan. 13: Exchanged contracts for the sale of "Goodinvest" for £120,000, the deposit of £12,000 being received by the firm for them to hold as stakeholders.

Jan. 14: Debts amounting to £2,424, together with funeral expenses of £775, are paid out of client account.

Jan. 20: Cheque for £1,297 received from the auctioneer in respect of the sale of household contents. Commission of £150 (including VAT) had already been deducted.

Jan. 21: Paid survey fee £276 (inclusive of VAT) in respect of the house "Epicentre" being purchased by Fissure, the local land charges search fee (personal inspection) of £24 being paid out of petty cash.

Jan. 22: The sum of £13,000 is transferred from the executors' designated deposit account to client current bank account.
Cheques are drawn in respect of the legacies and handed over to the legatees.
The executors agree to make an interim distribution to Fissure, and the sum of £10,000 is transferred to his client account. The firm then send a cheque for £10,000 to the solicitors acting for the vendor of the house "Epicentre," for them to hold as stakeholders, contracts being exchanged at the same time.

Jan. 27: Completed sale of "Goodinvest." The balance of the purchase money payable by the purchaser is £108,000. The mortgage is to be redeemed by a payment of £20,506 which is inclusive of accrued interest. The mortgagees (Crevice Building Society) are not clients of Tremor, Quake & Co. The purchaser brings two drafts, one payable direct to the mortgagees' solicitors and the other, for the balance, payable to Tremor, Quake & Co.

Paid estate agents' commission of £2,510 plus VAT.

Jan. 28: Transferred the sum of £80,000 from client current bank account to the executors' designated deposit account.

Jan. 29: The firm agrees the bills of costs for the sale of the house and the administration of the estate with the executors. Profit costs with regard to the sale are £600 (plus VAT), and with regard to the administration £900 (plus VAT), together with disbursements.

Feb. 1: All monies due to the firm by the executors are transferred to office account.

Feb. 4: The executors' designated deposit account is closed and the balance, including interest of £108, is transferred to client current bank account.

Feb. 5: The balance of monies held by the firm on behalf of the executors, including interest allowed by the firm of £194 (excluding the interest on the designated deposit account but including an amount in respect of interest on the deposit held by the firm as stakeholders), is transferred to the account of Fissure at the request of the executors. Fissure requests that the monies now due to him be held by the firm on general deposit account pending the completion of his purchase of the house "Epicentre."

You are required to show the ledger accounts of the executors of Chasm, deceased, and of Fissure, recording all the above transactions. Show also the cash account (NOT the designated deposit cash account), recording the entries for the month of January 1988. There is no need to complete the balance columns in the cash account.

Ignore all forms of taxation, except the stated amount of Inheritance Tax and VAT.

In making the necessary entries, it is important that the account in which the corresponding entry would be made is clearly identified by the appropriate entry in the details column.

2. Jack has practised as a solicitor for many years, and he decides that due to the expansion of business in his practice, it is necessary to admit a partner into the practice as from July 1, 1987. Jill becomes a partner, and the relevant parts of the partnership agreement relating to the preparation of the accounts, are as follows:

(a) The name of the firm is to be Jack & Jill.
(b) Jill is to be admitted a partner with effect from July 1, 1987.
(c) Interest is to be allowed on capital at the rate of 10 per cent. per annum.
(d) Jill is to be paid a salary of £8,000 per annum.
(e) Profits and losses are to be shared between the partners, as to Jack two thirds and Jill one third.
(f) Jill is to contribute the sum of £10,000 together with the lease of an office she owns (agreed value £15,000), towards her share of the capital.

The firm's bookkeeper produces the following list of balances, which he has extracted from the firm's books, for the year ended December 31, 1987:

	£
Profit Costs	324,786
Work in progress at 1 January 1987	32,874
Interest Receivable	22,946
Administrative and General Expenses	268,567
Miscellaneous Income	1,129
Motor Cars at cost	24,000
Library, Furniture and Computer at cost	34,000
Leasehold property at cost	34,000
Provision for depreciation accounts at 1st January 1987:	
Motor Cars	12,000
Library, Furniture and Computer	8,500
Cash at Bank—Clients' Account	
Current Account	34,876
Deposit Account	100,000
Designated Deposit Accounts	250,000
Cash at Bank—Office Account	6,952
Petty Cash	84
Due from Clients	9,765
Sundry Creditors	5,423
Due to Clients	384,876
Capital Accounts:	
Jack (at 1 January 1987)	60,000
Jill (at 1 July 1987)	25,000
Drawings:	
Jack	38,542
Jill	11,000

After the above list of balances had been prepared, the partners and the office accountant decided that the following adjustments were necessary:

(a) There are bills outstanding at December 31, 1987, in respect of Administrative and General Expenses, which have not yet been accounted for, and these amount to £1,242.

(b) It has been discovered that a cheque received (£240) from a client, has been returned by the paying bankers marked "refer to drawer." The cheque had been banked and recorded in the office books, on December 30, 1987. It has been decided that the amount should be written off as a bad debt as at December 31, 1987.

(c) Depreciation is to be charged (straight line basis) at the following rates:

Motor Cars	25 per cent per annum
Library, Furniture and Computer	25 per cent per annum

(d) Work in Progress at December 31, 1987, was valued at £44,862.

(e) The firm had paid a personal bill (£200) on behalf of Jack, and the amount has inadvertently been included in Administrative and General Expenses. No adjustment has yet been made in respect of this amount.

(f) Profits are to be allocated between partners on a time basis. (All calculations to be made in months.)

From the foregoing information, you are asked to prepare a Profit and Loss and Appropriation Account for the year ended December 31, 1987, together with a Balance Sheet as at that date. (Use the vertical form of presentation.)

Taxation (including VAT) is to be ignored, for the purpose of the preparation of these Accounts.

Movements on partners' current accounts must be shown in detail.

(Solicitors' Final Examination. Winter 1988)

Test Five

1. The following balances appeared in the relevant clients' ledger accounts of Oak, Poplar & Co., Solicitors, as at April 1, 1988:

Larch	Office Account	£nil	Client Account	£600
Aspen	Office Account	£43	Client Account	£20,232
Willow	Office Account	£nil	Client Account	£1,500

The firm deals with the following events during the months of April and May, 1988:

1988

Apr. 1: A designated deposit account is opened by the firm on behalf of Aspen, and the sum of £20,000 is transferred thereto, in accordance with his request.

Apr. 7: After receiving the agreement of Larch, the sum of £250 is transferred to the account of Maple Insurance Limited from the amount held on behalf of Larch in client account, being an insurance premium due this day.

Apr. 11: Cheque received from Alder, being the deposit on the sale of a house by Aspen, the firm to hold the sum (£5,500) as stakeholders.

Exchanged contracts for the sale of Aspen's house, and paid disbursements of £14 (no VAT) on his behalf, out of petty cash the same day.

Apr. 12: Poplar, a partner in the firm, is purchasing a cottage jointly with his wife and they have instructed the firm to act on their behalf in this matter. The firm pays the local land charges search fee (£14) re the cottage, from petty cash.

Apr. 15: A bill of costs is received from Wych Elm & Co., a firm of solicitors acting as agents on behalf of the firm in connection with the affairs of Willow. The bill shows profit costs of £800 (excluding VAT) and disbursements of £100 (no VAT). The firm pays the agents' bill and renders its own bill of costs to Willow, showing disbursements of £100 (no VAT) and profit costs of £1,200 plus VAT. Both the profit costs and the disbursements of the agent solicitors, are included in the foregoing amounts.

Apr. 18: Poplar hands over a cheque to the firm's cashier for £4,000, being the deposit on the cottage which he is purchasing jointly with his wife.

Apr. 20: Paid by cheque to Willow, the amount outstanding in his client account, together with interest allowed by the firm of £42. The account is then closed.

Apr. 25: Contracts are exchanged for the purchase of the Poplars' cottage, the deposit of £4,000 being paid to the vendor's solicitors as stakeholders.

Apr. 27: Banker's draft (£49,500) received from Horse Chestnuts, solicitors, on completion of the sale of Aspen's house. Paid estate agents' fees (£700 plus VAT) the same day, the invoice being addressed to Aspen.

Apr. 28: Aspen agrees with the bill of costs rendered by the firm, showing profit costs of £400 plus VAT and disbursements. The amount due to the firm is transferred to office account, and Aspen's designated deposit account is closed, interest of £83 having been credited thereto.

The balance of monies now held on behalf of Aspen, including interest allowed by the firm of £106 (inclusive of interest on the deposit held by the firm as stakeholders) is paid over by one cheque, thereby closing the client's ledger account.

Apr. 29: The net amount due to Maple Insurance Limited is paid, being the gross premium received (£250) less commission of £37, the client (Larch) having agreed with the firm's retention of that amount. The account is then closed.

May 3: Larch requests that the firm send a cheque for £1,000 to Rowan, to whom he owes money. The firm sends the cheque, and later the same day, a cheque for £400 is received from Larch in partial satisfaction, together with a cheque for £250 drawn by Spruce (a debtor of Larch) payable to Larch. The latter cheque is indorsed over to Oak, Poplar & Co.

May 9: The bank notifies the firm that the cheque from Spruce has been returned unpaid by the paying bankers.

You are required to show all the relevant entries in the accounts in the clients' ledger (including a shakeholder account, if necessary), recording the above transactions. It is important that the account in which the corresponding entry would be made, is clearly identified by the appropriate entry in the details column. All accounts are to be balanced.

Ignore all forms of taxation, except VAT.

2. The partnership agreement of Sherry and Brandy, who are practising solicitors, shows the following details which are relevant to the preparation of their annual accounts:

(a) Profits and losses are to be shared between the partners, as to Sherry three quarters and Brandy one quarter, after allowing a salary of £24,000 per annum for Brandy, and providing for interest on capital.
(b) Interest is to be allowed on capital at the rate of 10 per cent. per annum.
(c) The sum of £4,000 per annum is to be transferred from Brandy's current account to his capital account, such transfer to cease once the balance on the latter account reaches the sum of £40,000.

The firm's accountant produces the following information, which he has extracted from the firm's books, for the year ended April 30, 1988:

	£
Freehold Premises	80,000
Motor Cars at cost	30,000
Furniture, Library and Equipment at cost	14,600
Computer and Ancillary Equipment at cost	8,400
Provision for depreciation accounts at 1 May 1987:	
Motor Cars	18,000
Furniture, Library and Equipment	7,300
Computer and Ancillary Equipment	2,100
Amount due to Clients	765,987

Cash at Bank—Clients' Account:

Current Account	65,987
Deposit Account	700,000
Amount due from Clients	53,567
Cash at Bank—Office Account	7,617
Petty Cash Balance	123
Capital Accounts:	
Sherry	80,000
Brandy	30,000
Current Accounts:	
Sherry	8,342 (credit)
Brandy	654 (credit)
Drawings:	
Sherry	47,326
Brandy	22,768
Sundry Creditors	11,890
Profit Costs	367,875
Work in hand at 1 May 1987	21,426
Interest Received	24,562
Administrative and General Expenses	264,896

After reviewing the above balances, the partners decide that the following adjustments are necessary:

(i) Depreciation is to be charged (straight line basis) at the following rates:

Motor Cars	20 per cent per annum
Furniture, Library and Equipment	10 per cent per annum
Computer and Ancillary Equipment	25 per cent per annum

(ii) Work in hand at April 30, 1988, was valued at £11,432.

(iii) There are bills outstanding at April 30, 1988, in respect of Administrative and General Expenses, which have not yet been accounted for, and these amount to £18,567.

(iv) It was agreed that the transfer of the sum of £4,000 from Brandy's current account to his capital account, should be effected on April 30, 1988, and that interest should not be allowed on that sum, in respect of the year ending on that date.

(v) It was discovered that Sherry had drawn two cheques on the office bank account, on April 29, 1988, without reference having been made to the accounts department. Consequently, no entries had been made in the books of account as at April 30, 1988. One cheque was in respect of a private debt of £1,000, the other cheque being the repayment of a rebate (£420) which had been allowed to a client who had previously paid his bill in full. No entry has yet been made in the books in respect of the rebate, and any VAT is to be ignored.

(vi) The freehold premises had been revalued at £100,000 on October 31, 1987, but the necessary entries had not yet been recorded in the books.

From the foregoing information, you are asked to prepare a Profit and Loss and Appropriation Account for the year ended April 30, 1988, together with a Balance Sheet as at that date. (Use the vertical form of presentation.)

Movements on partners' current accounts must be shown in detail.

Taxation (including VAT) is to be ignored, for the purpose of the preparation of these Accounts.

(Solicitors' Final Examination. Summer 1988)

Test Six

1. Cayenne decides to sell his house "Pailecroft" for £200,000, and purchase a
   cottage "Stillstand" for £100,000 together with an apartment in France for
   £50,000. There is a mortgage on "Pailecroft" of £30,000, the mortgagees
   being the Cloves Building Society. Both Cayenne and the Cloves Building
   Society instruct the same firm of solicitors, Garlics, to act on their behalf
   with regard to the purchase of "Stillstand" and the sale of "Pailecroft" and
   the redemption of the mortgage thereon. Garlics have agreed to provide
   advice generally, with regard to the purchase of the French property.

   The following events and transactions take place, and you are required to
   show the ledger accounts of Cayenne and the Cloves Building Society,
   making all the necessary entries to deal with the events and transactions,
   and to prepare a suitable financial statement showing any balance of money
   due to Cayenne after all the transactions have been completed. Cayenne's
   transactions are recorded in one ledger account.

   Ignore all forms of taxation, except Stamp Duty and VAT.

   In making the necessary entries, it is important that the account in which
   the corresponding entry would be made, is clearly identified by the appropriate entry in the details column.

   Oct. 3: Received cheque from Cayenne for £1,000 on account of costs
               generally.
   Oct. 6: Local land charges search fee re "Stillstand" (£16) is paid from
               petty cash.
   Oct. 10: Paid survey fee (£300 plus VAT) in respect of "Stillstand", the
               invoice being addressed to Garlics.
   Oct. 15: Cayenne is unable to find the deposit on "Stillstand" from his
               own resources, and after his employers have agreed to act as
               surety, Garlics agree to advance the deposit upon exchange of
               contracts, out of available practice monies.
   Oct. 17: Contracts are exchanged for the sale of "Pailecroft", the deposit
               of £20,000 being received by Garlics who are to act as stake-
               holders. On the same day, contracts are exchanged for the pur-
               chase of "Stillstand", the deposit of £10,000 being paid to the
               solicitors acting for the vendor of the house who are to act as
               stakeholders.
   Nov. 1: Sent completion statement to the purchaser's solicitors in
               respect of "Pailecroft" showing the balance due in respect of the
               purchase monies (£180,000).
   Nov. 5: Received completion statement in respect of "Stillstand", show-
               ing balance of purchase monies due (£90,000).
   Nov. 8: Received invoice from estate agent addressed to Cayenne, show-
               ing commission due in respect of the sale of "Pailecroft" £2,000
               plus VAT.
   Nov. 9: Sent bill of costs to Cayenne, showing total profit costs of £900
               exclusive of VAT (Purchase of "Stillstand" £400, Sale of "Paile-
               croft" £500). The profit costs for acting for the Cloves Building
               Society (to be borne by Cayenne) in the redemption of the mort-
               gage, amount to £20 exclusive of VAT.
   Nov. 15: Completed sale of "Pailecroft" and purchase of "Stillstand".
               Sent cheque for £30,263 redemption monies to Cloves Building
               Society, the appropriate amount together with a sum in respect
               of the redemption costs, having been transferred to the Society's
               ledger account.
               Paid Stamp Duty of £1,000.

Nov. 18: Paid estate agent's commission plus VAT.
Garlics, acting upon further instructions from Cayenne, send a cheque for £6,000 to Cayenne's grandson.

Nov. 20: Paid Land Registry fees of £160.
Transferred costs and disbursements from client account to office account.

Dec. 15: Sent bank draft to French law firm for £52,301, in respect of the purchase price of the French property together with their costs.

Dec. 16: Sent financial statement to Cayenne, together with a cheque for the balance of monies held on his behalf, including interest allowed by the firm of £424. The latter amount is inclusive of interest on the deposit held by the firm as stakeholders, and has been ascertained after making due allowance for interest payable by Cayenne on the amount advanced by the firm in respect of the deposit on "Stillstand".
The client's ledger account of Cayenne is then closed.

2. Water has been in practice as a solicitor for many years, and he decides to admit Air, his senior assistant, into the firm as a partner. Those parts of the partnership agreement which are relevant to the preparation of the annual accounts, are as follows:

(a) The name of the firm is to be Water and Air.
(b) Air is to be admitted into the firm as a partner, with effect from July 1, 1988.
(c) Profits and losses are to be shared between the partners, as to Water three fifths and Air two fifths, after allowing a salary of £20,000 per annum for Air and providing for interest on capital.
(d) Interest is to be allowed on capital at the rate of 10 per cent. per annum.
(e) The following business asset owned by Water, is to be revalued as at June 30, 1988, the new valuation to be entered into the books being:

Freehold Premises £120,000

(f) Air is to contribute the sum of £40,000 as his share of the capital of the firm.

The firm's accountant produces the following list of balances, for the year ended December 31, 1988:

	£
Capital Accounts:	
Water (at January 1, 1988)	80,000
Air (at July 1, 1988)	40,000
Cash at Bank—Clients' Account	
Deposit Account	500,000
Current Account	23,425
Office Account	14,723
Petty Cash Balance	60
Clients' Ledger Balances:	
Office Account	48,956
Clients' Account	523,425
Drawings:	
Water	51,000
Air	15,650
Profit Costs	422,563
Work in Progress at January 1, 1988	38,693
Interest Receivable	27,422
Sundry Creditors	16,342
Administrative and General Expenses	355,389

Freehold Premises	80,000
Furniture and Library at cost	12,200
Motor Cars at cost	36,340
Provision for Depreciation Accounts at January 1, 1988:	
Furniture and Library	4,880
Motor Cars	21,804
Bank Loan	40,000

At the commencement of the financial year, Water was appointed part-time legal adviser to a book publisher and the remuneration due in respect of the appointment, at December 31, 1988, amounts to £10,000. It has been agreed between the partners, that one half of the remuneration should be treated as partnership income and should be taken into account in determining the profits and losses for the year ended December 31, 1988. Of the total amount due in respect of the appointment, £6,000 had been received by Water in July 1988, being paid into his personal bank deposit account. The remaining sum due (£4,000) was received and paid into the firm's bank account in January 1989.

Subsequent to the extraction of the above balances, it has been discovered that a cheque received (£300) from a client has been returned by the paying bankers marked "refer to drawer". The cheque had been banked and recorded in the office books on December 29, 1988. It has been decided that the amount should be written off as a bad debt, as at December 31, 1988.

The following additional information is pertinent:

(a) Depreciation is to be charged at the following rates (straight line basis):

Furniture and Library	10 per cent per annum
Motor Cars	20 per cent per annum

(b) The new valuation for the freehold property as at 1 July 1988, has not yet been recorded in the partnership books.
(c) There are bills outstanding at December 31, 1988 in respect of Administrative and General Expenses, which have not yet been accounted for, and these amount to £5,755.
(d) The firm have paid a personal bill (£400) on behalf of Water, and the amount has inadvertently been included in Administrative and General Expenses. No adjustment has yet been made in respect of this amount.
(e) Work in Progress at December 31, 1988, is valued at £24,240.
(f) Profits are to be allocated between partners on a time basis. (All calculations to be made in months.)

From the foregoing information, prepare a Profit and Loss and Appropriation Account for the year ended December 31, 1988, together with a Balance Sheet as at that date. (Use the vertical form of presentation.)

Movements on partners' current accounts must be shown in detail.

Taxation (including VAT) is to be ignored, for the purpose of the preparation of these Accounts.

(Solicitors' Final Examination. Winter 1989)

APPENDIX

ANSWERS

SECTION ONE

THE GENERAL RUNNING OF THE BUSINESS

Chapter 2

Page 17.

13. (1)

Cash			Alice	
1	6		6	1
2	7		7	2
3	8		8	3
10	13		13	10
11	14		14	11
12	15		15	12
16	18		18	16
17	19		19	17
	20		20	

13. (2) (a)

Purchases		Sales		Bill	
21			26	26	21
22			27	27	22
23			28	28	23
31			34	34	31
32			35	35	32
33			36	36	33

13. (2) (b)

Purchases		Sales		Carol	
41			42	42	41
43			44	44	43
45					45

13. (3) (a)

Purchases		Cash		Dick			
51			51	Cash	51	Purchases	51
52			52		52		52
53			53		53		53

13. (3) (b)

Cash		Sales		Ellen			
56			56	Sales	56	Cash	56
57			57		57		57
58			58	·	58		58

13. (4)

Purchases		Sales		Cash		Fred		George	
61			62	64	63	63	61	62	64
65			66	68	67	67	65	66	68
69			70				69	70	

Chapter 3

Page 24.

12.   (1)

Cash

	10,000		8,000
	900		470
	60		100
		Balance	2,390
	10,960		10,960
Balance	2,390		

X				Y			
	470		400		600		60
Balance	630		700			Balance	540
	1,100		1,100		600		600
		Balance	630	Balance	540		

Capital   Dr. —   *Purchases*   Dr. 400. 700.   *Sales*   Dr. —
         Cr. 10,000   Cr. —   Cr. 600. 900.

Premises   Dr. 8,000   *Wages*   Dr. 100.
          Cr. —   Cr. —

12.   (2)

Cash

	5,000		2,000
	250		1,500
			400
			500
			300
			100
		Balance	450
	5,250		5,250

Balance 450

Furniture & Fittings Dr. 2,000.   *Van* Dr. 1,500.   *Tools* Dr. 400.
              Cr. —   Cr. —   Cr. —

Rent Dr. 500.   *Electricity* Dr. 300.   *Paint* Dr. 100.
     Cr. —   Cr. —   Cr. —

Capital   Dr. —   *Income* Dr. —
          Cr. 5,000.   Cr. 250.

Debit Balances   Cash 450. Fixtures & Fittings 2,000. Van 1,500.
                 Tools 400. Rent 500. Electricity 300. Paint 100.

Credit Balances   Capital 5,000. Income 250.

Page 26.

19. (1)   *Purchases*   Dr. 50. 230.   *Sales* Dr. —   *X* Dr. 40. 190.
                         Cr. —   Cr. 100, 180, 42.   Cr. 50. 230.

           Cash   Dr. 70. 42. 120.   *Z* Dr. 180.   *Y* Dr. 100.
                         Cr. 40. 190.   Cr. 120.   Cr. 70.

          Trial Balance Dr. Purchases 280. Y 30. Z 60. Cash 2.
                     Cr. Sales   322. X 50.

                TOTAL = 372.

19. (2)   *Cash*   Dr. 5,000. 13,000. 1,000. 1,500.
                         Cr. 4,000. 10,000.

           Capital   Dr. —   *Purchases* Dr. 10,000. 4,000.
                         Cr. 5,000.   Cr. —

          S. Ltd.   Dr. 10,000.   *A.* Dr. 1,000.   *B.* Dr. 2,000.
                         Cr. 10,000.   Cr. 1,000.   Cr. 1,500.

          Sales   Dr. —
                         Cr. 13,000. 1,000. 2,000.

          Trial Balance Dr. Cash   6,500. Purchases 14,000. B 500.
                     Cr. Capital 5,000. Sales   16,000.

                TOTAL = 21,000.

19. (3)   *Cash*   Dr. 1,500. 3,000. 2,000. 4,000. 750.
                         Cr. 500. 750. 1,500. 25. 150. 1,500.

          Capital   Dr. —   *Loan*   Dr. —
                         Cr. 1,500.   Cr. 3,000.

          Rent   Dr. 500   *Fixtures and Fittings* Dr. 750
                         Cr. —   Cr. —

          Purchases   Dr. 1,500. 2,000.
                         Cr. —

          Sales   Dr. —
                         Cr. 2,000. 4,000. 500. 250.

          Electricity   Dr. 25   *Wages* Dr. 150.
                         Cr. —   Cr. —

          Rachel   Dr. 500. 250.   *Tom* Dr. 1,500.
                         Cr. 750.   Cr. 2,000.

          Trial Balance Dr. Cash. 6,825. Rent 500. Fixtures & Fittings 750.
                        Purchases 3,500. Wages 150. Electricity 25.
                        Cr. Capital 1,500. Loan 3,000. Sales 6,750. Creditors
                        500.

                TOTAL = 11,750.

19.   (4)   *Cash*   Dr. 2,000. 490.
                          Cr. 100. 200. 10. 500. 600. 10.

            Capital   Dr. —   *Rent* Dr. 100.
                          Cr. 2,000.   Cr. —

            Furniture   Dr. 200.
                          Cr. —

            Purchases   Dr. 600. 700. 800.
                          Cr. —

            A   Dr. 500.
                          Cr. 600. 800.

            Sales   Dr. —
                          Cr. 500. 300.

            X   Dr. 500, 300. *B* Dr. 600. *Wages* Dr. 10. 10.
                          Cr. 490.   Cr. 700.   Cr. —

            Trial Balance Dr. Cash 1,070. Rent 100. Furniture 200. Purchases
                          2,100. Debtors (X) 310. Wages 20.
                          Cr. Capital 2,000. Creditors (A and B) 1,000. Sales
                          800.
                          TOTAL = 3,800.

19.   (5)   *Cash*   Dr. 5,000. 130. 240. 230.
                          Cr. 700. 1,200. 800. 900. 300.

            Capital   Dr. —   *Rent* Dr. 700.
                          Cr. 5,000.   Cr. —

            Fixtures   Dr. 1, 200.   *Van* Dr. 900.
                          Cr. —   Cr. —

            Purchases   Dr. 800. 300. 420.
                          Cr. —

            Sales   Dr. —
                          Cr. 130. 230. 240.

            O. Penn   Dr. 230. *R. Street* Dr.
                          Cr. 230.   Cr. 420.

            Trial Balance Dr. Cash 1,700. Rent 700. Fixtures 1,200. Van
            as at   900. Purchases 1,520.
            30 Sept.
                          Cr. Capital 5,000. Sales 600. Creditors (R. Street)
                          420.
                          TOTAL = 6,020.

19.   (6)   *Trial Balance* Dr. Rent 620. Furniture 250. Rates 35. Sundry
                          Expenses 12. Purchases 3,100. Debtors 915. Cash
                          908.
                          Cr. Capital 2,200. Sales 2,800. Creditors 840.
                          TOTAL = 5,840.

19.   (7)   *Trial Balance* Dr. Rates 3,000. Premises 28,000. Motor Vehicles
            as at   13,000. Fixtures 1,800. Wages 14,000. Purchases
            31 Dec.   30,000. Postages & Telephones 900. Lighting
                          and Heating 2,800. Debtors 8,600. Cash 2,400.
                          Cr. Capital 40,000. Loan 10,000. Sales 50,000
                          Creditors 4,500.
                          TOTAL = 104,500.

Chapter 4

Page 34.

8. (1)   *Trial Balance*   Dr. Salaries 42,000. Postages 1,020. Rates 4,160. Furniture and Fittings 11,000. Premises 33,000. Debtors 3,000. Cash in Bank 180. Cash in Hand 40.

Cr. Capital 60,000. Creditors 2,400. Costs 32,000.

TOTAL = 94,400.

8. (2)   *Trial Balance*   Dr. Fixtures and Fittings 24,000. Machinery and Equipment 17,100. Motor Cars 12,000. Salaries 19,200. Rent and Rates 18,000. Light and Heat 2,600. Interest on Loan 2,400. Bad Debts 580. Debtors 620.

Cr. Capital 30,000. Loan from George 15,000. Costs 46,500. Interest Received 300. Bank Overdraft 4,210. Creditors 490.

TOTAL = 96,500.

Chapter 5

Page 43.

23. (1)   Profit and Loss Account

	£	£
Costs		7,000
Administration Expenses	3,000	
Financial Expenses	2,000	
Miscellaneous Expenses	500	5,500
NET PROFIT		1,500

23. (2)   Profit and Loss Account for the 6 months ending March 31

	£	£
COSTS		32,000
EXPENSES		
Salaries	15,000	
Stationery	500	
Postages and Telephones	1,600	
Fares	700	
Rent	2,000	
Electricity	200	
Rates	300	
Sundry Expenses	130	
		20,430
NET PROFIT		11,570

23. (3)   Profit and Loss Account for the 6 months ending December 31

INCOME	£	£
Costs	19,000	
Commissions Received	200	
Interest Received	500	
Investment Income	300	
		20,000
EXPENSES		
Salaries	9,000	
Postages and Telephones	600	
Fares	400	
Rates	100	
Rent	900	
Electricity	800	
Interest Paid	80	
Sundry Expenses	320	
		12,200
NET PROFIT		7,800

23. (4)   Balance Sheet as at

EMPLOYMENT OF CAPITAL	£	£
Fixed Assets	700	
Cash	600	
		1,300
CAPITAL EMPLOYED		
Capital	1,000	
Loan	300	
		1,300

23. (5)   Profit and Loss Account for the

INCOME	£	£
Costs		210
EXPENSES		
Administration	100	
Financial	40	
Miscellaneous	20	160
NET PROFIT		50

Balance Sheet as at

CAPITAL EMPLOYED	£	£
Capital	1,000	
Plus Net Profit	50	
	1,050	
Less Drawings	200	850
Loan		300
		1,150

EMPLOYMENT OF CAPITAL
  Fixed Assets   700
  Current Assets
    Debtors   700
    Cash   150
                                               ———
                                               850
  Less Current Liabilities
    Creditors   400
    Net Current Assets   ———   450
                                                                ———
                                                              1,150
                                                              ═════

23. (6)   Profit and Loss Account for year ending December 31

       Costs   19,157
  Less Rent and Rates   854
       Light and Heat   422
       Wages   3,164
       Insurances   105
       Motor Expenses   1,133   5,678
                                              —————   ——————
       Net Profit   13,479
                                                             ══════

                   Balance Sheet as at December 31

EMPLOYMENT OF CAPITAL
  Fixed Assets
    Premises   50,000
    Fixtures & Fittings   11,000
    Vans   10,166   71,166
                                           ——————

  Current Assets
    Debtors   3,672
    Cash   3,347
                                           ——————
                                            7,019
  less   Current Liabilities
    Creditors   1,206   5,813
                                           ——————   ——————
                                                            76,979
                                                            ══════

CAPITAL EMPLOYED
  Capital as at
  Jan. 1.   65,900
  Plus Net Profit   13,479
                                           ——————
                                           79,379
    Less Drawings   2,400   76,979
                                           ——————   ══════

23. (7)   Profit & Loss Account for year ending December 31

INCOME	£	£
Costs	41,000	
Commission Received	3,000	
		44,000

EXPENSES		
Salaries and Wages	7,000	
Rates	3,800	
Lighting and Heating	4,100	
Stationery	5,000	
Postages & Telephones	2,400	
Interest on Loan	1,200	
Bad Debts	500	
		24,000
NET PROFIT		20,000

Balance Sheet as at December 31

EMPLOYMENT OF CAPITAL

Fixed Assets	£		
Premises		30,000	
Machinery and Equipment		13,000	
Furniture and Fittings		18,000	
			61,000
Current Assets			
Debtors		4,000	
less Current Liabilities			
Creditors	2,000		
Bank Overdraft	1,000	3,000	
Net Current Assets			1,000
			62,000

CAPITAL EMPLOYED

Capital		
Balance as at Jan. 1	50,000	
plus Net Profit	20,000	
	70,000	
less Drawings	18,000	
		52,000
Loan		10,000
		62,000

23. (8)   Profit and Loss Account for year ending December 31

INCOME	£	£
Costs	12,000	
Investment Income	2,500	14,500

EXPENSES		
Salaries	8,000	
Postages and Telephones	700	
Rates	50	
Rent	900	
Fares	150	
Light and Heat	250	
Bank Charges	100	
Audit Fees	700	
Sundry Expenses	200	11,050
NET PROFIT		3,450

Balance Sheet as at December 31

CAPITAL EMPLOYED	£	£
Capital	25,000	
plus Net Profit	3,450	
	28,450	
less Drawings	2,800	25,650

EMPLOYMENT OF CAPITAL		
Fixed Assets		
Machinery	12,200	
Furniture and Fittings	9,400	
Investments	3,000	24,600
Current Assets		
Debtors	1,780	
Cash (Office Account)	470	
	2,250	
less Current Liabilities		
Creditors	1,200	
Net Current Assets		1,050
CLIENT ACCOUNT		
Cash in bank	8,100	
less Due to clients	8,100	—
		25,650

Chapter 6

Page 57.

37.   (1) *Depreciation (Furniture)*   Dr. —   Depreciation   Dr. —
                                         Cr. 1,260   (Library)   Cr. 105

           Profit & Loss   Dr. Depreciation 1,365.
                                         Cr. —

           Balance Sheet (Extract)

                                         Furniture   7,000
                              Less Depreciation   1,260

                                                                           5,740
                                         Library   2,100
                              Less Depreciation   105   1,995

37.   (2) *Motor Cars*   Dr. Balance 8,000. Cash 9,000.
                                         Cr. —

           Depreciation (Motor Cars)   Dr. —
                                         Cr. Balance 800. Profit & Loss 1,700.

           Profit & Loss   Dr. Depreciation 1,700.
                                         Cr. —

           Balance Sheet (Extract)

                                         Motor Cars   17,000
                              Less Depreciation   2,500

                                                                          14,500

37.   (3) *Machinery*   Dr. Balance 16,000. Cash 15,000.
                                         Cr. Disposal 12,000.

           Depreciation   Dr. Balance 2,400.
                                         Cr. Balance 2,800. Profit & Loss 1,900.

           Machinery Disposal   Dr. Machinery 12,000. Profit 400.
                                         Cr. Cash 10,000. Depreciation 2,400.

           Profit & Loss   Dr. Depreciation 1,900.
                                         Cr. Profit on Disposal 400.

           Balance Sheet (Extract)

                                         Machinery   19,000
                              Less Depreciation   2,300

                                                                          16,700

37.   (4)   Electricity

           | Balance b/d | 1,400 | P & L | 1,550 |
           | A/COS | 150 | | |
           | | ----- | | ----- |
           | | 1,550 | | 1,550 |
           | | | A/COS | 150 |

37. (5)   Rent & Rates

Balance b/d	1,000	P.I.A.	100	$[200 \times \frac{1}{2}]$
A/COS	2,500	P & L	3,400	
	3,500		3,500	
P.I.A.	100	A/COS	2,500	$[3,000 \times \frac{5}{6}]$

37. (6)   Stationery

Balance b/d	520	Stock	33
		P & L	487
	520		520
Stock	33		

37. (7) *Costs*   Dr. P & L 15,200
Cr. Balance 15,000. W in H 200.

Debit Balance b/d 200

37. (8) *Costs*   Dr. W in H 1,300. P & L 21,600.
Cr. Bills delivered 21,000. W in H 1,900.

Debit Balance b/d 1,900.

37. (9) *Bad Debts*   Dr. Carol 40. Dick 70. Provision 20.
Cr. P & L 130.

Credit Balance b/d 20

37. (10) *Bad Debts*   Dr. Write Offs 800, Provision 60.
Cr. Bad Debt Received 31. P & L 829.

Credit Balance b/d 60

37. (11)   Profit and Loss Account for the year ending 31/12/81

	£	£
INCOME		
Costs	24,000	
Work in Hand	3,471	27,471
EXPENSES		
Rent & Rates	2,412	
Light & Heat	2,136	
Wages	9,492	
Insurances	473	
Bad Debts	490	
Depreciation	4,000	19,003
NET PROFIT		8,468

Balance Sheet as at 31/12

EMPLOYMENT OF CAPITAL

Fixed Assets	£	£	£
Premises		32,000	
Fixtures & Fittings	20,000		
Depreciation	8,000	12,000	44,000
Current Assets			
Work in Hand		3,471	
Debtors	11,016		
Provision	50	10,966	
Prepayments		150	
Cash		1,429	
		16,016	
Current Liabilities			
Creditors	13,618		
Accounts outstanding	435	14,053	
Net Current Assets			1,963
			45,963
CAPITAL EMPLOYED			
Capital			
Balance as at 1/1		44,695	
N.P.		8,468	
		53,163	
less Drawings		7,200	
			45,963

37.   (12)

INCOME

	£	£	£
Costs	60,000		
plus Work in Hand	17,500		
		77,500	
Interest Received		17,500	
Profit on Sale of Equipment		500	
			95,500
EXPENSES			
Wages		42,750	
Rates		600	
General Expenses	19,940		
	1,620	21,560	
Insurances		485	
Stationery	2,300		
Stock	200	2,100	
Bad Debts	6,000		
	1,040	7,040	
Postages		525	
Depreciation			
Furniture	3,000		
Machinery	7,000	10,000	
			85,060
			10,440

CAPITAL EMPLOYED

Capital	£	£	£
Balance as at January 1		60,000	
plus Net Profit		10,440	
		70,440	
less Drawings		8,000	
			62,440

EMPLOYMENT OF ASSETS

Fixed Assets			
Premises		30,600	
Machinery & Equipment	35,000		
less Depreciation	23,300	11,700	
Furniture	15,000		
less Depreciation	8,000	7,000	
			49,300
Current Assets			
Work in Hand		17,500	
Stationery Stock		200	
Debtors	20,780		
Less Provision	1,040	19,740	
Cash in Bank			
(Office Account)		1,610	
		39,050	
less Current Liabilities			
Creditors	24,290		
Accounts Outstanding	1,620		
		25,910	
Net Current Assets			13,140
			62,440

Machinery	Dr. Balance b/d 32,000. Suspense 10,000. Cr. Disposal 7,000. Balance c/d 35,000.
Depreciation (Machinery)	Dr. Disposal 4,200. Balance c/d 23,300. Cr. Balance b/d 20,500. P & L 7,000.
Machinery Disposal	Dr. Machinery 7,000. P & L 500. Cr. Cash 3,300. Depreciation 4,200.

Chapter 7

Page 63.

6. (1)   Profit & Loss Account for the [period] ending

		£
	INCOME	100,000
less	EXPENSES	88,000
	N.P.	12,000
	A$\frac{1}{2}$	6,000
	B$\frac{1}{4}$	3,000
	C$\frac{1}{4}$	3,000
		12,000

6. (2)   Profit & Loss Account for the [period] ending

		£	£
	INCOME		75,000
less	EXPENSES		63,000
	NET PROFIT		12,000
	INTEREST ON CAPITAL		
	A 720		
	B 480	1,200	
	SALARIES		
	A 2,000		
	B 2,500	4,500	
	BALANCE OF PROFIT		
	A 4,200		
	B 2,100	6,300	
			12,000

6. (3)   Profit and Loss Account for the [period] ending

		£	£
	INCOME		9,000
less	EXPENSES		11,000
	NET LOSS		2,000

Appropriation Account for the [period] ending

	£	£
INTEREST ON CAPITAL		
A	150	
B	50	200
SALARY A		800
		1,000
SHARE OF LOSS		
A ($\frac{1}{2}$)	(1,500)	
B ($\frac{1}{2}$)	(1,500)	(3,000)
		(2,000)

6. (4)   APPROPRIATION for the 6 months ending June 30

SHARE OF PROFIT	£	£	£
$A\frac{1}{2}$		2,500	
$B\frac{1}{4}$		1,250	
$C\frac{1}{4}$		1,250	5,000

APPROPRIATION for the 6 months ending December 31

INTEREST ON CAPITAL			
B	400		
C	300		
D	300	1,000	
BALANCE OF PROFIT			
$B\frac{2}{5}$	1,600		
$C\frac{2}{5}$	1,600		
$D\frac{1}{5}$	800	4,000	5,000
			10,000

6. (5)   Profit & Loss Account for the [period] ending

INCOME	£	£
Costs	5,000	
Work in Hand	1,000	
		6,000

Less   EXPENSES

	£	£
Salaries	200	
General Expenses	560	
Rent and Rates	300	
Financial Expenses	40	
		1,100
NET PROFIT		4,900

INTEREST ON CAPITAL

	£	£
A	300	
B	200	
		500
SALARY—C		400

BALANCE OF PROFIT

	£	£
$A\frac{1}{2}$	2,000	
$B\frac{1}{4}$	1,000	
$C\frac{1}{4}$	1,000	
		4,000
		4,900

Balance Sheet as at [date]

CAPITAL EMPLOYED	£	£
Capital Accounts		
A	3,000	
B	2,000	
C	2,000	7,000
Current Accounts		
A	500	
B	200	
C	100	800
		7,800
EMPLOYMENT OF CAPITAL		
Fixed Assets		6,000
Current Assets		
Work in Hand	1,000	
Debtors	600	
Cash	400	
	2,000	
less *Current Liabilities*		
Creditors	200	
Net Current Assets		1,800
		7,800

CURRENT ACCOUNTS

	A	B	C
	£	£	£
Balance	100	200	300
Interest	300	200	—
Salary	—	—	400
Profit	2,000	1,000	1,000
	2,400	1,400	1,700
— Drawings	1,900	1,200	1,600
	500	200	100

6.   (6)   Profit & Loss Account for the year ending December 31

INCOME	£	£
Costs	185,000	
Work in hand	15,000	
		200,000
less EXPENSES		170,000
NET PROFIT		30,000

APPROPRIATION for the 3 months ending March 31

SALARIES	£	£		£
A	500			
B	750	1,250		
BALANCE OF PROFIT				
A$\frac{1}{2}$	3,125			
B$\frac{1}{2}$	3,125	6,250		7,500

APPROPRIATION for the 9 months ending December 31

INTEREST ON CAPITAL			
A	2,400		
B	2,400		
C	240	5,040	
BALANCE OF PROFIT			
A $\frac{2}{5}$	6,984		
B $\frac{2}{5}$	6,984		
C $\frac{1}{5}$	3,492	17,460	22,500
			30,000

Balance Sheet as at December 31

CAPITAL EMPLOYED		
Capital Accounts	£	£
A	40,000	
B	40,000	
C	4,000	84,000
Current Accounts		
A	1,009	
B	3,259	
C	732	5,000
Long Term Liabilities		
Loan		5,000
		94,000

EMPLOYMENT OF CAPITAL		
Fixed Assets		70,000
Current Assets		
Work in hand	15,000	
Debtors	17,000	
Cash	1,000	
	33,000	
less *Current Liabilities*		
Creditors	9,000	
Net Current Assets		24,000
		94,000

	£ A	£ B	£ C
Salary	500	750	—
N.P.	3,125	3,125	—
Interest	2,400	2,400	240
N.P.	6,984	6,984	3,492
	13,009	13,259	3,732
Drawings	12,000	10,000	3,000
	1,009	3,259	732

6. (7)   Profit & Loss Account for 6 months ending May 30

	INCOME	£	£	£
	Costs	22,960		
	Work in hand	7,500	30,460	
	Insurance commissions		470	30,930
less	EXPENSES			
	Wages		12,560	
	Rent and Rates		2,520	
	General expenses		3,680	
	Agency expenses		730	
	Depreciation			
	Library	500		
	Furniture	560	1,060	20,550
				10,380
	NET PROFIT			
	Grace		5,190	
	Leslie		5,190	
				10,380

Balance Sheet as at May 30

CAPITAL EMPLOYED			
Capital Accounts			
Grace		5,000	
Leslie		2,500	7,500
Current Accounts			
Grace	5,190		
less	190	5,000	
Leslie	5,190		
less	820	4,370	9,370
			16,870

EMPLOYMENT OF CAPITAL

	Fixed Assets	£	£	£
	Furniture	5,600		
less	Depreciation	560	5,040	
	Library	2,750		
less	Depreciation	500	2,250	7,290
	Current Assets			
	Work in hand		7,500	
	Debtors		830	
	Payments in advance		350	
	Cash in Bank		850	
	Cash in hand		50	9,580
	Client Account			
	Bank balances		11,240	
less	Due to clients		11,240	—
				16,870

6. (8)   Alpha and Beta

Profit & Loss Account for 6 months ending December 31

	£	£
INCOME		
Costs	24,000	
Deposit Interest Received	4,000	
Insurance Commission Received	500	
Investment Income	200	
		28,700
EXPENSES		
Salaries	10,000	
Rent & Rates	5,500	
Light & Heat	1,200	
General Expenses	4,600	
Deposit Interest Payable	200	
Depreciation	800	
		22,300
		6,400
NET PROFIT		
Alpha	4,800	
Beta	1,600	
		6,400

Balance Sheet as at December 31

	£	£
CAPITAL EMPLOYED		
Capital Accounts		
Alpha	3,000	
Beta	1,000	4,000
Current Accounts		
Alpha	800	
Beta	− 200	600
		4,600

EMPLOYMENT OF CAPITAL

		£	£
Fixed Assets			
Fixtures		5,200	
less Depreciation		3,200	
		2,000	
Investments		1,600	3,600
Current Assets			
Debtors		1,500	
Cash in Bank		500	
		2,000	
less Current Liabilities			
Creditors		1,000	
Net Current Assets			1,000
Client Account			
Bank Balances		70,000	
Less Due to clients		70,000	—
			4,600

Alpha Current Account		Beta Current Account	
	£		£
N.P.	4,800	N.P.	1,600
— Drawings	4,000	— Drawings	1,800
	800	—	200

6. (9) Profit & Loss Account for the year ending December 31

			£
INCOME			
Costs		340,000	
Work in hand		80,000	
			420,000
less EXPENSES			
Loss on car	200		
General Expenses	376,200		
Depreciation			
Fixtures	3,600		
Library	2,800		
Car	1,800	8,200	384,600
			35,400
NET PROFIT			
Wendy			23,600
Tom			11,800
			35,400

Current Accounts

	Wendy		Tom
N.P.	23,600		11,800
Drawings	21,500		13,300
	2,100		1,500 DR

Balance Sheet as at December 31

EMPLOYMENT OF CAPITAL

	Fixed Assets	£	£	£
	Freeholds		30,000	
	Fixtures	18,000		
less	Depreciation	7,000	11,000	
	Library	14,000		
less	Depreciation	6,000	8,000	
	Car	9,000		
less	Depreciation	1,800	7,200	
				56,200
	Current Assets			
	Work in Hand	80,000		
	Debtors	122,000		
	Cash	2,400		
		204,400		
less	*Current Liabilities*			
	Creditors	200,000		
	Net Current Assets			4,400
				60,600

CAPITAL EMPLOYED

	Capital Accounts		£	£
	Wendy		40,000	
	Tom		20,000	60,000
	Current Accounts			
	Wendy		2,100	
	Tom		1,500DR	600
				60,600

WORKINGS

Car Disposal   Dr. Car 7,500.
       Cr. Cash 3,800. Depreciation 3,500. P & L 200.

Page 69.

9. (1)   Revaluation Account

	£		£
Machinery	3,000	Freeholds	37,000
Balance	34,000		
	37,000		37,000
Alice $\frac{3}{4}$	25,500	Balance	34,000
Bill $\frac{1}{4}$	8,500		
	34,000		34,000

Freeholds	Dr Balance 15,000 Revaluation 37,000		
	Cr —		
Machinery	Dr Balance 8,000		
	Cr Revaluation 3,000		
Capital Alice	Dr —	Capital Bill	Dr —
	Cr Revaluation 25,500		Cr Revaluation 8,500

9. (2)   Revaluation Account

	£		£
Fixtures	1,000	Freeholds	20,000
Balance	21,000	Investments	2,000
	22,000		22,000
Carol	7,000	Balance	21,000
Dick	7,000		
Elaine	7,000		
	21,000		21,000

Freeholds	Dr. Balance 12,000 Revaluation 20,000.		
	Cr. —		
Investments	Dr. Balance 5,000 Revaluation 2,000.		
	Cr. —		
Cash	Dr. Capital Fred 3,000	Capital	Dr. —
	Cr. —	Fred	Cr. Cash 3,000
Capital	Dr. —	Fixtures	Dr. Balance 3,000
Carol	Cr. Revaluation 7,000		Cr. Revaluation 1,000

(Dick and Elaine are identical)

9. (3)   Revaluation Account

	£		£
Fixtures and Fittings	6,000	Premises	30,000
Balance	24,000		
	30,000		30,000
George $\frac{1}{2}$	12,000	Balance	24,000
Helen $\frac{1}{3}$	8,000		
Ian $\frac{1}{6}$	4,000		
	24,000		24,000

Capital Account—George

	£		£
Motor Cars	9,000	Balance	15,000
Debtors	7,000	Revaluation	12,000
Cash	11,000		
	27,000		27,000

Balance Sheet as at January 1

CAPITAL EMPLOYED	£	£
Capital Accounts		
Helen	20,000	
Ian	15,000	35,000
Current Accounts		
Helen	800	
Ian	200	1,000
		36,000

EMPLOYMENT OF CAPITAL		
Fixed Assets		
Premises	40,000	
Fixtures and Fittings	5,000	45,000
Current Assets		
Debtors	14,000	
Cash	500	
	14,500	
less *Current Liabilities*		
Creditors	23,500	
Net Current Liabilities		9,000
		36,000

Motor Cars	Dr. Balance 9,000	*Fixtures and*	Dr. Balance	11,000
	Cr. George 9,000	*Fittings*	Cr. Revaluation	6,000
Premises	Dr. Balance 10,000	Revaluation 30,000		
	Cr.—			
Debtors	Dr. Balance 21,000			
	Cr. George 7,000			
Cash	Dr. Balance 12,500			
	Cr. George Capital 11,000 George Current 1,000			
Capital	Dr. —			
Helen	Cr. Balance 12,000	Revaluation 8,000		
Capital	Dr. —			
Ian	Cr. Balance 11,000	Revaluation 4,000		

9. (4) Profit & Loss Account for the year ending December 31

		£
INCOME		200,000
EXPENSES		137,000
NET PROFIT		63,000

Appropriation Account for the 6 months ending June 30

Interest on Capital	£	£	
Jane (12% 45,000* ÷ 2)	2,700		
Kevin (12% 45,000* ÷ 2)	2,700	5,400	
Profit			
Jane ($\frac{1}{2}$)	13,050		
Kevin ($\frac{1}{2}$)	13,050	26,100	31,500

Appropriation Account for the 6 months ending December 31
Interest on Capital

Jane (12% 60,000* ÷ 2)	3,600		
Kevin (12% 60,000* ÷ 2)	3,600		
Lorna (12% 5,000 ÷ 2)	300	7,500	
Salary			
Lorna (£8,000 ÷ 2)		4,000	
Profit			
Jane (2/5)	8,000		
Kevin (2/5)	8,000		
Lorna (1/5)	4,000	20,000	31,500
			63,000

*Note these figures carefully.

Current Account Movements

	Jane	Kevin	Lorna
Balance	500	400	—
Interest to June 30	2,700	2,700	—
to December 31	3,600	3,600	300
Salary to December 31	—	—	4,000
Profit to June 30	13,050	13,050	—
to December 31	8,000	8,000	4,000
	27,850	27,750	8,300
Drawings	27,050	26,850	5,000
	800	900	3,300

Balance Sheet as at December 31

CAPITAL EMPLOYED	£	£
Capital Accounts		
Jane	60,000	
Kevin	60,000	
Lorna	5,000	125,000
Current Accounts		
Jane	800	
Kevin	900	
Lorna	3,300	5,000
		130,000

EMPLOYMENT OF CAPITAL		
Fixed Assets		
Premises	70,000	
Machinery	15,000	
Motor Cars	10,000	95,000
Current Assets	40,000	
less *Current Liabilities*	5,000	
Net Current Assets		35,000
		130,000

Premises   *Dr* Balance 40,000. Revaluation 30,000.
            Cr

Capital Jane   *Dr*   *Capital Lorna*   *Dr*
           Cr Balance 45,000. Revaluation 15,000.   *Cr* Cash 5,000.
(Kevin's Capital Account is identical).

Revaluation

Balance	30,000	Premises	30,000
	30,000		30,000
Jane ($\frac{1}{2}$)	15,000	Balance	30,000
Kevin ($\frac{1}{2}$)	15,000		
	30,000		30,000

Chapter 8

Page 72.

7. (1)   Balance as per Bank Statement 500. Unpresented Cheques 100 = 400
          + Late Credits 50 = Balance as per Cash Book. 450.

7. (2)   Balance as per Bank Statement 400. Unpresented Cheques 50 = 450
          Late Credits 100 = Balance as per Cash Book − 350.

7. (3)   *Cash Book*   Dr. Old Balance b/d 500
                         Cr. Bank Charges 60 Balance c/d 440

          BRS   Bank Balance 300. Unpresented Cheques 140 = 160.
                         Late Credits 280 = Cash Book Balance 440

7. (4)   *Cash Book*   Dr. Balance c/d 58
                         Cr. Old Balance b/d 40. Bank Charges 18

          BRS   Bank Balance 50. Unpresented Cheques 124 Late
                         Credits 16 = Cash Book Balance − 58

7. (5)   *Cash Book*   Dr. Old Balance b/d 3,000. Error 60.
                         Cr. Bank Charges 40. Standing Order 200. Error 100
                         = Balance c/d 2,720

          BRS   Bank Balance 4,000. Unpresented Cheques 1,550.
                         Late Credits 270 = Cash Book Balance 2,720

7. (6)   *Cash Book*   Dr. Error 50. Receipt 50. Balance c/d 2,090.
                         Cr. Old balance b/d 1,000. Bank Charges 500. Inter-
                         est paid 250. Cheque dishonoured 140. Error 200.
                         Error of addition 100.

          BRS   Bank Balance − 2,000. Unpresented Cheques 130.
                         Late Credits 40 = Cash Book Balance − 2,090.

7. (7)   *BRS*   Bank Balance − 6,000. Unpresented Cheques 368.
                         Late Credits 42 − Cash Book Balance − 6,326.

CASH

Balance c/d	6,326	Balance b/d	786[2]
		Bank Charges	520
		Interest Paid	700
		Direct Debit	4,320
	6,326		6,326
		Balance b/d	6,326[1]

[1] This is taken from the Bank Reconciliation Statement.
[2] This must be the opening balance, if the closing balance, after
making the necessary adjustments, is to be £6,326.
N.B. The Bank Reconciliation Statement was done first.

7. (8)

Cash Account

Date	Details	Dr £	Cr £	Balance £
March 31	Balance	878		878
	Standing bankers order		60	818
	Cheque returned		49	769
	Giro direct transfer	126		895

Bank Reconciliation Statement as at March 31, 1975

	£
Balance as per Bank Statement	227 DR
Unpresented Cheques	425
	652 DR
Late Credits	1,547
	895

Unpresented Cheques		*Late Credits*	
PCD	42	PTR	33
PDG	54	JNQ	101
KZ	89	DBM	678
KLO	240	Cash	235
	425	YU	500
			1,547

7. (9)

Cash Account

Date	Details	Dr £	Cr £	Balance £
Dec. 31, 1979	Balance	1,756		1,756
	Standing bankers order		120	1,636
	Cheque returned		98	1,538
	Giro direct transfer	252		1,790

Bank Reconciliation Statement as at December 31, 1979

	£
Balance as per Bank Statement	454 DR
Unpresented Cheques	850
	1,304 DR
Late Credits	3,094
	1,790

Unpresented Cheques		*Late Credits*	
DCP	84	TF	66
DPN	108	ND	202
ZK	178	LKJ	1,356
LKO	480	Cash	470
	850	POY	1,000
			3,094

Chapter 9

Page 77.

Jones

(1)   Profit and Loss Account for year ending December 31, 1982

	INCOME	£	£	£
	Costs	72,946		
	Work in Hand	2,348		
		75,294		
	Sundry rents received		1,000	
	Interest received		1,532	77,826
less	EXPENSES			
	General Expenses*		49,628	
	Loss on car		150	
	Depreciation			
	Cars (6,300 × 25%)	1,575		
	Fixtures, Furniture &			
	Library (4,000 × 15%)	600	2,175	51,953
	NET PROFIT			25,873

```
*  49,769
+     628
   -------
   50,397
-      74
   -------
   50,323
-     695
   -------
   49,628
```

Workings

Motor Cars

Bal. b/d.	8,300	Disposal of Car	2,000
		Bal. c/d.	6,300
	8,300		8,300
Bal. b/d.	6,300		

Disposal of Motor Car

Motor Cars	2,000	Capital	1,350
		Depreciation	500*
		Loss	150
	2,000		2,000

*£2,000 × 25% × 1.

Capital Account

Disposal of Car	1,350	Bal. b/d.	38,161
Bal. c/d.	36,811		
	38,161		38,161
		Bal. b/d.	36,811

Depreciation (Motor Cars)

Disposal of Car	500	Bal. b/d.	1,900
Bal. c/d.	2,975	Profit & Loss	1,575
	3,475		3,475
		Bal. b/d.	2,975

Balance Sheet as at December 31, 1982

CAPITAL EMPLOYED

		£	£	£
Capital Account				
Old Balance		36,811		
Net Profit		25,873		
		62,684		
Drawings		15,234		47,450

EMPLOYMENT OF CAPITAL

Fixed Assets				
Lease			14,000	
Fixtures, Furniture & Library	4,000			
less Depreciation	2,600		1,400	
Motor Cars	6,300			
less Depreciation	2,975		3,325	18,725
Current Assets				
Work in hand			2,348	
Stationery stock			74	
Debtors			11,428	
Prepayments			695	
Cash in bank			15,927	
Cash in hand			24	
			30,496	
less *Current Liabilities*				
Creditors		1,143		
Accounts outstanding		628	1,771	
Net Current Assets				28,725
Client Account				
Cash in bank			94,620	
less Due to Clients			94,620	—
				47,450

(2)   April Blossom & Co.

Profit and Loss Account for year ending June 30, 1976

Income	£	£	£
Costs			
Add: Work in progress	83,567		
June 30, 1976	2,126		
		85,693	
Interest Received		1,469	
			87,162
less **Expenditure**			
Administration		44,426	
General Expenses		16,059	
Depreciation		2,095	62,580
Net Profit			24,582

APPROPRIATIONS

Salary			
Smith			5,000
Interest on Capital			
Jones		750	
Smith		250	1,000
Share of Profit			
Jones $\frac{2}{3}$		12,388	
Smith $\frac{1}{3}$		6,194	18,582
			24,582

Current Account Movements

	Jones	Smith
Opening Balances	2,300	1,200
Add Salary	—	5,000
Interest on capital	750	250
Share of profit	12,388	6,194
	15,438	12,644
Less Drawings	14,500	9,000
Closing balances	938	3,644

Balance Sheet as at June 30, 1976

CAPITAL EMPLOYED	£	£	£
Capital Accounts			
Jones	15,000		
Smith	5,000	20,000	
Current Accounts			
Smith	3,644		
Jones	938	4,582	
			24,582

EMPLOYMENT OF CAPITAL			
Fixed Assets			
Lease		6,000	
Library		1,456	
Furniture	2,795		
Less Depreciation	705	2,090	
Motor Cars	13,030		
Less Depreciation	7,440	5,590	15,136
Current Assets			
Work in hand	2,126		
Debtors	8,042		
Bank-office account	1,356		
Petty Cash	14	11,538	
less *Current Liabilities*			
Creditors	842		
Accrued Expenses	1,250	2,092	
Net Current Assets			9,446
Client Account			
Current Account	6,219		
Deposit Account	84,567	90,786	
less Due to clients		90,786	—
			24,582

(3)   Olde, Rustred, Razor & Co.

Profit & Loss Account for the year ending December 31, 1985

INCOME	£	£	£
Costs	310,426		
less Work in hand 1/1/85	28,115		
	282,311		
plus Work in hand 31/12/85	32,174	314,485	
Interest Receivable		17,427	331,912
EXPENSES			
Administrative & General			
Expenses	226,327		
plus accounts outstanding	1,120		
plus allowance to Razor	315	227,762	
Bad Debts		750	
Depreciation			
Motor Cars	8,000		
Library, Furniture and			
Computer	4,800	12,800	241,312
NET PROFIT			90,600

Appropriation Account for the 6 months ending June 30, 1985

Salary			
Razor (12,000 ÷ 2)		6,000	
Interest on Capital			
Olde (10% 70,000 ÷ 2)	3,500		
Razor (10% 50,000 ÷ 2)	2,500	6,000	
Profit			
Olde ($\frac{2}{3}$)	22,200		
Razor ($\frac{1}{3}$)	11,100	33,300	45,300

Appropriation Account for the 6 months ending December 31, 1985

Olde ($\frac{1}{3}$)		15,100	
Razor ($\frac{1}{3}$)		15,100	
Rustred ($\frac{1}{3}$)		15,100	45,300
			90,600

As it's for 6 mths divide £90,600 by 2 & then share profits out for 6 mths—

Olde, Rustred, Razor & Co.

Balance Sheet as at December 31, 1985

EMPLOYMENT OF CAPITAL	£	£	£
Fixed Assets			
Freehold Land and Buildings		77,000	
Motor Cars	32,000		
less Depreciation	16,000	16,000	
Library, Furniture &			
Computer	24,000		
less Depreciation	16,800	7,200	100,200
Current Assets			
Work in hand		32,174	
Debtors		45,363	
Cash in bank		8,642	
Cash in hand		85	
		86,264	
Current Liabilities			
Creditors	11,129		
Accounts outstanding	1,120	12,249	
Net Current Assets			74,015
Client Account			
Cash in hand: Deposit Account	247,000		
Current Account	72,096	319,096	
less Due to clients		319,096	—
			174,215
CAPITAL EMPLOYED			
Capital Accounts			
Olde		70,000	
Razor		50,000	
Rustred		30,000	150,000
Current Accounts			
Olde		12,200	
Razor		6,915	
Rustred		5,100	24,215
			174,215

Current Account Movements

	Olde	Razor	Rustred
Balance	7,400	(600)	—
Salary to 30/6		6,000	—
Interest to 30/6	3,500	2,500	—
Profit to 30/6	22,200	11,100	
Profit to 31/12	15,100	15,100	15,100
Allowance to Razor		315	
	48,200	34,415	15,100
Drawings	36,000	27,500	10,000
	12,200	6,915	5,100

(4)   Alfred Basil Charles and Douglas

Profit & Loss Account for year ending June 30, 1964

		£
Income		39,320
less *Expenses*		30,800
		8,520

Appropriation Account for the 6 months ending December 31, 1963

	£	£	£
Interest on Capital			
Alfred (5% £6,200 ÷ 2)	155		
Basil (5% £4,400 ÷ 2)	110		
Charles (5% £3,000 ÷ 2)	75	340	
Profits			
Alfred ($\frac{3}{8}$)	1,470		
Basil ($\frac{3}{8}$)	1,470		
Charles ($\frac{2}{8}$)	980	3,920	
			4,260

Appropriation Account for the 6 months ending June 30, 1964

	£	£	£
Consultancy			
Alfred (£600 ÷ 2)		300	
Interest on Capital			
Basil (5% £4,400 ÷ 2)	110		
Charles (5% £3,000 ÷ 2)	75		
Douglas (5% £600 ÷ 2)	15	200	
Profits			
Basil ($\frac{2}{5}$)	1,504		
Charles ($\frac{2}{5}$)	1,504		
Douglas ($\frac{1}{5}$)	752	3,760	
			4,260
			8,520

Balance Sheet as at June 30, 1964

	£	£
CAPITAL EMPLOYED		
Capital Accounts		
Basil	4,400	
Charles	3,000	
Douglas	600	8,000
Current Accounts		
Basil	1,220	
Charles	820	
Douglas	144	2,184
Loan Account		
Alfred		4,960
		15,144

Partners' Current Account Movements

	Basil	Charles	Douglas
Balance	119	98	—
Interest to Dec. 31	110	75	—
Profit	1,470	980	—
Interest to June 30	110	75	15
Profit	1,504	1,504	752
	3,313	2,732	767
Drawings	2,093	1,912	623
	1,220	820	144

Movements on Alfred's Current Account

	£
Balance	135
Interest to December 31	155
Profit	1,470
Consultancy	300
	2,060
Drawings	1,200
	860

This is shown separately because Alfred is no longer a partner.

EMPLOYMENT OF CAPITAL

		£	£	£
	Fixed Assets			8,000
	Current Assets		11,644	
less	Current Liabilities			
	Creditors	3,640		
	Alfred (Current A/C)	860	4,500	
	Net Current Assets			7,144
				15,144

Workings

Capital Alfred

Cash	1,240	Balance b/d.	6,200
Balance c/d.	4,960		
	6,200		6,200
		Balance b/d.	4,960

SECTION TWO

THE HANDLING OF TRANSACTIONS ON
BEHALF OF CLIENTS

General Notes

1. Whenever possible, payments have been made of clients' money. It is not wrong, when clients' money is available, to make payments out of office money but, certainly where the sum involved is substantial, it is impractical to use office money.

2. This was a composite cheque which can either:
   (a) be split; or
   (b) paid into clients' bank account followed by a transfer from CLIENT ACCOUNT to OFFICE ACCOUNT.

3. All petty cash payments must be made out of office money. Clients' money thus could not have been used.

4. The Principal Method of payment has been used in this case, so the VAT item (after the costs charge) will also include the VAT on this payment. It would have been perfectly permissible in this case to use the Agency Method instead, in which case the amount debited to the ledger account when making the payment would also have included the VAT (and not the debit for the VAT after the costs debit).

5. This could not have been paid out of CLIENT ACCOUNT, because the Principal Method of payment is used.

6. This must be office money (Rule 9 (2) (SAR)).

Chapter 10

10. (1)   Client A/C

Cash		Alice	
30	20	20	30

10. (2)   Office A/C

Cash		Alice	
800	1,000	1,000	800

10. (3)   Client A/C

Cash		Alice	
70	50	50	70

Office A/C

Cash		Alice	
30	400	400	30

Chapter 12

Page 98.

11. (1)

		OFFICE ACCOUNT			CLIENT ACCOUNT		
Alpha							
		DR	CR	BALANCE	DR	CR	BALANCE
	Cash					800–	800–
	Cash				300–		500–
	Cash				400–		100–
	Cash				2–		98–

		OFFICE ACCOUNT			CLIENT ACCOUNT		
Cash							
		DR	CR	BALANCE	DR	CR	BALANCE
	Alpha				800		
	Alpha					300	
	Alpha					400	
	Alpha					2	

11. (2)

		OFFICE ACCOUNT			CLIENT ACCOUNT		
Beta							
		DR	CR	BALANCE	DR	CR	BALANCE
	Cash	6–		6–			
	Cash	700–		706–			
	Cash	45–		751–			
	Cash		300–	451–			

Cash

		OFFICE ACCOUNT			CLIENT ACCOUNT		
		DR	CR	BALANCE	DR	CR	BALANCE
Beta			6				
Beta			700				
Beta			45				
Beta		300					

11. (3)

Omega

	OFFICE ACCOUNT			CLIENT ACCOUNT		
	DR	CR	BALANCE	DR	CR	BALANCE
Cash					38–	38–
Cash				20–		18–
Cash				18–		—
Cash	16–		16–			
Cash		9–	7–			

Cash

	OFFICE ACCOUNT			CLIENT ACCOUNT		
	DR	CR	BALANCE	DR	CR	BALANCE
Omega				38		
Omega					20	
Omega					18	
Omega		16				
Omega	9					

Page 99.

16. (1)

		OFFICE ACCOUNT			CLIENT ACCOUNT		
Alpha							
		DR	CR	BALANCE	DR	CR	BALANCE
	P. Cash	4–		4–			

		OFFICE ACCOUNT			CLIENT ACCOUNT		
Beta							
		DR	CR	BALANCE	DR	CR	BALANCE
	P. Cash	3–20		3–20			

		OFFICE ACCOUNT			CLIENT ACCOUNT		
Gamma							
		DR	CR	BALANCE	DR	CR	BALANCE
	P. Cash	4–60		4–60			

Petty Cash				
		DR	CR	BALANCE
	Alpha		4	
	Beta		3–20	
	Gamma		4–60	

16. (2)

		OFFICE ACCOUNT			CLIENT ACCOUNT		
		Delta					
		DR	CR	BALANCE	DR	CR	BALANCE
P. Cash		6–		6–			
Cash						18–	18–
P. Cash		1–70^3		7–70			

* For meaning of superior figures throughout these answers see General Notes, page 261.

		DR	CR	BALANCE
		Petty Cash		
Delta			6–	
Delta			1–70	

Page 100.

20. (1)

		OFFICE ACCOUNT			CLIENT ACCOUNT		
		Alan					
		DR	CR	BALANCE	DR	CR	BALANCE
Cash						100–	100–
Cash					60–		40–
Cash		70–		70–			

20. (2)

		OFFICE ACCOUNT			CLIENT ACCOUNT		
Brian							
		DR	CR	BALANCE	DR	CR	BALANCE
Cash						200–	200–
Cash					30–		170–
Cash		400–		400–			
Cash					50–		120–

20. (3)

		OFFICE ACCOUNT			CLIENT ACCOUNT		
Charles							
		DR	CR	BALANCE	DR	CR	BALANCE
Cash						300–	300–
Cash					200–		100–
Cash		150–		150–			
Cash					75–		25–
Cash		30–		180–			

20. (4)

		OFFICE ACCOUNT			CLIENT ACCOUNT		
Donald							
		DR	CR	BALANCE	DR	CR	BALANCE
Cash						400–	400–
Cash					100–		300–
Cash		350–		350–			
Cash					150–		150–
Cash					40–		110–

Page 103.

24. (1)

		OFFICE ACCOUNT			CLIENT ACCOUNT		
Ethel							
		DR	CR	BALANCE	DR	CR	BALANCE
	Cash	100–		100–			
	Cash		70–	30–			
	Cash					40–	40–

24. (2)

		OFFICE ACCOUNT			CLIENT ACCOUNT		
Fred							
		DR	CR	BALANCE	DR	CR	BALANCE
	Cash	200–		200–			
	Cash		160–	40–			
	Cash					50–	50–
	Cash		30–	10–			

24. (3)

		OFFICE ACCOUNT			CLIENT ACCOUNT		
George							
		DR	CR	BALANCE	DR	CR	BALANCE
	Cash	300–		300–			
	Cash					400–	400–
	Cash		50–	250–			
	Cash	580–		830–			
	Cash		800–	30–			

Page 104.

31. (1) *Harry*   OFFICE A/C Dr. 60
                                Cr. 60
                    CLIENT A/C Dr. —
                                Cr. —

31. (2) *Ian*   OFFICE A/C Dr. 50.40
                                Cr. 90
                    CLIENT A/C Dr. —
                                Cr. —

31. (3) *Joan*   OFFICE A/C Dr. 400.650
                                Cr. 1,050
                    CLIENT A/C Dr. —
                                Cr. —

31. (4) *Kate*   OFFICE A/C Dr. 80.1,500
                                Cr. 1,580
                    CLIENT A/C Dr. —
                                Cr. —

Chapter 13

Page 106.

5. (1)

Alice (CL1)							
		OFFICE ACCOUNT			CLIENT ACCOUNT		
		DR	CR	BALANCE	DR	CR	BALANCE
(a)	Cash. You.					100–	100–
(b)	Costs	20–		20–			
(c)	Cash. Transfer		20–	—	20–		80–

Cash							
		OFFICE ACCOUNT			CLIENT ACCOUNT		
		DR	CR	BALANCE	DR	CR	BALANCE
(a)	Alice				100–		
(c)	Alice Transfer	20–				20–	

5. (2)

		OFFICE ACCOUNT			CLIENT ACCOUNT		
	Bill (CL2)						
		DR	CR	BALANCE	DR	CR	BALANCE
(a)	Cash. You.					300–	300–
(b)	Costs	50–		50–			
(c)	Cash.						
	Transfer		50–	—	50–		250–

		OFFICE ACCOUNT			CLIENT ACCOUNT		
	Cash						
		DR	CR	BALANCE	DR	CR	BALANCE
(a)	Bill				300–		
(b)	Bill. Transfer	50–				50–	

5. (3)

		OFFICE ACCOUNT			CLIENT ACCOUNT		
	Charles (CL3)						
		DR	CR	BALANCE	DR	CR	BALANCE
(a)	Cash. You.					600–	600–
(b)	Cash				70–		530–
(c)	Costs	80–		80–			
(d)	Cash.						
	Transfer		80–	—	80–		450–

Cash							
		OFFICE ACCOUNT			CLIENT ACCOUNT		
		DR	CR	BALANCE	DR	CR	BALANCE
(a)	Charles				600–		
(b)	Charles					70–	
(d)	Charles						
	Transfer	80–				80–	

5. (4)

Dennis (CL4)							
		OFFICE ACCOUNT			CLIENT ACCOUNT		
		DR	CR	BALANCE	DR	CR	BALANCE
(a)	Cash. You.					90–	90–
(b)	P. Cash	10–[3]		10–			
(c)	Costs	30–		40–			
(d)	Cash.						
	Transfer		40–	—	40–		50–

Cash							
		OFFICE ACCOUNT			CLIENT ACCOUNT		
		DR	CR	BALANCE	DR	CR	BALANCE
(a)	Dennis				90–		
(d)	Dennis.						
	Transfer	40–				40–	

5. (5)

		OFFICE ACCOUNT			CLIENT ACCOUNT		
	Ethel (CL5)						
		DR	CR	BALANCE	DR	CR	BALANCE
(a)	Cash					400–	400–
(b)	Cash				50–		350–
(c)	P. Cash	6–[3]		6–			
(d)	Costs	70–		76–			
(e)	Cash.						
	Transfer		76–	—	76–		274–

		OFFICE ACCOUNT			CLIENT ACCOUNT		
	Cash						
		DR	CR	BALANCE	DR	CR	BALANCE
(a)	Ethel				400–		
(b)	Ethel					50–	
(e)	Ethel						
	Transfer	76–				76–	

5. (6)

		OFFICE ACCOUNT			CLIENT ACCOUNT		
	Frances (CL6)						
		DR	CR	BALANCE	DR	CR	BALANCE
(a)	Cash					80–	80–
(b)	Cash				10–		70–
(c)	P. Cash	1–		1–			
(d)	Costs	20–		21–			
(e)	Cash.						
	Transfer		21–	—	21–		49–

		OFFICE ACCOUNT			CLIENT ACCOUNT		
	Cash						
		DR	CR	BALANCE	DR	CR	BALANCE
(a)	Frances				80		
(b)	Frances					10	
(e)	Frances. Transfer	21				21	

Page 109.

10. (1)

		OFFICE ACCOUNT			CLIENT ACCOUNT		
	Graham (CL7)						
		DR	CR	BALANCE	DR	CR	BALANCE
	Cash					40–	40– DR
	Cash				50–		10–
	Cash Transfer	10–		10–		10–	—

		OFFICE ACCOUNT			CLIENT ACCOUNT		
	Cash						
		DR	CR	BALANCE	DR	CR	BALANCE
	Graham				40		
	Graham					50	
	Graham Transfer		10		10		

10. (2)

Henry (CL8)							
		OFFICE ACCOUNT			CLIENT ACCOUNT		
		DR	CR	BALANCE	DR	CR	BALANCE
	Cash					700–	700– DR
	Cash				1,000–		300–
	Cash. Transfer	300–		300–		300–	—

Cash							
		OFFICE ACCOUNT			CLIENT ACCOUNT		
		DR	CR	BALANCE	DR	CR	BALANCE
	Henry				700		
	Henry					1,000	
	Henry. Transfer		300		300		

10. (3)

Ian (CL9)							
		OFFICE ACCOUNT			CLIENT ACCOUNT		
		DR	CR	BALANCE	DR	CR	BALANCE
	Cash					2,000–	2,000– DR
	Cash				2,500–		500–
	Cash. Transfer	500–		500–		500–	—

		OFFICE ACCOUNT			CLIENT ACCOUNT		
		\multicolumn{6}{c}{Cash}				
		DR	CR	BALANCE	DR	CR	BALANCE
	Ian				2,000		
	Ian					2,500	
	Ian. Transfer		500		500		

Page 111.

16. (1)

		OFFICE ACCOUNT			CLIENT ACCOUNT		
		\multicolumn{6}{c}{John (CL10)}				
		DR	CR	BALANCE	DR	CR	BALANCE
	Cash					40–	40–
	Kevin				20–		20–

		OFFICE ACCOUNT			CLIENT ACCOUNT		
		\multicolumn{6}{c}{Kevin (CL11)}				
		DR	CR	BALANCE	DR	CR	BALANCE
	John					20–	20–

16. (2)

		OFFICE ACCOUNT			CLIENT ACCOUNT		
		DR	CR	BALANCE	DR	CR	BALANCE
	Cash					700–	700–
	Mary				400–		300–

Lesley (CL12)

		OFFICE ACCOUNT			CLIENT ACCOUNT		
		DR	CR	BALANCE	DR	CR	BALANCE
	Lesley					400–	400–

Mary (CL13)

16. (3)

		OFFICE ACCOUNT			CLIENT ACCOUNT		
		DR	CR	BALANCE	DR	CR	BALANCE
(a)	Cash					300–	300–
(b)	Costs	40–		40–			
(c)	Cash				50–		250–
(d)	Cash.						
	Transfer		40–	—	40–		210–
(e)	Olive				210–		—

Nick (CL14)

Olive (CL15)							
		OFFICE ACCOUNT			CLIENT ACCOUNT		
		DR	CR	BALANCE	DR	CR	BALANCE
(e)	Nick					210–	210–

Cash							
		OFFICE ACCOUNT			CLIENT ACCOUNT		
		DR	CR	BALANCE	DR	CR	BALANCE
(a)	Nick				300		
(c)	Nick					50	
(d)	Nick. Transfer	40				40	

16. (4)

Peter (CL16)							
		OFFICE ACCOUNT			CLIENT ACCOUNT		
		DR	CR	BALANCE	DR	CR	BALANCE
	Balance					10–	10–
	Robert				5–		5–
							DR
	Robert				7–		2–
	Cash	2–		2–		2–	—

		OFFICE ACCOUNT			CLIENT ACCOUNT		
		Robert (CL17)					
		DR	CR	BALANCE	DR	CR	BALANCE
Peter						5–	5–
Peter						7–	12–

		OFFICE ACCOUNT			CLIENT ACCOUNT		
		Cash					
		DR	CR	BALANCE	DR	CR	BALANCE
Peter			2		2		

Chapter 14

Page 113.

(1)

		OFFICE ACCOUNT			CLIENT ACCOUNT		
		Alice (CL1)					
		DR	CR	BALANCE	DR	CR	BALANCE
	Cash	300–		300–			
	Cash					400–	400–
	Cash		50–	250–			
	Cash	580–		830–			
	Cash		800–	30–			

(2)

Barbara (CL2)							
		OFFICE ACCOUNT			CLIENT ACCOUNT		
		DR	CR	BALANCE	DR	CR	BALANCE
	Cash	50–		50–			
	Costs	40–		90–			
	Cash		90–	—			

(3)

Carol (CL3)							
		OFFICE ACCOUNT			CLIENT ACCOUNT		
		DR	CR	BALANCE	DR	CR	BALANCE
	P. Cash	1–		1–			
	Cash	4–		5–			
	Costs	50–		55–			
	Cash		55–	—			

(4)

Diana (CL4)							
		OFFICE ACCOUNT			CLIENT ACCOUNT		
		DR	CR	BALANCE	DR	CR	BALANCE
	Cash					100–	100–
	Costs	20–		20–			
	Cash.						
	Transfer		20–	—	20–		80–

(5)

Ellen (CL5)							
		OFFICE ACCOUNT			CLIENT ACCOUNT		
		DR	CR	BALANCE	DR	CR	BALANCE
	Cash					200–	200–
	Cash				30–		170–
	Costs	40–		40–			
	Cash. Transfer		40–	—	40–		130–

(6)

Kate (CL6)							
		OFFICE ACCOUNT			CLIENT ACCOUNT		
		DR	CR	BALANCE	DR	CR	BALANCE
	Cash					300–	300–
	P. Cash	4–[3]		4–			
	Cash				50–		250–
	Cash	600–		604–			
	Costs	70–		674–			
	Cash. Transfer		250–	424–	250–		—

(7)

Mary (CL7)							
		OFFICE ACCOUNT			CLIENT ACCOUNT		
		DR	CR	BALANCE	DR	CR	BALANCE
	Cash					600–	600–
	Sally				70–		530–
	Cash	540–		540–			
	Cash		60–	480–			
	Cash. Transfer		480–	—	480–		50–

(8)

		OFFICE ACCOUNT			CLIENT ACCOUNT		
		Penny (CL8)					
		DR	CR	BALANCE	DR	CR	BALANCE
Cash		50–		50–			
Cash						400–	400–
Cash					7–		393–
P. Cash		8–³		58–			
Costs		200–		258–			
Cash.							
Transfer			258–	—	258–		135–
Rachel					135–		—

Chapter 15

Page 123.

16. (1) *Cash*   Dr. —
                                   Cr. 50.5.40.4.30.3.

       Postages & Telephones   Dr. 50
                                   Cr. —

       Typewriters   Dr. 40
                                   Cr. —

       Stationery   Dr. 30
                                   Cr. —

       Customs & Excise   Dr. 5.4.3.
                                   Cr. —

16. (2) *Cash*   Dr. —
                                   Cr. 5.4.10.8.7–70.

       Fares   Dr. 5   *Postages*   Dr. 4
                      Cr. —   Cr. —

       Water Rates Dr. 10   *Interest*   Dr. 8
                      Cr. —   Cr. —

       Entertaining Dr. 7–70
                      Cr. —

Page 128.

29. (1)

Adam (CL1)							
		OFFICE ACCOUNT			CLIENT ACCOUNT		
		DR	CR	BALANCE	DR	CR	BALANCE
	Cash VAT	1–		1–			
	Cash VAT	2–		3–			
	P. Cash VAT	3–		6–			
	Cash VAT	4–		10–			
	P. Cash VAT	5–		15–			

Cash							
		OFFICE ACCOUNT			CLIENT ACCOUNT		
		DR	CR	BALANCE	DR	CR	BALANCE
	Adam		1				
	VAT		0–10				
	Adam		2				
	VAT		0–20				
	Adam		4				
	VAT		0–40				

Customs & Excise (NL11)				
		DR	CR	BALANCE
	Cash	0–10		0–10
	Cash	0–20		0–30
	P. Cash	0–30		0–60
	Cash	0–40		1
	P. Cash	0–50		1–50

Petty Cash			DR	CR	BALANCE
	Adam			3	
	VAT			0–30	
	Adam			5	
	VAT			0–50	

29. (2) *Adam*   OFFICE A/C   Dr. 1–10.2–20.3–30.4–40.5–50.
                                      Cr. —
                         CLIENT A/C   Dr. —
                                      Cr. —

         Cash   OFFICE A/C   Dr. —
                                      Cr. 1–10.2–20.4–40.
                         CLIENT A/C   Dr. —
                                      Cr. —

         Petty Cash   Dr. —
                         Cr. 3–30.5–50.

29. (3) *Bill*   OFFICE A/C   Dr. 1–.2–20.3–.4–40.5–.
                                      Cr. —
                         CLIENT A/C   Dr. —
                                      Cr. —

         Customs & Excise Dr. 0–10.0–30.0–50.
                            Cr. —

Cash		OFFICE ACCOUNT			CLIENT ACCOUNT		
		DR	CR	BALANCE	DR	CR	BALANCE
	Bill		1				
	VAT		0–10				
	Bill		2–20				
	Bill		5				
	VAT		0–50				

Petty Cash				
		DR	CR	BALANCE
	Bill		3	
	VAT		0–30	
	Bill		4–40	

29. (4)

Carol (CL3)							
		OFFICE ACCOUNT			CLIENT ACCOUNT		
		DR	CR	BALANCE	DR	CR	BALANCE
	Cash					400–	400–
	Cash VAT	50–[5]		50–			
	Cash				44–		356–
	Cash				30–		326–

Cash							
		OFFICE ACCOUNT			CLIENT ACCOUNT		
		DR	CR	BALANCE	DR	CR	BALANCE
	Carol				400		
	Carol		50				
	VAT		5				
	Carol					44	
	Carol					30	

Customs & Excise (NL11)				
		DR	CR	BALANCE
	Cash	5–		

29. (5)

Dick (CL4)							
		OFFICE ACCOUNT			CLIENT ACCOUNT		
		DR	CR	BALANCE	DR	CR	BALANCE
Cash						700–	700–
Cash					100–		600–
Cash VAT		20–[5]		20			
P. Cash		8–[3]		28–			
Cash					66–		534–
P. Cash VAT		4–[3, 5]		32–			

Cash							
		OFFICE ACCOUNT			CLIENT ACCOUNT		
		DR	CR	BALANCE	DR	CR	BALANCE
Dick					700		
Dick						100	
Dick			20				
VAT			2				
Dick						66	

Customs & Excise (NL11)				
		DR	CR	BALANCE
Cash		2–		
P. Cash		0–40		

Petty Cash				
		DR	CR	BALANCE
	Dick		8	
	Dick		4	
	VAT		0–40	

29. (6)

Edward (CL5)							
		OFFICE ACCOUNT			CLIENT ACCOUNT		
		DR	CR	BALANCE	DR	CR	BALANCE
	Cash					600–	600–
	Cash				440–		160–
	P. Cash	$3-^3$		3–			
	Cash				150–		10–
	Cash VAT	$10-^5$		13–			
	Cash	50–		63–			

Cash							
		OFFICE ACCOUNT			CLIENT ACCOUNT		
		DR	CR	BALANCE	DR	CR	BALANCE
	Edward				600		
	Edward					440	
	Edward					150	
	Edward		10				
	VAT		1				
	Edward		50				

Customs & Excise (NL11)				
		DR	CR	BALANCE
	Cash	1–		

Petty Cash				
		DR	CR	BALANCE
	Edward		3	

Page 130.

34. (1)   *Fred*   OFFICE A/C   Dr. 70.7.
                                        Cr. 77.
                              CLIENT A/C   Dr. —
                                          Cr. —

34. (2)   *George*   OFFICE A/C   Dr. 90.9.
                                          Cr. 99.
                              CLIENT A/C   Dr. —
                                          Cr. —

34. (3)   *Harold*   OFFICE A/C   Dr. 40.60.6.
                                          Cr. 106.
                              CLIENT A/C   Dr. —
                                          Cr. —

34. (4)   *Ian*   OFFICE A/C   Dr. 80.120.12.
                                          Cr. 212.
                              CLIENT A/C   Dr. —
                                          Cr. —

Page 130.

37. (1)   *Jane*   OFFICE A/C   Dr. 10.60.7.
                                          Cr. 77.
                              CLIENT A/C   Dr. —
                                          Cr. —

37. (2)   *Kate*   OFFICE A/C   Dr. 20.70.9
                                          Cr. 99.
                              CLIENT A/C   Dr. —
                                          Cr. —

37. (3)   *Lucy*   OFFICE A/C   Dr. 3.80.8–30.
                                  Cr. 91–30.
                     CLIENT A/C   Dr. —
                                  Cr. —

37. (4)   *Mary*   OFFICE A/C   Dr. 20.30.40.7.
                                  Cr. 97.
                     CLIENT A/C   Dr. —
                                  Cr. —

37. (5)   *Nancy*   OFFICE A/C   Dr. 90.10.20.11.
                                  Cr. 131.
                     CLIENT A/C   Dr. —
                                  Cr. —

37. (6)   *Olivia*   OFFICE A/C   Dr. 1.20.3.4.50.7–30.
                                  Cr. 85–30.
                     CLIENT A/C   Dr. —
                                  Cr. —

Page 134.

43. (1)

Peter (CL16)							
		OFFICE ACCOUNT			CLIENT ACCOUNT		
		DR	CR	BALANCE	DR	CR	BALANCE
	Cash VAT	100–					
	VAT	10–		110–			
	Cash.						
	Humphrey		110–[6]				

43. (2)

		OFFICE ACCOUNT			CLIENT ACCOUNT		
	Rachel (CL17)						
		DR	CR	BALANCE	DR	CR	BALANCE
May							
1	Cash					800–	800–
2	Cash VAT	300–[5]		300–			
3	VAT	30–		330–			
3	Cash. Transfer		330–	—	330–		470–

43. (3)

		OFFICE ACCOUNT			CLIENT ACCOUNT		
	Stephen (CL18)						
		DR	CR	BALANCE	DR	CR	BALANCE
July							
1	Cash. VAT	80–		80–			
5	Cash. You					700–	700–
6	Cash. VAT	60–[5]		140–			
8	VAT	14–		154–			
	Cash. Transfer		154–	—	154–		546

Chapter 16

Page 142.

7. (1) *Dust*   OFFICE A/C   Dr. 400.40.
                               Cr. 20.2.
                 CLIENT A/C   Dr. —
                               Cr. —

7. (2) *Lizzie*   OFFICE A/C   Dr. 47.
                               Cr. 47.
                 CLIENT A/C   Dr. —
                               Cr. 13.

7. (3)

		OFFICE ACCOUNT			CLIENT ACCOUNT		
		DR	CR	BALANCE	DR	CR	BALANCE
	Lizzie (CL2)						
	Balance	47–		47–			
	Cash					60–	60–
	Cash. Transfer		47–	—	47–	—	13–

7. (4)

		OFFICE ACCOUNT			CLIENT ACCOUNT		
		DR	CR	BALANCE	DR	CR	BALANCE
	Meff (CL3)						
	Costs	800					
	VAT	80		880			
	Abatement		50				
	VAT		5	825			
	Cash		825	—		75–	75–

7. (5)

		OFFICE ACCOUNT			CLIENT ACCOUNT		
		DR	CR	BALANCE	DR	CR	BALANCE
	Meff (CL3)						
	Costs	800–					
	VAT	80–		880–			
	Abatement		50–				
	VAT		5–	825–			
	Cash					900–	900–
	Cash. Transfer		825–	—	825–		75–

7. (6)

Saunders (CL4)							
		OFFICE ACCOUNT			CLIENT ACCOUNT		
		DR	CR	BALANCE	DR	CR	BALANCE
(b)	Cash. You. Cheque indorsed to Fry.				600–	600–	

Cash							
		OFFICE ACCOUNT			CLIENT ACCOUNT		
		DR	CR	BALANCE	DR	CR	BALANCE
(b)	Saunders. Cheque indorsed to Fry.				600–	600–	

NOTE: (a) No double-entries needed. See p. 140.

7. (7)

Griffiths (CL5)							
		OFFICE ACCOUNT			CLIENT ACCOUNT		
		DR	CR	BALANCE	DR	CR	BALANCE
	Cash. You. Cheque indorsed to Hare. Cash. You. Cash. Cheque dishonoured				8,000– 200–	8,000– 200–	200– —

Cash							
		OFFICE ACCOUNT			CLIENT ACCOUNT		
		DR	CR	BALANCE	DR	CR	BALANCE
	Griffiths. Cheque indorsed to Hare. Griffiths Griffiths Cheque dishonoured				8,000 200	8,000 200	

7. (8)

Rudge (CL6)							
		OFFICE ACCOUNT			CLIENT ACCOUNT		
		DR	CR	BALANCE	DR	CR	BALANCE
May 1 2 5	Cash. You. Cash. Cash. Cheque dishonoured Cash. Transfer	1,000–		1,000–	1,000– 5,000–	5,000– 1,000–	5,000– 4,000– DR 1,000– —

Cash							
		OFFICE ACCOUNT			CLIENT ACCOUNT		
		DR	CR	BALANCE	DR	CR	BALANCE
May 1 2 5	Rudge Rudge Rudge. Cheque dishonoured Rudge. Transfer		1,000		5,000 1,000	1,000 5,000	

Chapter 17

Page 143.

(1)

Bill (CL2)							
		OFFICE ACCOUNT			CLIENT ACCOUNT		
		DR	CR	BALANCE	DR	CR	BALANCE
Cash						400–	400–
Cash					50–		350–
P. Cash		6–		6–			
Costs		70–					
VAT		7–		83–			
Cash.							
Transfer			83–		83–		267–

(2)	*Carol*	OFFICE A/C	Dr. 80.90.2.10.300.40.
			Cr. 522.
		CLIENT A/C	Dr. —
			Cr. —
(3)	*David*	OFFICE A/C	Dr. 3.400.55.60.700.110–30.
			Cr. 1,328–30.
		CLIENT A/C	Dr. —
			Cr. —
(4)	*Ethel*	OFFICE A/C	Dr. 88.9.125.20.3.42.17.
			Cr. 304.
		CLIENT A/C	Dr. —
			Cr. —

(5)

George (CL7)						
	OFFICE ACCOUNT			CLIENT ACCOUNT		
	DR	CR	BALANCE	DR	CR	BALANCE
Cash. You.					70–	70–
Cash				8–		62–
Cash				9–90		52–10
Cash. VAT	10–^{5}		10–			
Costs	20–					
VAT	3–		33–			
Cash.						
Transfer		33–	—	33–		19–10

(6)

Henry (CL8)						
	OFFICE ACCOUNT			CLIENT ACCOUNT		
	DR	CR	BALANCE	DR	CR	BALANCE
Cash. You.					80–	80–
Cash. VAT	20–^{5}		20–			
P. Cash	1–^{3}		21–			
Cash				11–		69–
Costs	30–					
VAT	5–		56–			
Cash.						
Transfer		56–	—	56–		13–

(7)

		OFFICE ACCOUNT			CLIENT ACCOUNT		
		Kate (CL10)					
		DR	CR	BALANCE	DR	CR	BALANCE
	Cash	80–		80–			
	Cash. VAT.	90–		170–			
	Costs	100–					
	VAT	21–*		291–			
	Cash. You.					311–	311–
	Cash. VAT.	20–[5]		311–			
	Cash.						
	Transfer		311–	—	311–		—

* See page 131.

(8)

		OFFICE ACCOUNT			CLIENT ACCOUNT		
		Linda (CL11)					
		DR	CR	BALANCE	DR	CR	BALANCE
	Cash. You.					300–	300–
	Cash. VAT	4–		4–			
	VAT	0–40*		4–40			
	Cash.						
	Transfer		4–40		4–40		295–60
	Cash				5–50		290–10
	Costs	60–					
	VAT	6–		66–			
	Cash.						
	Transfer		66–	—	66–		224–10
	Cash				70–		154–10

* See page 132.

(9)

		OFFICE ACCOUNT			CLIENT ACCOUNT		
		Phantom Co. Ltd. (CL12)					
		DR	CR	BALANCE	DR	CR	BALANCE
Apr							
4	Cash. Documents. VAT	10*[4]		10			
9	Cash. You.					200	200
May							
8	Cash. Accountant. Witness fee				88**		112
26	Cash. Jakes. Transcripts				44**		68
31	Costs	500		510			
	VAT	51***		561			
June							
21	Cash. You.		493[6]	68			
	Cash. Transfer.		68	—	68		—

* Principal Method. If it had been an input of Phantom Co. Ltd., the Agency Method would have been used.

** Agency Method. Payments made using the Principal cannot be paid out of clients' money, whereas Agency Method payments can.

*** Taxable supplies by Carambas to Phantom Co. Ltd. are Costs £500 (*exclusive* of VAT) plus the £10 payment for documents, *i.e.* £510 @ 10% = £51 VAT.

(10)

		OFFICE ACCOUNT			CLIENT ACCOUNT		
		Cashe, decd. (CL13)					
		DR	CR	BALANCE	DR	CR	BALANCE
Nov							
1	Balance					84	84
3	Cash. Disbursements	126*		126			
20	Cash. Completion					31,710	31,794
27	Tree. Transfer				200		31,594

* The £84 could now be transferred from CLIENT to OFFICE ACCOUNT.

Another way of dealing with this would be to draw 2 cheques: £84 on CLIENT ACCOUNT, £42 on OFFICE ACCOUNT.

Guy Forkes (CL14)							
		OFFICE ACCOUNT			CLIENT ACCOUNT		
		DR	CR	BALANCE	DR	CR	BALANCE
Nov							
1	Balance					100	100
5	Cash. Disbursement				22		78
6	Costs	80		80			
	VAT	8		88			
	Cash. Transfer		78	10	78		—
28	Cash. You		10^6	—			

Fred (CL15)							
		OFFICE ACCOUNT			CLIENT ACCOUNT		
		DR	CR	BALANCE	DR	CR	BALANCE
Nov							
8	Cash. You.					450	450
16	Cash. Surveyor.				100		350
17	Cash. Cheque dishonoured.				450		100 DR
	Cash. Transfer.	100		100		100	—

Brown (CL16)							
		OFFICE ACCOUNT			CLIENT ACCOUNT		
		DR	CR	BALANCE	DR	CR	BALANCE
Oct	Costs. Agreed fee.	60		60			
	VAT	6		66			
	Cash. You		66	—			
Nov 23	Abatement		20	20CR			
	VAT		2	22CR			
	Cash. You.	22		—			

The balance on the account at the start of November is nil. When the fee was agreed with Brown the client ledger should have been debited with the fee plus VAT and when the money due was received from Brown the client ledger should have been credited.

No entries are needed to record the cheque for £1,243 as this was payable direct to Brown (see page 140).

The amount sent to Brown is the £22 owing to Brown on OFFICE ACCOUNT as a result of the abatement.

Tree (CL17)							
		OFFICE ACCOUNT			CLIENT ACCOUNT		
		DR	CR	BALANCE	DR	CR	BALANCE
Nov 27	Cash	1,200		1,200			
	Cash. You.		1,000⁶	200			
	Cashe decd. Transfer					200*	200
	Cash. Transfer		200	—	200		—

* Step 1. A Ledger Transfer from Cashe decd. to Tree.
  2. A Cash Transfer of the money due from CLIENT ACCOUNT TO OFFICE ACCOUNT.

		OFFICE ACCOUNT			CLIENT ACCOUNT		
		Cash Sheet					
		DR	CR	BALANCE	DR	CR	BALANCE
Nov							
3	Cashe decd. Disburse-ments		126				
5	Forkes. Disbursements					22	
6	Forkes. Transfer	78				78	
8	Fred				450		
16	Fred. Surveyor					100	
17	Fred. Cheque dishonoured					450	
	Fred. Transfer		100		100		
20	Cashe decd. Completion				31,710		
23	Brown		22				
27	Tree		1,200				
	Tree	1,000					
	Tree. Transfer	200				200	
28	Forkes	10					

Chapter 18

Page 148.

7. (1)

Laurence (CL2). On deposit Jan 3. Removed Sep. 3							
		OFFICE ACCOUNT			CLIENT ACCOUNT		
		DR	CR	BALANCE	DR	CR	BALANCE
Jan 2	Cash. You.					5,000–	5,000–
Sept 1	Deposit Cash Interest					30–	5,030–
4	Cash. You.				5,030–		—

Cash							
		OFFICE ACCOUNT			CLIENT ACCOUNT		
		DR	CR	BALANCE	DR	CR	BALANCE
Jan 2	Laurence				5,000		
3	Deposit Cash. Re. Laurence					5,000	
Sept 3	Deposit Cash. Re. Laurence				5,030		
4	Laurence					5,030	

Deposit Cash Re Laurence							
		OFFICE ACCOUNT			CLIENT ACCOUNT		
		DR	CR	BALANCE	DR	CR	BALANCE
Jan 3	Cash				5,000		5,000
Sept 1	Laurence Interest				30		5,030
3	Cash					5,030	—

7. (2)

Barnaby (CL3). On deposit Feb. 1. Removed Oct. 2.							
		OFFICE ACCOUNT			CLIENT ACCOUNT		
		DR	CR	BALANCE	DR	CR	BALANCE
Feb 1	Cash. You.					2,000	2,000–
Aug 1	Deposit Cash. Interest					42–	2,042–
Oct 2	Cash. Jacob				2,000–		42–
3	Cash. Interest					18–	60–
4	Cash. You.				60–		—

Cash		OFFICE ACCOUNT			CLIENT ACCOUNT		
		DR	CR	BALANCE	DR	CR	BALANCE
Feb 1	Barnaby Deposit. Cash. Re.				2,000*		
	Barnaby					2,000	
Oct 2	Deposit Cash. Re. Barnaby				2,042		
	Barnaby Cheque to Jacob					2,000	
3	Barnaby Interest				18		
4	Barnaby					60	

* NOTE: This was paid into current account and then put on deposit. It could have been paid directly into the deposit account with no need for the transfer.

Deposit Cash. Barnaby		OFFICE ACCOUNT			CLIENT ACCOUNT		
		DR	CR	BALANCE	DR	CR	BALANCE
Feb 1	Cash				2,000		2,000
Aug 1	Barnaby Interest				42		2,042
Oct 2	Cash					2,042	—

Violet (CL4). On deposit Mar. 1. Removed April 3.							
		OFFICE ACCOUNT			CLIENT ACCOUNT		
		DR	CR	BALANCE	DR	CR	BALANCE
Mar							
1	Cash. You.					4,500–	4,500–
Apr							
1	Deposit						
	Cash.						
	Interest					14–	4,514–
2	Costs	20–					
	VAT	2–		22–			
4	Cash. You.				4,492–		
	Cash.						
	Transfer		22–	—	22–		—

Cash							
		OFFICE ACCOUNT			CLIENT ACCOUNT		
		DR	CR	BALANCE	DR	CR	BALANCE
Mar							
1	Violet				4,500		
1	Deposit						
	Cash. Re.						
	Violet					4,500	
Apr							
3	Deposit						
	Cash. Re.						
	Violet				4,514		
4	Violet.					4,492	
	Violet.						
	Transfer	22				22	

Deposit Cash. Violet							
		OFFICE ACCOUNT			CLIENT ACCOUNT		
		DR	CR	BALANCE	DR	CR	BALANCE
Mar 1	Cash.				4,500		4,500
Apr 1	Violet. Interest				14		4,514
3	Cash.					4,514	—

Page 152.

15. (1)

Laurence (CL2)							
		OFFICE ACCOUNT			CLIENT ACCOUNT		
		DR	CR	BALANCE	DR	CR	BALANCE
	Cash. You.					5,000–	5,000–
	Cash. You. Refund (Plus Interest £30)				5,000–		—

Cash							
		OFFICE ACCOUNT			CLIENT ACCOUNT		
		DR	CR	BALANCE	DR	CR	BALANCE
	Laurence				5,000		
	Laurence. Refund Deposit Interest Payable					5,000	
	Laurence		30				

15. (2)

Barnaby (CL3)						
	OFFICE ACCOUNT			CLIENT ACCOUNT		
	DR	CR	BALANCE	DR	CR	BALANCE
Cash. You.					7,000–	7,000–
Cash. X.						
(Interest						
£60 sent to						
client)				7,000–		—

Cash						
	OFFICE ACCOUNT			CLIENT ACCOUNT		
	DR	CR	BALANCE	DR	CR	BALANCE
Barnaby				7,000		
Barnaby						
Cheque to						
X					7,000	
Deposit						
Interest						
Payable Re.						
Barnaby		60				

15. (3)

Sue (CL3)						
	OFFICE ACCOUNT			CLIENT ACCOUNT		
	DR	CR	BALANCE	DR	CR	BALANCE
Cash. You.					5,000–	5,000–
Cash.						
Interest.					30–	5,030–
Cash. You.				5,030–		—

Cash						
	OFFICE ACCOUNT			CLIENT ACCOUNT		
	DR	CR	BALANCE	DR	CR	BALANCE
Sue				5,000		
Interest		30				
Payable Sue						
Sue Interest					30	
Sue					5,030	

15. (4)

Violet (CL4)						
	OFFICE ACCOUNT			CLIENT ACCOUNT		
	DR	CR	BALANCE	DR	CR	BALANCE
Cash. You.					4,500–	4,500–
Cash.				4,400–		100–
Costs.	120–					
VAT	12–		132–			
Cash.						
Interest.					43–	143–
Cash.						
Transfer		132–	—	132–		
Cash. You.				11–		—

Page 154.

22. (1)

Cash						
	OFFICE ACCOUNT			CLIENT ACCOUNT		
	DR	CR	BALANCE	DR	CR	BALANCE
Balance				20,000		20,000
D. Cash.						
Gen. Deposit					15,000	5,000
Interest						
Received	52					
D. Cash						
Gen. Deposit				2,500		7,500
Interest						
Received	34					

		OFFICE ACCOUNT			CLIENT ACCOUNT		
		— Deposit Cash. General Deposit					
		DR	CR	BALANCE	DR	CR	BALANCE
Cash					15,000		15,000
Cash						2,500	12,500

		Deposit Interest Receivable (PL6)		
		DR	CR	BALANCE
Cash			52–	52–
Cash			34–	86–

22. (2)

		OFFICE ACCOUNT			CLIENT ACCOUNT		
		— Cash					
		DR	CR	BALANCE	DR	CR	BALANCE
Balance					18,000		18,000
D. Cash							
General						14,000	4,000
A.					8,300		12,300
A. Refund						8,300	4,000
Deposit							
Interest							
Payable							
Re. A.			58				
Deposit							
Interest							
Received		108					

22. (3)

Adams (CL1) (a) On deposit. (d) Withdrawn							
		OFFICE ACCOUNT			CLIENT ACCOUNT		
		DR	CR	BALANCE	DR	CR	BALANCE
(a)	Cash. You.					4,500–	4,500–
(d)	Deposit Cash						
	Interest					100–	4,600–
(d)	Cash. You.				4,600–		—

Cash							
		OFFICE ACCOUNT			CLIENT ACCOUNT		
		DR	CR	BALANCE	DR	CR	BALANCE
(a)	Adams Deposit Cash Re.				4,500		
	Adams					4,500	
(b)	Deposit Interest Received	70					
(c)	Brown Interest Paid Re.					500	
	Brown		25				
(d)	Deposit Cash. Re. Adams				4,600		
	Adams					4,600	

Brown (CL2)							
		OFFICE ACCOUNT			CLIENT ACCOUNT		
		DR	CR	BALANCE	DR	CR	BALANCE
	Balance					500–	500–
(c)	Cash. You. (plus interest £25)				500–		—

22. (4)

Date	Details	OFFICE ACCOUNT			CLIENT ACCOUNT		
		Cash					
		DR	CR	BALANCE	DR	CR	BALANCE
May							
1	Dep. Cash General					30,000	
2	Simon				10,000		
	Dep. Cash Simon					10,000	
3	Andrew.				20,000		
Sept							
1	Deposit Interest Received	35					
2	Deposit Cash. Re. Simon				10,025		
	Simon Refund					10,025	
3	Interest Paid Re. Andrew		15				
	Andrew Interest				15		
	Andrew						20,015

22. (5)

On deposit May 1. Removed: Oct. 31.

Date	Details	OFFICE ACCOUNT			CLIENT ACCOUNT		
		Swanning (CL3)					
		DR	CR	BALANCE	DR	CR	BALANCE
May							
1	Cash. You.					10,000	10,000
Oct.							
31	Dep. Cash Interest					500	10,500
Nov.							
1	Cash. Taxhaven Ltd.				10,500		—

Martin (CL4)							
Date	Details	OFFICE ACCOUNT			CLIENT ACCOUNT		
		DR	CR	BALANCE	DR	CR	BALANCE
July 1	Cash. Debtor					2,000	2,000
Oct 1	Cash. Debtor					2,000	4,000
Dec. 31	Costs	40		40			
	VAT	4		44			
	Cash. Interest.					150*	4,150
	Cash. Transfer		44	—		44	4,106
	Cash. You.				4,106		—

* Interest   10% 2,000 × 6/12 = 100
              10% 2,000 × 3/12 = 50
                          ——
                         150

The other entries will be
(a) **CREDIT** cash — **DEBIT** Interest Payable — **OFFICE ACCOUNT** and
(b) **DEBIT** cash — **CLIENT ACCOUNT** — this is the other half of the double entry for this item (see page 150).

Chapter 19

Page 158.

5. (1)   *Simon*   OFFICE A/C   Dr. 300.400.70.
                                    Cr. 770[6]
                     CLIENT A/C   Dr. —
                                    Cr. —

5. (2)   *Andrew*   OFFICE A/C   Dr. 108*. 10–80.   *Costs 100
                                  Cr. 118–80.   Sundries   8
                                                          108
                     CLIENT A/C   Dr. —
                                    Cr. —

NOTE: The £3 fares is debited to the Fares Account.

Appendix

Page 159.

10. (1)   *James*   OFFICE A/C   Dr. 50.70.7.
                                        Cr. 127 (Mick).
                           CLIENT A/C   Dr. —
                                        Cr. —

10. (2)   *Matthew*   OFFICE A/C   Dr. 10.40.4.
                                        Cr. 39–60 (Paul). 14–40 (You).
                           CLIENT A/C   Dr. —
                                        Cr. —

10. (3)   *John*   OFFICE A/C   Dr. 30.80.8
                                        Cr. 110 (Luke). 8 (You).
                           CLIENT A/C   Dr. —
                                        Cr. —

Page 161.

12. (1)   *Philip*   OFFICE A/C   Dr. 50.70.7.
                                        Cr. (Bartholomew) 127.
                           CLIENT A/C   Dr. —
                                        Cr. —

          Bartholomew   OFFICE A/C   Dr. (Philip) 127.
                                        Cr. 127.
                           CLIENT A/C   Dr. —
                                        Cr. —

12. (2)   *Thomas*   OFFICE A/C   Dr. 10.40.4.
                                        Cr. (Jude) 54.
                           CLIENT A/C   Dr. —
                                        Cr. —

          Jude   OFFICE A/C   Dr. 20.50.5. (Thomas) 54.
                                        Cr. 129.
                           CLIENT A/C   Dr. —
                                        Cr. —

Page 165.

16. (1)   *Peter & Co*   OFFICE A/C   Dr. 19.1–90.
                                        Cr. 20–90.
                           CLIENT A/C   Dr. —
                                        Cr. —

16. (2)   *Benjamin &*   OFFICE A/C   Dr. 6.28–50.2–85.
          Co.   Cr. 37–35.
                           CLIENT A/C   Dr. —
                                        Cr. —

16. (3)   *Jeremy*   OFFICE A/C   Dr. 10.33.60.6.
                                     Cr. 109.
                       CLIENT A/C   Dr. —
                                     Cr. —

> NOTE: The £19 VAT exclusive, paid to the Agents
> is debited on the Agency Expenses Account.

16. (4)   *Jackson*   OFFICE A/C   Dr. 50.6.80.13.
                                     Cr. 149.
                       CLIENT A/C   Dr. —
                                     Cr. —

          Agency   Dr. 28–50
          Expenses   Cr. —

16. (5)   *Tom*   OFFICE A/C   Dr. 7.9.40.4.
                                     Cr. 60.
                       CLIENT A/C   Dr. —
                                     Cr. —

          Agency   Dr. 17–10.
          Expenses   Cr. —

16. (6) (a)

		OFFICE ACCOUNT			CLIENT ACCOUNT		
		DR	CR	BALANCE	DR	CR	BALANCE
Jan							
2	Cash. You.						
	On account					75–	75–
4	Cash					900–	975–
9	Cash.						
	Bland & Co.						
	Counsel	15–*		15–			
	VAT						
10	Costs	95–**					
	VAT	11–		121–			
	Cash.						
	Transfer		121–	—	121–		854
	Cash. You.				854–		—

* The Principal Method was used because the tax invoice was addressed to you.
The VAT is debited to Customs & Excise account — see page 127.
** Our costs   £40
     Agents' costs £55
                    ─────
                    £95

Customs & Excise		DR	CR	BALANCE
Jan				
9	Cash. Bland & Co.	6–50*		
10	Thomasina		11–	

* Costs £50 + Counsel £15 = £65 × 10% = £6.50

Agency Expenses (NL20)		DR	CR	BALANCE
Jan				
9	Cash. Bland & Co. Re. Thomasina	50–		

16. (6) (b)

A. Solicitor (CL100)		OFFICE ACCOUNT			CLIENT ACCOUNT		
		DR	CR	BALANCE	DR	CR	BALANCE
Jan							
5	Cash. Counsel	16–50*		16–50			
8	Costs	50–					
	VAT	5–		71–50			
11	Cash. You.		71–50	—			

* Agency Method. The tax invoice is NOT addressed to Bland & Co.

Page 168.

21. (1)

Gamma Insurance Co. (CL20)							
		OFFICE ACCOUNT			CLIENT ACCOUNT		
		DR	CR	BALANCE	DR	CR	BALANCE
	Cash					34–	34–
	Commission	5–		5–			
	Cash.						
	Transfer		5–	—	5–		
	Cash. You.				29–		—

21. (2)

Zeta Insurance Co. (CL21)							
		OFFICE ACCOUNT			CLIENT ACCOUNT		
		DR	CR	BALANCE	DR	CR	BALANCE
	Delta						
	Transfer					41–	41–
	Commission	16–		16–			
	Cash.						
	Transfer		16–	—	16–		
	Cash. You.				25–		—

21. (3)

Sigma Insurance Co. (CL22)							
		OFFICE ACCOUNT			CLIENT ACCOUNT		
		DR	CR	BALANCE	DR	CR	BALANCE
	Commission	7–		7–			
	Cash.						
	Premium					28–	28–
	Commission	5–		12–			
	Cash. You.				16–		
	Cash						
	Transfer		12–	—	12–		—

Appendix

21. (4)

Nonpay Insurance Co. Ltd. (CL24)							
Date	Details	OFFICE ACCOUNT			CLIENT ACCOUNT		
		DR	CR	BALANCE	DR	CR	BALANCE
Jan 2	Balance Cash.	43		43			
	Brown					104	104
17	Commission Cash.	15		58			
	Transfer Cash. You.		58	—	58 46		46 —

Black (CL25)							
Date	Details	OFFICE ACCOUNT			CLIENT ACCOUNT		
		DR	CR	BALANCE	DR	CR	BALANCE
Jan 7	Savall B.S. Transfer	22		22			

Savall Building Society (CL26)							
Date	Details	OFFICE ACCOUNT			CLIENT ACCOUNT		
		DR	CR	BALANCE	DR	CR	BALANCE
Jan 7	Costs	20		20			
	VAT	2		22			
	Black. Transfer		22	—			

White (CL28)							
Date	Details	OFFICE ACCOUNT			CLIENT ACCOUNT		
		DR	CR	BALANCE	DR	CR	BALANCE
Jan 10	Cash					1,250	1,250
	Costs	40		40			
	VAT	4		44			

Yellow (CL27)							
Date	Details	OFFICE ACCOUNT			CLIENT ACCOUNT		
		DR	CR	BALANCE	DR	CR	BALANCE
Jan 14	Cash. Counsel VAT	100		100			
	Costs Our work 100 Agents' work 120	220		320			
	VAT. 320 @ 10%	32		352			
18	Cash. You.					364	364
	Cash. Agents. Court fee	12		364			
	Cash. Transfer		364	—	364		—

Cash							
Date	Details	OFFICE ACCOUNT			CLIENT ACCOUNT		
		DR	CR	BALANCE	DR	CR	BALANCE
Jan							
2	Nonpay.				104		
10	White				1,250		
17	Nonpay.						
	Transfer	58				58	
	Nonpay					46	
18	Yellow				364		
	Agency						
	Expenses						
	120						
	− 20		100				
	VAT		10				
	Yellow.						
	Court fee		12				
	Yellow.						
	Transfer	364				364	

Chapter 20

Page 179.

17. (1)   Statement

Oliver. Sale of Whiteacre

	£		£
Discharge of mortgage	20,000	Deposit	6,000
Mortgagee's costs	33	Sale	54,000
Costs	140		
VAT	14		
BALANCE DUE	39,813		
	60,000		60,000

17. (2)   Statement

Robert. Purchase of . . .

Search	15	You	7,000
Deposit	7,000	Mortgage advance	30,000
Completion	63,000	BALANCE DUE	33,535
Mortgagee's costs	66		
Costs	340		
VAT	34		
L.R. Fees	80		
	70,535		70,535

17. (3)   Statement

Sarah. Sale of Greenacre. Purchase of Blueacre

PURCHASE of Blueacre	£	£	£
Payments			
Search	10		
Deposit	11,000		
Completion	99,000		
Search	8		
Costs	450		
VAT	45		
Stamp duty	550		
Mortgage costs	99*		
		111,162	
Receipts			
On account	11,000		
Mortgage advance	20,000		
		31,000	
			80,162
SALE of Greenacre			
Receipts			
Deposit	8,000		
Completion	72,000		
		80,000	
Payments			
Mortgage redemption	9,230		
Costs	350		
VAT	35	9,615	
			70,385
BALANCE DUE from you			9,777

* Any price quoted is deemed to include VAT unless the contrary is made clear.

Page 180.

18. (1)

		OFFICE ACCOUNT			CLIENT ACCOUNT		
		Albert (CL1)					
Date	Details	DR	CR	BALANCE	DR	CR	BALANCE
Jan 2	Cash. Deposit					2,000−	2,000−
Feb 1	Cash. Completion					18,000−	20,000−
2	Costs	300−					
	VAT	30−		330−			
	Cash. Transfer		330−	—	330−		
	Cash. You.				19,670−		—

18. (2)

		OFFICE ACCOUNT			CLIENT ACCOUNT		
		Brian (CL2)					
Date	Details	DR	CR	BALANCE	DR	CR	BALANCE
Sept 1	Cash. Search	1.85		1.85			
Oct 14	P. Cash. Search	1.50		3.35			
15	Costs	200−					
	VAT	20−		223.35			
29	Cash. You*		223.35[2]			9,000−[2]	9,000−
Nov 1	Cash. Completion			—	9,000−		—

* For meaning of superior figures throughout these answers see General Notes, page 257.

18. (3)

		OFFICE ACCOUNT			CLIENT ACCOUNT		
		Charles (CL3)					
Date	Details	DR	CR	BALANCE	DR	CR	BALANCE
May 1	P. Cash. Search	1.85		1.85			
16	Cash. You. Deposit					1,800–	1,800–
	Cash. Deposit				1,800–		—
June 9	Costs	135–					
	VAT	13.50		150–35			
19	Cash. You.		150.35*			16,240²	16,240–
24	Cash. Completion				16,200–	—	40–
25	Cash. L.R. Fees				40–		—

* Of the £16,390.35, only £150.35 is office money. The £40 in respect of the Land Registry fees is clients' money, since payment has not yet been made.

18. (4)

		OFFICE ACCOUNT			CLIENT ACCOUNT		
		\multicolumn{6}{c}{William (CL4)}				
Date	Details	DR	CR	BALANCE	DR	CR	BALANCE
Jan							
13	Cash. Search	4–		4–			
19	Cash. You.					3,000–	3,000–
22	Cash. Survey Fee	165–**		169–			
27	Cash. Deposit				3,000–		
Feb							
12	Cash. Search	2–		171–			
13	Costs	200–					
	VAT	20–		391–			
5	Cash. You.		391–[2]	—		27,072–*	27,072–
17	Cash. Completion				27,000–		172–
20	Cash. Stamp Duty				72–		—

* This includes the stamp duty to be paid later.
** The £3,000 in CLIENT ACCOUNT is to be used for paying the deposit and the solicitor is not authorised to use it to pay for another item.

18. (5)

Date	Details	OFFICE ACCOUNT			CLIENT ACCOUNT		
		DR	CR	BALANCE	DR	CR	BALANCE
Jan							
2	P. Cash. Search	6–		6–			
10	P. Cash. Search	4–		10–			
20	Costs	150–					
	VAT	15–		175–			
30	Cash. You.		175–[2]			1,055–[2]	1,055–
Feb							
10	Cash. Vendors' Solicitors Completion				1,055–*		—

Edward (CL5) table.

* Note:

Completion Moneys		9,000.00
Mortgage Advance	8,000.00	
Less	55.00	7,945.00
		1,055.00

18. (6)

Date	Details	OFFICE ACCOUNT			CLIENT ACCOUNT		
		DR	CR	BALANCE	DR	CR	BALANCE
Feb							
8	Costs	50–					
	VAT	5–		55–			
9	Cash. You.					8,000–[2]	8,000–
10	Cash. Completion				7,945–		
	Cash. Transfer		55–	—	55–		—

Fishy Building Society (CL6) table.

18. (7)

Date	Details	OFFICE ACCOUNT			CLIENT ACCOUNT		
		DR	CR	BALANCE	DR	CR	BALANCE
Apr							
1	Cash Search	7–		7–			
May							
8	Costs	400–					
	VAT	40–		447–			
17	Cash. You.		447–	—		8,077–[2]	8,077–
19	Cash. Vendors Solicitors. Completion				8,077–*		—

Table title: George (CL7)

* Note:

Completion			23,000.00
Mortgage		15,000.00	
Less		77.00	14,923.00
			8,077.00

Date	Details	OFFICE ACCOUNT			CLIENT ACCOUNT		
		DR	CR	BALANCE	DR	CR	BALANCE
May							
8	Costs	70–					
	VAT	7–		77–			
18	Cash. You.					15,000–[2]	15,000–
19	Cash. Vendor's Solicitors.* Completion				14,923–		77
	Cash. Transfer		77–	—	77–		—

Table title: Grim Building Society (CL8)

* The £14,923 could be transferred to George's account, which would then be debited with the total purchase money of £23,000.

18. (8)

Henry (CL8)							
Date	Details	OFFICE ACCOUNT			CLIENT ACCOUNT		
		DR	CR	BALANCE	DR	CR	BALANCE
June							
1	P. Cash. Search	3–		3–			
20	Cash. You. Deposit indorsed to Vendor's Solicitors.				5,000–	5,000–	
30	P. Cash. Search	4–		7–			
July							
1	Costs	200–		207–			
	VAT	20–		227–			
	Ink B.S.	33–		260–			
15	Cash. You.		260–[2]	—		35,120–[2]	35,120–
16	Cash. Completion				35,000*		120–
17	Cash. Stamp Duty				100–		
18	Cash. L.R. Fees				20–		—

Ink Building Society (CL10)							
Date	Details	OFFICE ACCOUNT			CLIENT ACCOUNT		
		DR	CR	BALANCE	DR	CR	BALANCE
July							
1	Costs	30–		30–			
	VAT	3–		33–			
	Henry		33				
15	Cash. You.					10,000–	10,000–
16	Cash. Vendor's Solicitors.* Completion				10,000–		

* The £10,000 could be transferred to Henry's account, which would be debited with the total purchase money of £45,000.

18. (9)

		\multicolumn{6}{c}{John (CL12)}					

		OFFICE ACCOUNT			CLIENT ACCOUNT		
Date	Details	DR	CR	BALANCE	DR	CR	BALANCE
June							
1	Cash. Completion					9,000–	
	Stakeholder. Transfer					1,000–	10,000–
	Kate. Transfer				5,000–		5,000–
2	Costs	50–					
	VAT	5–					
	Kate. Transfer	22–		77–			
	Cash. Transfer		77–	—	77–		
	Cash. You.				4,923–		—

		\multicolumn{6}{c}{Kate (CL13)}					

		OFFICE ACCOUNT			CLIENT ACCOUNT		
Date	Details	DR	CR	BALANCE	DR	CR	BALANCE
June							
1	John. Transfer					5,000–	5,000–
2	Costs	20–					
	VAT	2–		22–			
	John. Transfer		22–	—			
	Cash. You.				5,000–		—

Stakeholder (CL11)							
Date	Details	OFFICE ACCOUNT			CLIENT ACCOUNT		
		DR	CR	BALANCE	DR	CR	BALANCE
May 1	Cash. Purchaser's Solicitors. Re. John					1,000–	1,000–
June 1	John. Transfer				1,000–		—

18. (10)

Mary (CL14)							
Date	Details	OFFICE ACCOUNT			CLIENT ACCOUNT		
		DR	CR	BALANCE	DR	CR	BALANCE
Jan 2	Cash. Search	4–		4–			
Feb 2	Cash. Deposit	2,000–		2,004–			
15	Cash. You. On Account.					5,500–*	5,500–
Mar 1	Cash. Sale					13,500–	19,000–
	Purchase				18,000–		1,000–
2	Cash. Stamp Duty.				180–		
	Cash. L.R. Fees				70–		750–
3	Cash. Noddy & Co. Deposit					1,100–	1,850–
8	Costs.	150–					
	VAT	15–		2,169–			
	Cash. Transfer.		1,850–	319–	1,850–		—

* This could have been split. If so, it would have meant that there was insufficient clients' money on Mar. 1 to pay £18,000, so that office money would have had to be used.

18. (11)   Statement

Harvey. Purchase of "Bumper Hall Pen"

Jan. 3	Search	2	Jan. 2	On account	1,500
3	Survey fee	50	Mar.	Mortgage advance	12,000
Feb. 4	Deposit	1,400			
Mar.6	Costs	150			13,500
	VAT	22–50		BALANCE DUE	844–50
	Mortgage costs	55			
Mar.	Rail ticket	25			
	Completion	12,600			
	L. Registry fees	40			
		14,344–50			14,344–50

Harvey (CL15)							
Date	Details	OFFICE ACCOUNT			CLIENT ACCOUNT		
		DR	CR	BALANCE	DR	CR	BALANCE
Jan							
2	Cash. You.					1,500–	1,500–
3	P. Cash. Search	2–		2–			
Feb							
3	Cash. S & Co. Survey. VAT	50–		52–			
4	Cash. V & Co. Deposit				1,400–		100–
Mar							
6	Costs	150–		202–			
	VAT	22–50		224–50			
	Facey B.S.	55–		279–50			
16	Cash. You.		279–50	—		565–	665–
18	Cash. B. Rail Ticket				25–		640–
20	Facey B.S. Transfer. Mortgage					12,000–	12,640–
	Cash. V & Co. Completion				12,600–		40–
23	Cash. L. Registry fees				40–		—

```
        * Taxable Items
           Costs                  150–
           Survey fee              50–
           Fares (see page 157)    25–
                                  225 @ 10% = 22–50
```

Facey Building Society (CL16)							
Date	Details	OFFICE ACCOUNT			CLIENT ACCOUNT		
		DR	CR	BALANCE	DR	CR	BALANCE
Mar 6	Costs	50–		50–			
	VAT	5–		55–			
	Harvey.		55–	—			
17	Cash. You.					12,000–	12,000–
20	Harvey. Transfer				12,000–		—

18. (12)   Statement

Dick. Sale of "The Habendum." Purchase of "The Testatum"

PURCHASE of the Testatum	£	£	£
Payments			
Search	10		
Completion	52,200		
Costs	400		
VAT	40		
Mortgage costs	115		
L.R. Fees	440		
		53,205	
Receipts			
Mortgage advance		15,000	38,205
SALE of The Habendum			
Receipts			
Completion		36,000	
Payments			
Mortgage redemption	3,000		
Mortgage costs	22		
Costs	200		
VAT	20	3,242	
			32,758
			5,447
less Received on account			5,000
BALANCE DUE from you			447

| \multicolumn{10}{c}{Mrs. Dick (CL17)} |

Date	Details	OFFICE ACCOUNT			CLIENT ACCOUNT		
		DR	CR	BALANCE	DR	CR	BALANCE
Mar 1	P. Cash. Search	10–		10–			
May 1	Cash. You.					5,000–	5,000–
5	Cash. Completion of sale.					36,000–	41,000–
	Gibson B.S. Transfer. Mortgage redemption				3,000–		38,000–
	Cash. Completion purchase				37,755–*		245–
8	Costs. Purchase 400 Sale 200	600–					
	VAT	60–					
	Gibson B.S. Transfer Mortgage costs	22–		692–			
	Cash. Transfer		245–	447–	245–		—

```
    *  Completion Money                          52,200
       Mortgage                    15,000
       Less Costs         115
             L.R. Fees    440        555         14,445
                          ———        ———         ———
                                                 37,755
                                                 ———
```

Gibson B.S. (CL18)							
Date	Details	OFFICE ACCOUNT			CLIENT ACCOUNT		
		DR	CR	BALANCE	DR	CR	BALANCE
May 5	Mrs. Dick Transfer Mortgage redemption Cash. You.				3,000–	3,000–	3,000– —
8	Costs. VAT Mrs. Dick Transfer	20– 2–	22–	22– —			

18. (13)   Statement

Hotspur. Sale of "Blackwater." Purchase of "Greenmead"

PURCHASE of Greenmead	£	£	£
Payments			
Searches	4		
Deposit	6,500		
Costs	74		
VAT	7–40		
Mortgage costs	17–60		
Search	1		
Completion	58,500		
S. Duty	325		
L.R. Fees	20		
		65,449	
Receipts			
Mortgage advance	25,000		
less deductions	160	24,840	
			40,609
SALE of Blackwater			
Receipts			
Deposit	4,000		
Completion	36,000		
		40,000	
Payments			
Costs	60		
VAT	6		
		66	
			39,934
BALANCE DUE from you			675

		OFFICE ACCOUNT			CLIENT ACCOUNT		
Date	Details	DR	CR	BALANCE	DR	CR	BALANCE
Aug.							
31	Cash. Search	3		3			
	Cash. Search	1		4			
Sept.							
17	Cash. Deposit. Sale					4,000	4,000
	Cash. Transfer. Loan to Hotspur	2,500*		2,504		2,500	6,500
	Cash. Deposit. Purchase				6,500		—
30	Costs	134		2,638			
	VAT	13–40		2,651–40			
	Whinshire B.S. Transfer Mortgage costs	17–60		2,669			
Oct.							
12	Cash. You.		675	1,994			
16	P. Cash. Search	1–		1,995			
18	Cash. Completion. Sale					36,000	36,000
	Whinshire B.S. Transfer					24,840	60,840
	Cash. Completion. Purchase				58,500		2,340
19	Cash. Stamp duty				325		2,015
	L.R. Fees				20		1,995
30	Cash. Transfer		1,995	—	1,995		—

* Alternatively (a) two cheques could have been drawn: one on OFFICE ACCOUNT for £2,500, one on CLIENT ACCOUNT for £4,000; or

(b) £6,000 could have been drawn on OFFICE ACCOUNT and then the £4,000 transferred from CLIENT to OFFICE ACCOUNT.

Whinshire Building Society							
Date	Details	OFFICE ACCOUNT			CLIENT ACCOUNT		
		DR	CR	BALANCE	DR	CR	BALANCE
Sept. 30	Costs.	16		16			
	VAT	1–60		17–60			
	Hotspur. Transfer		17–60				
Oct. 17	Cash. You.					24,840	24,840
18	Hotspur. Transfer				24,840		—

18. (14) Norman. Purchase and Sale of "Treetops". Purchase of "Windy Ridge"

PURCHASE of Windy Ridge	£	£	£
Payments			
Search	5		
Costs	180		
VAT	18		
L.R. Fees	500		
Mortgage costs	33		
Completion	45,010		
		45,746	
Receipts			
Mortgage advance		30,000	
			15,746
PURCHASE and SALE of Treetops			
Receipts			
Completion of sale		35,000	
Payments			
Search	4		
Deposit	2,500		
Costs	160		
VAT	16		
Completion of purchase	22,500		
		25,180	
			9,820
BALANCE DUE from you			5,926

Date	Details	OFFICE ACCOUNT			CLIENT ACCOUNT		
		DR	CR	BALANCE	DR	CR	BALANCE

Norman. Purchase and sale of "Tree Tops." Purchase of "Windy Ridge"

Date	Details	OFFICE ACCOUNT DR	OFFICE ACCOUNT CR	OFFICE ACCOUNT BALANCE	CLIENT ACCOUNT DR	CLIENT ACCOUNT CR	CLIENT ACCOUNT BALANCE
Nov. 30	Cash. Search	4		4			
Jan. 2	Cash. Deposit. T. Tops	2,500		2,504			
11	Cash. Search	5		2,509			
Feb. 10	Costs. T. Tops 160 W. Ridge 180	340		2,849			
	VAT	34		2,883			
20	Cash. You.		2,883	—		3,043	3,043
28	Cash. Sale of T. Tops					12,500*	15,543
	Cash. Purchase of W. Ridge				15,043		500
	Cash. L.R. Fees				500		—

* See Notes 3 and 4.

NOTES

1. January 10
   Norman pays the estate agents direct: no entries.

2. Rent
   Norman must indemnify the Vendor for rent paid in advance in respect of the period from completion to the next rent day: *i.e.*

$$\frac{10}{12} \times 12 = £10$$

3. Sale of Treetops   35,000
   Purchase of Treetops   22,500
   ───────
                             12,500

4. February 28: Completion
   "Treetops"
   The purchase and sub-sale are completed simultaneously. You will instruct Oliver's solicitors to provide two drafts ("split drafts"), one for £35,000 in favour of the vendor's solicitors (the balance required to complete Norman's purchase) and one for £12,500 in your favour (the balance of the sub-sale price).

   n.b. It is assumed throughout that the purchase and sub-sale of "Treetops" are completed before the purchase of "Windy Ridge" so that you are in funds and that the net proceeds from the sale of Treetops were banked before the completion money for the purchase of Windy Ridge was withdrawn. If this is not possible, provided the completion of Treetops took place first, you could deal with the transaction as follows:—

   (1) Draw a draft for £2,543 from the bank — this would alter the balance in the client account dated Feb. 28 to £500. The entry provided in the ledger account now comes BEFORE the completion of T. Tops.

   (2) Complete Treetops but do not bank the net proceeds of sale — the credit entry of £12,500 in the client column would still remain.

   (3) On completion of Windy Ridge hand over the draft of £2,543 and indorse over the draft of £12,500 received in respect of Windy Ridge — there would then be a debit entry in the client column dated Feb. 28 of £12,500 to record the indorsed draft.

Date	Details	OFFICE ACCOUNT			CLIENT ACCOUNT		
		DR	CR	BALANCE	DR	CR	BALANCE
Feb. 28	Cash. Purchase of W.R. Cash. Draft indorsed purchase W.R. Sale T. Tops				2,543 12,500	 12,500	500

"Windy Ridge"

Completion Money		45,010
Mortgage advance	30,000	
Costs	33	29,967
		15,043

18. (15)   Financial Statement

Pearl. Sale of Millstone and Purchase of Avarest

	£	£	£
PURCHASE of Avarest			
Purchase price		75,000	
Searches	19		
Costs	300		
VAT	30		
Survey fee	220		
Stamp duty	750		
L.R. fees	125		
Repayment of loan plus interest	7,594		
		9,038	
		84,038	
Less Received on account	500		
Loan	7,500	8,000	
			76,038
SALE of Millstone			
Sale price		150,000	
Less			
Costs	400		
VAT	40		
Mortgage redemption costs	22		
Mortgage redemption	25,724		
Estate agent's commission	1,650	27,836	
AMOUNT AVAILABLE ON SALE			122,164
Balance held			46,126

Client: Pearl
Matter: Purchase of "Avarest" Sale of "Millstone" and Advice re: Spanish property

Date	Details	OFFICE ACCOUNT DR	CR	BALANCE	CLIENT ACCOUNT DR	CR	BALANCE
1987							
Apr.							
3	Cash. You.					500	500
6	Petty Cash. Land Charges search	14		14			
10	Cash. Survey fee VAT	200		214			
15	Cash. Brite Emerald Finance Co. Ltd. Loan					7,500	8,000
17	Cash. Vendor's solicitors. Deposit on purchase				7,500		500
May							
8	Costs: Purchase 300 / Sale 400	700		914			
	VAT (700 + 200 = 900 @ 10%)	90		1,004			
13	Coral B.S. Transfer mortgage costs	22		1,026			
15	P. Cash—Land charges search	5		1,031			
15	Cash. Completion "Millstone"					135,000	135,500
	Stakeholder. Deposit					15,000	150,500
	Coral Mortgage redemption				25,724		124,776
	Cash—Vendor's solicitors. Completion "Avarest"				67,500		57,276
	Cash—Brite Emerald Finance Co. Ltd. Loan & interest				7,594		49,682
	Cash—Stamp duty				750		48,932
	Cash—Land Registry Fees				125		48,807
18	Cash—Estate agents				1,650		47,157
	Cash—Pearl's grandson				3,000		44,157
20	Cash—Transfer		1,031	—	1,031		43,126
June							
15	Cash—Spanish firm				41,623		1,503
16	Cash—Transfer interest					449	1,952
	Cash—You				1,952		—

Coral Building Society. Mortgage Redemption							
Date	Details	OFFICE ACCOUNT			CLIENT ACCOUNT		
		DR	CR	BALANCE	DR	CR	BALANCE
May 8	Costs	20		20			
	VAT	2		22			
	Pearl tfr. of redemption costs		22	—			
15	Pearl— mortgage redemption					25,724	25,724
	Cash. You.				25,724		—

Chapter 22

Page 189.

1.

Trial Balance as at December 31

	DR	CR
Capital		32,864
Drawings	8,290	
Debtors	9,529	
Creditors		8,012
Rent and Rates	980	
Light and Heat	359	
Salaries and Wages	37,952	
Bad Debts	322	
Insurances	142	
General Expenses	1,039	
Bank Balance	2,237	
Library	7,500	
Depreciation		2,700
Deposit Interest Paid	1,058	
Freeholds	22,000	
Fixtures	5,000	
Depreciation		2,300
Deposit Interest Received		1,000
Costs		49,532
	96,408	96,408

Profit and Loss Account for year ending December 31

	£	£	£
INCOME			
Costs	49,532		
Work in hand	8,204	57,736	
Deposit Interest Received		1,000	58,736
less **EXPENSES**			
Rent and Rates		940	
Light and Heat		441	
Salaries and Wages		37,952	
Bad Debts		917	
Insurances		79	
General Expenses		1,039	
Deposit Interest Paid		1,121	
Depreciation			
(Library)	1,500		
(Fixtures)	500	2,000	44,489
NET PROFIT			14,247

Balance Sheet as at December 31

	£	£	£
CAPITAL EMPLOYED			
Capital			
Balance as at January 1		32,864	
Net Profit		14,247	
		47,111	
less Drawings		8,290	
			38,821
EMPLOYMENT OF CAPITAL			
Fixed Assets			
Freeholds		22,000	
Fixtures and Fittings	5,000		
less Depreciation	2,800	2,200	
Library	7,500		
less Depreciation	4,200	3,300	27,500
Current Assets			
Work in hand		8,204	
Debtors	9,529		
less Provision	595	8,934	
Prepayments		40	
Cash in bank		2,237	
		19,415	
less Current Liabilities			
Creditors	8,012		
Accounts outstanding	82	8,094	
Net Current Assets			11,321
			38,821

2.   Profit and Loss Account for the year ending

INCOME	£	£
Costs		48,500
Insurance Commission		300
Interest Receivable		4,200
		53,000

less EXPENDITURE		
Interest Payable	1,400	
Salaries	10,000	
Rent	8,200	
Stationery	3,800	
Light & Heat	2,900	
Depreciation	3,700	30,000
NET PROFIT		23,000

APPROPRIATIONS

Interest on Capital	£	£
A	2,500	
B	500	3,000
Balance of Profit		
A	12,000	
B	8,000	20,000
		23,000

Balance Sheet as at

EMPLOYMENT OF CAPITAL		
FIXED ASSETS	£	£
Premises		11,400
Furniture	7,000	
less Depreciation	2,100	4,900
Library	12,000	
less Depreciation	3,000	9,000
		25,300

CURRENT ASSETS		
Work in hand	4,000	
Stationery	400	
Debtors	2,000	
Payments in advance	300	
Cash	5,200	
	11,900	

CURRENT LIABILITIES			
Creditors	600		
Accounts Outstanding	100	700	11,200

CLIENT ACCOUNT		
Bank balances	50,000	
less Due to Clients	50,000	—
		36,500

CAPITAL EMPLOYED

		£	£
Capital Accounts			
A		25,000	
B		5,000	30,000
Current Accounts			
A		3,500	
B		3,000	6,500
			36,500

	A	*B*
Interest on Capital	2,500	500
N.P.	12,000	8,000
	14,500	8,500
less Drawings	11,000	5,500
	3,500	3,000

3.   Profit and Loss Account for year ending December 31

INCOME	£	£	£
Costs	185,280		
Plus Work in Hand	17,628	202,908	
Deposit Interest Received		8,913	
Investment Income		563	212,384

less EXPENSES			
Salaries		107,288	
Postages and Telephones		8,102	
Stationery		1,950	
Fares		5,200	
Rent and Rates		27,300	
Light and Heat		12,674	
Deposit Interest Paid		600	
Bad Debts		1,452	
Depreciation		1,800	
Sundry Expenses		4,768	171,134
NET PROFIT			41,250

Interest on Capital		£	£
	A	1,600	
	B	800	
	C	640	
	D	400	3,440
Salaries			
	B	5,000	
	C	5,000	
	D	5,000	15,000
Balance of Profit			
	A$\frac{3}{10}$	6,843	
	B$\frac{3}{10}$	6,843	
	C$\frac{3}{10}$	6,843	
	D$\frac{1}{10}$	2,281	22,810
			41,250

CURRENT ACCOUNTS

	A	B	C	D
N.P.	6,843	6,843	6,843	2,281
Salaries	—	5,000	5,000	5,000
Interest	1,600	800	640	400
	8,443	12,643	12,483	7,681
Drawings	5,107	9,009	7,800	6,000
	3,336	3,634	4,683	1,681

Balance Sheet as at December 31

CAPITAL EMPLOYED		£	£
Capital Accounts			
	A	20,000	
	B	10,000	
	C	8,000	
	D	5,000	43,000
Current Accounts			
	A	3,336	
	B	3,634	
	C	4,683	
	D	1,681	13,334
Long Term Liabilities			
	Loan		7,000
			63,334

EMPLOYMENT OF CAPITAL

	£	£	£
Fixed Assets			
Leasehold Premises	8,000		
less Depreciation	1,600	6,400	
Furniture & Fittings	6,000		
less Depreciation	1,200	4,800	
Machinery & Equipment	4,000		
less Depreciation	800	3,200	
Investments		14,800	29,200

		£	£	£
Current Assets				
Work in hand		17,628		
Debtors	19,035			
less Provision	121	18,914		
Payments in advance		4,550		
Cash in hand		42		
		41,134		
Current Liabilities				
Creditors	5,200			
Accounts Outstanding	900			
Bank overdraft	900	7,000		
NET CURRENT ASSETS				34,134
				63,334

4.   Profit and Loss Account for year ending December 31

INCOME		£	£
Costs		36,619	
Commissions Received		1,320	
Rent Received		7,200	
Deposit Interest Received		740	45,879
less EXPENSES			
Salaries		27,000	
Postages and Telephones		1,820	
Stationery		1,236	
Agency Expenses		210	
Fares		1,090	
Rates		2,800	
Light and Heat		1,300	
Bank Charges		270	
Insurance		1,522	
Audit Fees		450	
Deposit Interest Paid		320	
Bad Debts		710	
Professional Subscriptions		330	
Courses		1,060	
Depreciation			
Furniture	155		
Library	90		
Motor Cars	650	895	41,013
NET PROFIT			4,866
SALARIES			
A		3,000	
B		3,000	6,000
less NET LOSS			
A($\frac{1}{2}$)		567	
B($\frac{1}{2}$)		567	1,134
			4,866

CURRENT ACCOUNTS

	A	B
Drawings	5,981	5,920
Net Loss	567	567
	6,548	6,487
Salaries	3,000	3,000
	3,548	3,487

Balance Sheet as at December 31

CAPITAL EMPLOYED	£	£	£
Capital Accounts			
A		9,000	
B		7,000	16,000
less Current Accounts			
A		3,548	
B		3,487	7,035
			8,965

EMPLOYMENT OF CAPITAL

Fixed Assets

Freeholds		10,600	
Furniture & Fittings	3,100		
less Depreciation	635	2,465	
Library	1,800		
less Depreciation	190	1,610	
Motor Cars	2,600		
less Depreciation	650	1,950	16,625

Current Assets

Work in Hand		3,200	
Debtors	1,400		
less Provision	60	1,340	
Prepayments		150	
		4,690	

less Current Liabilities

Bank Overdraft	6,950		
Creditors	5,300		
Accounts Outstanding	100	12,350	
			7,660
			8,965

5.   Profit and Loss Account for year ending December 31 1977

INCOME	£	£	£
Costs	32,311		
Work in hand	9,340	41,651	
Profit on sale of premises		6,000	
			47,651

less EXPENSES			
General Expenses		12,990	
Light and Heat		999	
Wages		8,420	
Rates		700	
Bad Debts		2,150	
Depreciation		300	
			25,559
NET PROFIT			22,092

Balance Sheet as at December 31 1977

CAPITAL EMPLOYED		£	£
Capital			
Balance as at January 1		48,745	
Net Profit		22,092	
		70,837	
less Drawings		9,922	60,915

EMPLOYMENT OF CAPITAL

Fixed Assets			
Premises		35,000	
Fixtures and Fittings		9,150	
Motor Cars	3,000		
less Depreciation	300	2,700	46,850

Current Assets			
Work in Hand		9,340	
Debtors	10,000		
less Provision	1,500	8,500	
Prepayments		225	
Cash		7,000	
		25,065	
less *Current Liabilities*			
Creditors		11,000	
Net Current Assets			14,065
			60,915

WORKINGS

Rates

Jan. 1 Cash apportionment	CB	150	Sept. 1 Cash refund	CB	50
April 1 Cash	CB	300	Dec. 31 paid in advance	c/d	225
Sept. 1 Cash to vendor	CB	75	Dec. 31 Profit & Loss		700
Oct. 1 Cash	CB	450			
		975			975
31 Dec. Paid in advance	b/d	225			

Bad Debts

Jan. 31 Mr. A	250	Jan. 1 provision b/d	800
May 31 Mr. B	200		
Dec. 31 Mr. C	750		
Dec. 31 Mr. D	250		
Dec. 31 provision c/d	1,500	Dec. 31 Profit & Loss	2,150
	2,950		2,950
		Dec. 31 provision b/d	1,500

Sale of Premises

Sept. 1 Premises	32,000	Sept. 1 Cash	38,000
Profit	6,000		
	38,000		38,000

Premises

Jan. 1 Cash	32,000	Sept. 1 Sale of Premises	32,000
Sept. 1 Cash	35,000	Dec. 1 Balance c/d	35,000
	67,000		67,000
Dec. 31 Balance b/d	35,000		

6.   Bank Reconciliation Statement as at January 1

Balance as per bank statement	£4,956	Dr
Add: Unpresented Cheques	£ 974	
	£5,930	Dr
Less: Late Credits	£1,240	
	£4,690	DR

For Information

Cash Book				Bank Charges	Rent		
Bal. 4,690	Bal.	2,590	Cash 400		Bal. 6,400	Bal. 8,100	
	Charges	400			Cash 1,700		
	Rent	1,700					
4,690		4,690			8,100	8,100	
	Bal.	4,690			Bal. 8,100		

TRIAL BALANCE as at 31/12

		DR	CR
PL1	Capital		60,000
2	Drawings	4,000	
NL 1	Bad Debts	100	
2	Investment Income		20
3	Agency Expenses Paid	300	
4	Deposit Interest Paid	4,000	
5	Deposit Interest Received		2,300
6	Light and Heat	4,730	
7	Costs		15,000
8	Rent and Rates	8,100	
9	Salaries	8,750	
10	Fixtures and Fittings	12,000	
11	Leasehold Premises	35,000	
12	Library	3,000	
13	Bank Charges	400	
	Creditors		2,000
CL	Debtors	3,600	
CB	Overdraft		4,690
PCB	Cash in Hand	30	
		84,010	84,010

Profit and Loss Account for 6 months ending December 31

		£	£	£
INCOME				
	Costs	15,000		
	Work in hand	4,000	19,000	
	Investment Income		20	
	Deposit Interest Received		2,300	21,320
less EXPENSES				
	Bad Debts		300	
	Agency Expenses		300	
	Deposit Interest Paid		4,000	
	Light and Heat		4,960	
	Rent and Rates		6,500	
	Salaries		8,750	
	Bank Charges		400	
	Depreciation			
	Lease	2,800		
	Library	300	3,100	28,310
NET LOSS				6,990

Balance Sheet as at December 31

EMPLOYMENT OF CAPITAL	£	£	£
Fixed Assets			
Leaseholds	35,000		
less Depreciation	2,800	32,200	
Fixtures & Fittings		12,000	
Library	3,000		
less Depreciation	300	2,700	46,900
Current Assets			
Work in hand		4,000	
Debtors	3,600		
less Provision	200	3,400	
Prepayment		1,600	
Cash in hand		30	
		9,030	
Current Liabilities			
Creditors	2,000		
Outstanding accounts	230		
Overdraft	4,690	6,920	
Net Current Assets			2,110
			49,010
CAPITAL EMPLOYED			
Capital			
Balance as at 1st July		60,000	
less			
Net Loss	6,990		
Drawings	4,000	10,990	
			49,010

7. Profit and Loss Account for the 6 months from
    October 6, 1981 to April 5, 1982

	£	£	£
INCOME			
Costs			89,100
less: Work in Hand at 6th October			7,100
			82,000
plus: Work in Hand at 5th April			8,200
			90,200
less **EXPENSES**			
General Expenses		66,860	
Bad Debts		2,500	
Loss on Sale of fixtures		20	
Depreciation		1,700	
Interest on Loan		1,120	
			72,200
NET PROFIT			18,000
Annuity			3,000
Balance of Profit			
B$\frac{3}{5}$		9,000	
C$\frac{2}{5}$		6,000	15,000
			18,000

Balance Sheet as at April 5

CAPITAL EMPLOYED		
Capital Accounts		
B	12,000	
C	8,200	20,200
Current Accounts		
B	1,500	
C	1,000	2,500
Loan Account		
A		12,000
		34,700

EMPLOYMENT OF CAPITAL

Fixed Assets		£	£	£
	Leaseholds	28,000		
less	Depreciation	1,000	27,000	
	Fixtures	3,500		
less	Depreciation	1,120	2,380	
				29,380
Current Assets				
	Work in hand		8,200	
	Debtors	4,200		
	less Provision	400	3,800	
	Cash		120	
			12,120	
less Current Liabilities				
	Creditors		6,800	
Net Current Assets				5,320
				34,700

CURRENT ACCOUNTS

		B	C
	Net Profit	9,000	6,000
less	Balance	7,500	5,000
		1,500	1,000

Capital Account A

1979						
5 Oct.	Cash Repayment	1,000		Balance	17,000
	Balance	16,000			
		17,000			17,000
1980					
5 April	Cash Repayment	4,000	5 Oct.	Balance	16,000

Fixtures				Depreciation			
Balance	3,000	Disposal	500	Disposal	280	Balance	700
Cash	1,000	Balance	3,500	Balance	1,120	P & L	700
	4,000		4,000		1,400		1,400
Balance	3,500					Balance	1,120

Fixtures Disposal

Fixtures	500	Cash	200
		Depreciation	280
		Loss	20
	500		500

8.   Profit and Loss Account for the year ending December 31

INCOME		£	£
	Costs	465,000	
	Work in Hand at December 31	35,000	500,000
EXPENSES			
	General Expenses	439,000	
plus	Accounts Outstanding	900	
		439,900	
less	Prepayments	300	
			439,600
NET PROFIT			60,400

Appropriation Account for the 3 months ending March 31

Interest on Capital		£	
A	$(10\% \ 18{,}000 \div 4)$	450	
B	$(10\% \ 18{,}000 \div 4)$	450	900
Profit			
A	$(\frac{1}{2})$	7,100	
B	$(\frac{1}{2})$	7,100	14,200
			15,100

Appropriation Account for the 9 months ending December 31

Interest on Capital			
A	$(10\% \ 20{,}000 \times \frac{3}{4})$	1,500	
B	$(10\% \ 20{,}000 \times \frac{3}{4})$	1,500	
C	$(10\% \ \ 4{,}000 \times \frac{3}{4})$	300	3,300
Profit			
A	2/5	16,800	
B	2/5	16,800	
C	1/5	8,400	42,000
			45,300
			60,400

CURRENT ACCOUNT MOVEMENTS

		A	B	C
Balance		2,000	1,600	—
Interest	to March 31	450	450	—
	to Dec. 31	1,500	1,500	300
Profit	to March 31	7,100	7,100	—
	to Dec. 31	16,800	16,800	8,400
		27,850	27,450	8,700
Drawings		26,000	26,000	6,000
		1,850	1,450	2,700

Balance Sheet as at December 31

CAPITAL EMPLOYED		£	£	£
Capital Accounts				
	A		20,000	
	B		20,000	
	C		4,000	44,000
Current Accounts	A		1,850	
	B		1,450	
	C		2,700	6,000
				50,000

EMPLOYMENT OF CAPITAL		£	£
Fixed Assets			
Premises		15,000	
Furniture & Fittings		5,000	20,000
Current Assets			
Work in Progress		35,000	
Debtors		4,000	
Prepayments		300	
		39,300	
less Current Liabilities			
Creditors	2,000		
Accounts Outstanding	900		
Overdraft	6,400	9,300	
Net Current Assets			30,000
			50,000

Capital A

		£
Balance b/d	18,000	
Revaluation	2,000	

Revaluation

	£		£
Furniture	1,500	Premises	5,500
Balance	4,000		
	5,500		5,500
A	2,000	Balance	4,000
B	2,000		
	4,000		4,000

9.

	Cash		
The Law Society	1,234	Balance	2,646
Balance c/d	1,600	Standing Order	120
		Charges	68
	2,834		2,834
		Balance b/d	1,600

Bank Reconciliation Statement as at July 31

	£
Balance as per bank statement	268
Unpresented Cheques	1,910
	− 1,642
Late Credits	42
	− 1,600

Using the Vertical presentation, the Cash Account would look as follows:

	Cash			
Date	Details	DR	CR	BALANCE
	Balance		2,646	2,646
	The Law Society	1,234		1,412
	Standing Order		120	1,532
	Charges		68	1,600

10.

N.U. Ltd. Company formation (CL1)							
Date	Details	OFFICE ACCOUNT			CLIENT ACCOUNT		
		DR	CR	BALANCE	DR	CR	BALANCE
	Cash. IRC. Capital Duty	300–		300–			
	Cash. Registration fee	50–		350–			
	Costs	200–					
	VAT	20–		570–			
	Cash. You.		570–[2]	—		40–[2]	40–
	Cash. Stationers				40–		—

11.

Albert Hill (CL2)							
		OFFICE ACCOUNT			CLIENT ACCOUNT		
		DR	CR	BALANCE	DR	CR	BALANCE
	Cash. Police Report	7–		7–			
	Cash. Medical Report.	30–		37–			
	Cash. Defendant					1,500–	1,500–
	Costs	75–					
	VAT	7.50		119.50			
	Cash. You.				1,380.50		119.50
	Cash. Transfer		119.50	—	119.50		—

12.

		OFFICE ACCOUNT			CLIENT ACCOUNT		
		Bill (CL3)					
		DR	CR	BALANCE	DR	CR	BALANCE
Cash.							
Court Fees		20–		20–			
Cash.							
Counsel.							
VAT		30–[4]		50–			
P. Cash.							
Witness.		5–		55–			
Costs		50–					
VAT		8–		113–			
Cash.							
Charles'							
Solicitor						2,094.50	2,094.50
Cash							
Transfer			113–		113–		1,981.50
Cash. You					1,981.50		—

13.

Romeo (CL4)							
		OFFICE ACCOUNT			CLIENT ACCOUNT		
		DR	CR	BALANCE	DR	CR	BALANCE
May							
1	Cash. You.					40–	40–
4	Cash. Enquiry Agent.				30–	—	10–
10	Cash. Court Fees	20–		20–			
June							
10	Cash. Witness Fee	22–					
	Cash. VAT Counsel	50–		92–			
July							
1	Costs	75–					
	VAT	12.50		179.50			
20	Cash. Juliet's Solicitors		124.50*	55–			
26	Cash. Transfer		10–	45–	10–		—
Aug							
1	Cash. You.		45–[6]	—			
	* Costs	55					
	Counsel	40					
		95					
	VAT	9.50					
	Court Fees	20					
		124.50					

NOTE: Fred & Co.'s fees, on payment, are debited to Agency Expenses Account.

14.

Desmond (CL5)							
		OFFICE ACCOUNT			CLIENT ACCOUNT		
		DR	CR	BALANCE	DR	CR	BALANCE
Jan							
2	Cash. You.					400–	400–
3	P. Cash.						
	Court Fee	10–		10–			
Feb							
3	Cash.						
	Enquiry						
	Agent.						
	VAT	30–[5]		40–			
4	Cash.						
	Witness				22–		378–
5	Cash.						
	Witness				9–		369–
Apr							
18	Costs	200–					
	VAT	29–		269–			
	Interest						
	Payable						
	Account		31–**	238–			
29	Cash. You.					1,356.20[2]	1,725.20
May							
1	Cash.						
	Percy's						
	Solicitors				1,427.20*		298–
2	Cash.						
	Counsel.						
	VAT	60[5]		298–			
3	Cash						
	Transfer		298–	—	298–		—

NOTE: April 18. The VAT includes the tax on Counsel's fees paid on May 2.

* The invoice of Percy's solicitor is addressed to Percy, not you. Thus, you could not use the Principal Method.

** In this case no Cash Sheet entries are made but merely DR Interest Payable Account.

15.

George (CL6)

		Details	OFFICE ACCOUNT			CLIENT ACCOUNT		
			DR	CR	BALANCE	DR	CR	BALANCE
May 30	Cash. X & Co. Valuation. VAT		200–		200–			
June 1	Cash. Newspaper Adverts		7–		207–			
2	Cash. George's Bank. Loan						1,200–	1,200–
3	Cash. Probate Fees		10–		217–			
	Cash. IRC. CTT					1,200–		—
July 20	Cash. Building Society						3,400–	3,400–
21	Cash. George's Bank						800–	4,200–
22	Cash. Life Policy						4,200–	8,400–
24	Cash. IRC. Tax Arrears					600–		
	Cash. George's Bank					1,200–		6,600–
Aug. 2	Cash. Legacy. Ethel					1,000–		
	Frank					1,000–		4,600–
31	Costs	300–	330–					
	General Disbursements	30–						
	VAT		53–		600–			
	Cash. Transfer			600–		600–		
	Cash. George's Son					2,000–		
	Cash. George's Daughter					2,000–		—

16.

Cash

Date	Details	OFFICE ACCOUNT			CLIENT ACCOUNT		
		DR	CR	BALANCE	DR	CR	BALANCE
April							
11	Tempest & Flood Insurance. Premium				40		
15	Tempest & Flood Insurance					38	
	Tempest & Flood Insurance. Transfer	2				2	
May							
8	Dodds & Co. Enquiry agent		20				
	VAT		2				
15	Dodds & Co	66					
16	Margaret				5,000		
18	Margaret					4,846	
	Margaret Transfer	154				154	
20	Margaret Transfer		11		11		

WORKINGS

Margaret

		OFFICE ACCOUNT			CLIENT ACCOUNT		
		DR	CR	BALANCE	DR	CR	BALANCE
May							
16	Cash. You.					5,000	5,000
18	Costs	140		140			
	VAT	14		154			
	Cash. You.				4,846		154
	Cash. Transfer		154	—	154		—
20	Abatement		10	10^{CR}			
	VAT		1	11^{CR}			
	Cash. Transfer	11		—		11	11

On May 20th the entries were made to record the abatement which resulted in the ledger account of Margaret having a credit balance in the OFFICE ACCOUNT. Normally such a balance would indicate a breach of Solicitors Accounts Rules (see page 100). In this case I do not think you have broken the rules. However you do now hold OFFICE ACCOUNT £11 which belongs to Margaret. (In retrospect what you did was to transfer £11 too much to OFFICE ACCOUNT on May 18th.) I think you should immediately either send an office account cheque for £11 to Margaret or transfer £11 from OFFICE ACCOUNT to CLIENT ACCOUNT. This would mean that you are now holding £11 in CLIENT ACCOUNT on Margaret's behalf for return to her or for any other use on her behalf. This is what I have shown in the answer.

17.

Cash

Date	Details	OFFICE ACCOUNT			CLIENT ACCOUNT		
		DR	CR	BALANCE	DR	CR	BALANCE
Sept.							
5	Tom. On account				800		
6	Tom					63	
7	Jones Family Trust				4,270		
8	Simon	57[6]					
9	Michael. House Purchase	12,340					
12	Tom. Cheque dishonoured					800	
	Tom. Rectification of breach		63		63		
13	Jones Family Trust					2,500	
	Jones Family Trust. Transfer to Trust Bank Account					1,770	
14	Nancy. Cheque indorsed				8,000–*	8,000–*	

* See pages 140 and 141.

Cash

Date	Details	OFFICE ACCOUNT			CLIENT ACCOUNT		
		DR	CR	BALANCE	DR	CR	BALANCE
May							
3	Bill. Interest	40					
	Bill. Transfer		40				
4	Deposit. Cash. General deposit				500		
5	Interest Payable Re. Christine		42				
	Christine Interest payable				42		
	Christine					6,042	
8	Peter. On account				200		
9	Robert. On account				14,000		
	Deposit Cash. Specially designated Re. Robert					14,000	
15	Stephen					8,000	
16	Interest Payable Re. Stephen		50		200		
17	Ethel. On account		30				
	Ethel. Stationers' fees						
	VAT		3				
18	Ethel Transfer	33				33	
19	Frances. Agreed fee.	20					
20	Peter		120			200	
22	Peter	40					
30	Interest Receivable				85		
	Interest Receivable Transfer	85				85	

NOTES:

May 1 & 2. No entries in the Firm's Books.

May 3. Clients' money wrongly paid into office bank account, and transferred under Rule 7 (c) (SAR) to the specially designated bank account if so desired.

May 18: Before this entry is made, the VAT of £3 must be debited to Ethel's account (see page 132). If no tax invoice for the £3 had been issued then only £30 could have been transferred.

May 19: The £20 includes the VAT because unless it is otherwise stated any price quoted is deemed to include the VAT.

19.

Cash

Date	Details	OFFICE ACCOUNT			CLIENT ACCOUNT		
		DR	CR	BALANCE	DR	CR	BALANCE
(a)	Stakeholder. Lucy & King. Re. Quentin				710		
(b)	Ian. Current Account. Marshire CC. Salary	75*					
(c)	Ian & Jane Ltd. Litigation				18		
(d)	Zebedee. L.R. Fees		20–75				
(e)	Oliver Trust. Violet					800	
(f)	Susan. Agreed Fee	30					
(g)	Pauline. Re. Fish Hall	62–85			550[2]		
	Pauline. Completion of Fish Hall					550	
	S. Building Society. Completion of Fish Hall					4,400	
(hi)	Rotten Insurance Co. Re. Nancy		47–50				
	Nancy. Transfer	45				45**	
(hii)	Marshire RDC. Rates		82–80				
	Ian Current A/C		44–50				

* Whether the credit is on Ian's current account or the firm's Costs account depends on the partnership agreement.

** There was insufficient clients' money. The full amount was drawn on OFFICE ACCOUNT which was then partially reimbursed by a transfer from CLIENT ACCOUNT. As an alternative, two cheques could have been drawn (see the answer to question 18 on page 361—May 20).

20.

Pauline and Robert. *Re* Simon deceased (CL8)

Date	Details	OFFICE ACCOUNT			CLIENT ACCOUNT		
		DR	CR	BALANCE	DR	CR	BALANCE
Feb							
1	Cash. The Bank. Re. CTT					4,000–	4,000–
3	Cash. IRC, CTT.				4,000–		—
3	Cash. Probate Fees	38–		38–			
20	Agreed Fee	90.91					
	VAT	9.09		138–			
Mar							
22	Cash Deposit					4,800–	4,800–
25	Cash. Investments					700–	5,500–
26	Cash. Funeral Expenses				125–		
	Cash. Debts				3,100–		2,275–
April							
22	Cash. Completion of Sale					43,200–	45,475–
	Cash. You.				3,800–		41,675–
May							
3	Costs	400–					
	VAT	40–		578–			
	Cash. Timothy. Legacy				5,000–		
	Cash. Transfer		578–	—	578–		
	Cash. William				36,097–		—

21.   Statement

Sale of The Count House. Purchase of Tangerine Cottage

PURCHASE of Tangerine Cottage	£	£	£
Payments			
Deposit	3,000		
Completion	27,000		
L.R. Fees	80		
Costs	300		
VAT	32		
General disbursements	20		
Mortgage Costs	33		
		30,465	
Receipts			
Mortgage advance		25,000	
			5,465
SALE of The Count House			
Receipts			
Deposit	1,580		
Completion	14,220		
		15,800	
Payments			
Mortgage redemption	10,187		
Costs	200		
VAT	20		
		10,407	
			5,393
BALANCE DUE from you			72

Mr. Hare. Sale of the Count House. Purchase of Tangerine Cottage (CL9)

Date	Details	OFFICE ACCOUNT			CLIENT ACCOUNT		
		DR	CR	BALANCE	DR	CR	BALANCE
June 2	Cash. Deposit Tangerine Cottage	3,000–		3,000–			
29	Plenty B.S. Transfer. Mortgage Advance					25,000–	25,000–
30	Cash. Completion. Tangerine Cottage	2,000–		5,000–	25,000–		—
	Cash. Completion. The Count House					4,033–	4,033–
	Stakeholder, Transfer					1,580–	5,613–
July 1	Cash. Transfer		5,000–	—	5,000–		613–
18	Cash. L.R. Fees				80–		533–
28	Costs	520		520			
	VAT	52–		572–			
	Plenty B.S.	33		605			
Aug. 1	Cash. Transfer		533–	72–	533–		—

22.   Statement

Simpson. Sale of Bolt House. Purchase of Dyer Hall

	£	£	£
PURCHASE of Dyer Hall			
Payments			
Deposit	5,000		
Searches	5		
Completion	45,000		
Costs	250		
VAT	25		
Mortgage costs	55		
		50,335	
Receipts			
On account	5,000		
Mortgage advance	40,000		
		45,000	
			5,335
SALE of Bolt House			
Receipts			
Deposit	4,000		
Completion	36,000		
		40,000	
Payments			
Mortgage redemption	35,000		
Costs	150		
VAT	15		
		35,165	
			4,835
			500
less Received on account generally			300
BALANCE DUE from you			200

Simpson, Sale of Bolt House. Purchase of Dyer Hall (CL10)

Date	Details	OFFICE ACCOUNT			CLIENT ACCOUNT		
		DR	CR	BALANCE	DR	CR	BALANCE
Mar 1	Cash. You. Deposit. Dyer Hall					5,000–	5,000–
2	Cash. Vendor's Solicitors. Deposit				5,000–		—
3	Cash. Search	2–		2–			
May 25	P. Cash. Search	3–		5–			
June 1	Cash. You. On account					300–	300–
3	Cash. Purchaser's Solicitors. Completion. Bolt House. Stakeholder. Transfer					1,000–*	
	Cash. Vendor's Solicitors. Completion Dyer Hall				5,000–	4,000–	5,300–
6	Costs	400–					300–
	VAT	40–					
	Mercer B.S. Transfer. Costs	55–		500–			
	Cash. Transfer		300–	200–	300–		—

* The purchaser's solicitor brought 2 drafts to completion as follows:

Mortgage Redemption (payable to mortgagees solicitors)	35,000
Balance payable to you	1,000
TOTAL	36,000

The Mercer Building Society (CL 12)

Date	Details	OFFICE ACCOUNT			CLIENT ACCOUNT		
		DR	CR	BALANCE	DR	CR	BALANCE
June							
1	Cash. You.				40,000–		40,000–
3	Cash. Vendor's Solicitors. Completion					40,000–	—
6	Costs	50–					
	VAT	5–		55–			
	Simpson. Transfer		55–	—			

Stakeholder (CL11)

Date	Details	OFFICE ACCOUNT			CLIENT ACCOUNT		
		DR	CR	BALANCE	DR	CR	BALANCE
April							
1	Cash. Re. Dyer Hall				4,000–		4,000–
June							
3	Simpson. Transfer					4,000–	—

23. Statement

Jack. Sale of the Manor House. Purchase of Half Moon Street

PURCHASE of Half Moon Street	£	£	£
Payments			
Search	10		
Costs. Sale	140		
Costs. Mortgage	66		
VAT	14		
Completion	27,000		
		27,230	
Receipts			
Mortgage advance		18,000	
			9,230
SALE of the Manor House			
Receipts			
Deposit	2,000		
Completion	18,000		
		20,000	
Payments			
Mortgage redemption	13,000		
Costs	100		
VAT	10		
		13,110	
			6,890
BALANCE DUE from you			2,340

Jack. Sale of the Manor House. Purchase of Half Moon Street (CL13)

Date	Details	OFFICE ACCOUNT			CLIENT ACCOUNT		
		DR	CR	BALANCE	DR	CR	BALANCE
Mar 3	Cash. Search	10–		10–			
Apr 1	Costs	240–		250–			
	VAT	24–		274–			
	Ernest B.S.	66–		340–			
11	Cash. You.		340–	—		2,000–[2]	2,000–
12	Cash. Purchaser's Solicitors. Completion. The Manor House.					5,000–	
	Stakeholder. Transfer					2,000–	9,000–
	Cash. Vendor's Solicitors. Completion Half Moon Street				9,000–		—

Ernest Building Society (CL14)

Date	Details	OFFICE ACCOUNT			CLIENT ACCOUNT		
		DR	CR	BALANCE	DR	CR	BALANCE
Apr 1	Costs	60–		60–			
	VAT	6–		66–			
	Jack		66–	—			
	Cash. You.					18,000–	18,000–
11	Cash. Purchaser's Solicitors. Completion The Manor House					13,000–	31,000–
12	Cash. Vendor's Solicitors. Completion. Half Moon Street				18,000–		
	Cash. You.				13,000–		—

Stakeholder CL(11)

Date	Details	OFFICE ACCOUNT			CLIENT ACCOUNT		
		DR	CR	BALANCE	DR	CR	BALANCE
Mar 1	Cash. Re. The Manor House.					2,000–	2,000–
Apr 12	Jack. Transfer.				2,000–		—

24.   Statement

Sale of Heartbreak House. Purchase of Horseback Hall

PURCHASE of Heartbreak House	£	£	£
Payments			
Search	10		
Costs	400		
VAT	40		
Completion	27,000		
L.R. Fees	120		
		27,570	
Receipts			
Mortgage	13,000		
less Mortgage costs	270		
		12,730	
			14,840
SALE of Horseback Hall			
Receipts			
Completion		22,500	
Payments			
Mortgage redemption	10,000		
Costs	300		
VAT	30		
		10,330	
			12,170
			2,670
BRIDGING LOAN			
Loan from bank		10,000	
less Repayment of loan		10,000	—
BALANCE DUE from you			2,670

Ellie. Sale of Heartbreak House. Purchase of Horseback Hall (CL15)

Date	Details	OFFICE ACCOUNT			CLIENT ACCOUNT		
		DR	CR	BALANCE	DR	CR	BALANCE
Apr 10	Cash. Search	10–		10–			
May 25	Costs	700–					
	VAT	70–		780–			
Jun 1	Cash. You.		780–	—		1,890–[2]	1,890–
	Cash. Ellie's Bank					10,000–	11,890–
Jun 2	Cash. Hector B.S. Redemption of Mortgage. Heartbreak House.				10,000–		1,890–
Jun 3	Cash. Purchaser's Solicitors. Completion. Heartbreak House; Indorsed over					14,270–	
	Cash. Net Purchase Moneys					8,230–	24,390–
	Cash. Vendor's Solicitors. Completion. Horseback Hall, Indorsed over				14,270–		
	Cash. Ellie's Bank				10,000–		120–
Jun 4	Cash. Land Registry Fees				120–		—

NOTE: May 25. The item of disbursements (£130) refers to the search (£10) and the Land Registry fees (£120) paid on May 25 and June 3 respectively.

June 3. Completion of Heartbreak House. The purchaser's solicitors were asked to provide two drafts and the first one for £14,270 was indorsed over to the vendor's solicitors on completion of Horseback Hall.

* 11.30 Complete sale. Receive 2 drafts from purchaser's
solicitors both payable to you   Draft 1   14,270

                                                          2   8,230

                                                                          22,500

12.30 Complete purchase. Draft (*i.e.* £14,270) indorsed over.

2.00 Balance banked *i.e.* Draft 2 (£8,230).

Test One

1.

Executors of Saturn decd. Administration of estate (CL.1)

Date	Details	OFFICE ACCOUNT			CLIENT ACCOUNT		
		DR	CR	BALANCE	DR	CR	BALANCE
Mar.							
9	Cash. Transfer to ins. co.	95		95			
14	Cash. Probate fees.	70		165			
26	Cash. Constellation B.S.					590	590
27	Saturn. Transfer					1,219	1,809
	Cash. Staty adverts				22		1,787
	P. Cash. Advert	12		177			
29	Cash. Pluto Ins.					6,342	8,129
30	Cash. Debts				1,500		6,629
	Cash. Funeral Expenses				1,000		5,629
	Neptune. Transfer				4,000		1,629
April							
3	P. Cash. Office copy entries	5		182			
12	Cash. Share transfer fees	3		185			
May							
2	Cash. Completion sale					63,000	64,629
	Stakeholder. Transfer					7,000	71,629
9	Costs						
	Sale 440						
	Admin. 700	1,140		1,325			
	VAT	114		1,439			
	Neptune. Transfer				36,146		35,483
16	Cash. Transfer		1,439	—	1,439		34,044
17	Cash. Interest					567	34,611
	Neptune. Transfer				34,611		—

		OFFICE ACCOUNT			CLIENT ACCOUNT		
Date	Details	DR	CR	BALANCE	DR	CR	BALANCE
Mar. 1	Balance			15			
30	Executors of Saturn Transfer					4,000	4,000
	Cash. Deposit				4,000		—
April 26	Costs	300		315			
	VAT	30		345			
	P. Cash. Search	1		346			
30	Cash. Aries' Bank Loan					36,000	36,000
	Cash. Completion				36,000		—
May 2	Cash. Stamp duty	400		746			
	Cash. L.R. fees	70		816			
9	Exors. of Saturn. Transfer					36,146	36,146
	Cash. Aries' Bank				36,146		—
17	Exors. of Saturn. Transfer					34,611	34,611
	Cash. Transfer		816	—	816		33,795*

Table title: **Neptune. Purchase of "Wild Leap" (CL.2)**

NOTES
* This could be placed on deposit
March 14 (£16,700) and 19 (£1,234): No entries needed.

2 *Brown*

Profit and Loss Account for year ending May 31, 1987

INCOME	£	£	£
Costs	129,818		
less work in progress at			
1st June 1988	14,322		
	115,469		
add work in progress at			
31st May 1987	16,217		
		131,713	
Interest received		7,896	
Miscellaneous Income	2,330		
less received in advance	100	2,230	
			141,839
EXPENSES			
General Expenses		91,466	
Bad debts		770	
Loss on sale of car		250	
Depreciation			
Cars	5,000		
Furniture etc.	2,200	7,200	99,686
NET PROFIT			42,153

Balance Sheet as at May 31, 1987

	£	£	£
CAPITAL EMPLOYED			
Capital		58,125*	
plus net profit		42,153	
		100,278	
less drawings		34,100	
Loan			66,178
			15,000
			81,178

EMPLOYMENT OF CAPITAL

Fixed Assets

Lease		30,000	
Cars	20,000		
less depreciation	15,000	5,000	
Furniture etc.	22,000		
less depreciation	13,200	8,800	
			43,800

Current Assets

Work in hand		16,217	
Debtors		26,331	
Cash		2,289	
Petty cash		50	
		44,887	

less Current Liabilities

Creditors	7,013		
Accounts outstanding	496	7,509	
Net Current Assets			37,378

Client Account

Cash in bank—Deposit Account	150,000		
—Current Account	31,440	181,440	
less due to clients		181,440	—
NET ASSETS			81,178

*63,125	
−	5,000
	58,125

Test Two

Cash Account

1.

Date	Details	OFFICE ACCOUNT DR	OFFICE ACCOUNT CR	OFFICE ACCOUNT BALANCE	CLIENT ACCOUNT DR	CLIENT ACCOUNT CR	CLIENT ACCOUNT BALANCE
Oct.							
2	Bull Dogge	16			68		
4	Estate of John decd.						
6	George		146				
10	Black		963		500		
12	Pink. From Green				800		
14	Estate of John				400		
15	Peter				15,678		
	D. Cash. Re. Peter					15,678	
18	Pink					702	
	Agency Expenses		60				
	VAT		6				
	Pink. Disbursement	98					
	Pink. Transfer		10			98	
19	Stakeholder. Clarence	996			2,000		
24	George	24			226		
	Harold	11					
25	Bull Dogge. Transfer					11	
	Bull Dogge.					57	
31	Harold. Cheque dishonoured		24		226	226	

Bull Dogge Co. Ltd. (CL1)							
Date	Details	OFFICE ACCOUNT			CLIENT ACCOUNT		
		DR	CR	BALANCE	DR	CR	BALANCE
Oct.							
	Balance			16			
2	Cash. You		16	—		68	68
25	Costs	10		10			
	VAT	1		11			
	Cash. Transfer		11	—	11		57
	Cash. You				57		—

Estate of John decd. (CL2)							
Date	Details	OFFICE ACCOUNT			CLIENT ACCOUNT		
		DR	CR	BALANCE	DR	CR	BALANCE
Oct.							
	Balance						83
4	Cash	146		146			
14	Cash. N.						
	Saving Bank					400	483

George (CL3)							
Date	Details	OFFICE ACCOUNT			CLIENT ACCOUNT		
		DR	CR	BALANCE	DR	CR	BALANCE
Oct.							
6	Cash	963		963			
	Costs	30		993			
	VAT	3		996			
24	Cash. You		996	—			

\multicolumn{9}{c|}{Black (CL4)}

Date	Details	\multicolumn{3}{c}{OFFICE ACCOUNT}	\multicolumn{3}{c}{CLIENT ACCOUNT}
		DR	CR	BALANCE	DR	CR	BALANCE
Oct. 10	Cash. You White. Transfer				500	500	500 —

\multicolumn{9}{c|}{White (CL5)}

Date	Details	\multicolumn{3}{c}{OFFICE ACCOUNT}	\multicolumn{3}{c}{CLIENT ACCOUNT}
		DR	CR	BALANCE	DR	CR	BALANCE
Oct. 10	Black. Transfer					500	500

\multicolumn{9}{c|}{Pink (CL6)}

Date	Details	\multicolumn{3}{c}{OFFICE ACCOUNT}	\multicolumn{3}{c}{CLIENT ACCOUNT}
		DR	CR	BALANCE	DR	CR	BALANCE
Oct. 12	Cash. Green					800	800
	Costs	80		80			
	VAT	8		88			
18	Cash. You				702		98
	Cash. Disbursement	10		98			
	Cash. Transfer		98	—	98		—

Peter (CL7) On deposit : Oct. 15							
Date	Details	OFFICE ACCOUNT			CLIENT ACCOUNT		
		DR	CR	BALANCE	DR	CR	BALANCE
Oct. 15	Cash. Sale of Shares					15,678	15,678

Stakeholder (CL8)							
Date	Details	OFFICE ACCOUNT			CLIENT ACCOUNT		
		DR	CR	BALANCE	DR	CR	BALANCE
Oct. 19	Cash. Clarence Re. Richard					2,000	2,000

Harold (CL9)							
Date	Details	OFFICE ACCOUNT			CLIENT ACCOUNT		
		DR	CR	BALANCE	DR	CR	BALANCE
Oct. 19	P. Cash	24		24			
24	Cash. You		24	—		226	226
31	Cash. Cheque dishonoured	24		24	226		—

2. Shrimp and Whelk

Profit and Loss Account for the year ending June 30, 1986

	£	£	£
Profit costs			284,596
less work in hand at 30.6.85			22,993
			261,603
add work in hand at 30.6.86			12,293
			273,896
Trade Association fee			2,000
Interest received			14,986
			290,882
Less expenses:			
Administration & General Expenses		208,412	
Bad debts		80	
Depreciation:			
Furniture & Library	840		
Cars	3,750	4,590	213,082
NET PROFIT			77,800

Appropriation Account

	£	£	£
Six months to 31.12.85			
Profit			
Shrimp		38,900	
			38,900
Six months to 30.6.86			
Salary			
Whelk		6,000	
Interest on capital			
Shrimp	3,000		
Whelk	1,500	4,500	
Profit			
Shrimp	17,040		
Whelk	11,360		
		28,400	
			38,900
			77,800

Shrimp and Whelk

Balance sheet as at June 30, 1986

	£	£	£
CAPITAL EMPLOYED			
Capital Accounts			
Shrimp		60,000	
Whelk		30,000	90,000
Current Accounts			
Shrimp		16,840	
Whelk		9,360	26,200
Long Term Liabilities			
Bank Loan			20,000
			136,200
EMPLOYMENT OF CAPITAL			
Fixed Assets			
Premises		80,000	
Furniture & Library	8,400		
less Depreciation	3,360	5,040	
Motor Cars	18,750		
less Depreciation	11,250	7,500	92,540
Current Assets			
Work in hand		12,293	
Debtors		35,242	
Cash		8,885	
Petty cash		45	
		56,465	
less Current Liabilities			
Creditors	8,942		
Expenses accrued due	3,863	12,805	
Net Current Assets			43,660
Cash at Bank—Client Account			
Deposit Account		300,000	
Current Account		47,586	
		347,586	
Less Due to Clients		347,586	—
			136,200

Movements on Current Accounts

	Shrimp	*Whelk*
Salary		6,000
Interest on Capital	3,000	1,500
Share of net profit	55,940	11,360
	58,940	18,860
less drawings	42,100	9,500
	16,840	9,360

Test Three

Black Bobb & Co.

Smith. Purchase of "The Padd." Sale of "Coslot"

1.

Date	Details	OFFICE ACCOUNT			CLIENT ACCOUNT		
		DR	CR	BALANCE	DR	CR	BALANCE
Nov. 3	P. Cash. Search	2		2			
9	Cash. Survey fee	165		167			
16	Cash. Nonsuch Bank					2,500	2,500
20	Cash. Deposit The Padd				2,500		—
Dec. 8	Costs	230		397			
	VAT	23		420			
11	Cash. You					3,150	3,150
14	Cash. Completion Sale					14,400	17,550
	Stakeholder. Transfer					1,600	19,150
	High Rate B.S. Transfer					6,956	26,106
	Cash. Completion Purchase				22,500		3,606
	Cash. Nonsuch Bank				2,500		1,106
	Cash. S. Duty				250		856
	Cash. L.R. Fees				51		805
15	Cash. Estate Agents fees				385		420
31	Cash. Transfer		420	—	420		—

Statement

Purchase of "The Padd". Sale of "Coslot"

PURCHASE of The Padd	£	£	£
Payments			
Search	2		
Survey fee	165		
Deposit	2,500		
Completion	22,500		
Mortgage costs	44		
Stamp duty	250		
L.R. fees	51		
Costs	140		
VAT	14		
		25,666	
Receipts			
Mortgage advance		7,000	
			18,666
SALE of Coslot			
Receipts			
Deposit	1,600		
Completion	14,400	16,000	
Payments			
Costs	90		
VAT	9		
Estate agents' commission	385		
		484	15,516
			3,150
BRIDGING LOAN			
Loan		2,500	
less Repaid		2,500	
			—
BALANCE DUE from you			3,150

		OFFICE ACCOUNT			CLIENT ACCOUNT		
Date	Details	DR	CR	BALANCE	DR	CR	BALANCE

Brown's Solicitors

		OFFICE ACCOUNT			CLIENT ACCOUNT		
Date	Details	DR	CR	BALANCE	DR	CR	BALANCE
Nov.							
3	Cash	11		11			
15	Cash. Bungo					2,400	2,400
18	Costs	130		141			
	VAT	13		154			
	Cash. You				2,246		154
Dec.							
31	Cash. Transfer		154		154		—

2.   Pen, Ink and Paper

Profit and Loss Account for the year ending June 30, 1982

Appropriation Account for the 6 months ending December 31, 1981

	£	£	£
INTEREST ON CAPITAL			
Pen (10% 40,000 ÷ 2)	2,000		
Ink (10% 20,000 ÷ 2)	1,000	3,000	
SALARY Ink (12,000 ÷ 2)		6,000	
PROFITS			
Pen (3/5)	9,600		
Ink (2/5)	6,400	16,000	25,000

Appropriation Account for the 6 months ending June 30, 1982

SALARIES			
Pen (20,000 ÷ 2)	10,000		
Ink (15,000 ÷ 2)	7,500		
Paper (10,000 ÷ 2)	5,000	22,500	
PROFITS			
Pen (2/5)	1,000		
Ink (2/5)	1,000		
Paper (1/5)	500	2,500	25,000
			50,000

Balance Sheet as at June 30, 1982

CAPITAL EMPLOYED	£	£
Capital Accounts		
Pen	40,000	
Ink	20,000	
Paper	10,000	70,000
Current Accounts		
Pen	2,900	
Ink	3,500	
	6,400	
less Paper	500	5,900
		75,900

Current Account Movements

		Pen	Ink	Paper
Interest	to 31/12/81	2,000	1,000	—
Salary	to 31/12/81		6,000	
Profit	to 31/12/81	9,600	6,400	
Salaries	to 30/6/82	10,000	7,500	5,000
Profit	to 30/6/82	1,000	1,000	500
		22,600	21,900	5,500
less Balance	at 30/6/82	19,700	18,400	6,000
		2,900	3,500	(500)

EMPLOYMENT OF CAPITAL	£	£
Sundry Assets		80,500
less Sundry Liabilities		4,600
		75,900
Client Account		
Cash in bank	87,322	
less Due to clients	87,322	—
		75,900

3.

Cash Account				
Date	Details			
		DR	CR	BALANCE
April 30	Balance			642
	Giro direct transfer	323		965
	Cheque returned		87	878
	Standing bankers order		300	578
	Correction of error		200	378

Bank Reconciliation Statement as at April 30

	£
Balance as per Bank Statement	(247)
Unpresented Cheques	(596)
	(843)
Late Credits	1,221
	378

Unpresented Cheques	*Late Credits*
323	345
273	876
596	1,221

Test Four

1.

Executors of Chasm Deceased (CL.1)

		OFFICE ACCOUNT			CLIENT ACCOUNT		
		Jan 12 £23,400 on deposit / 22 £13,000 removed			Jan 28 £80,000 on deposit / Feb 4 £90,400 removed		
Date	Details	DR	CR	BALANCE	DR	CR	BALANCE
1987 Dec. 10	Cash. **Transfer to Insurance Co.					4,876	4,876
11	Cash. Probate fees					507	5,383
1988 Jan. 5	Cash. Adverts. VAT	245		245			
5	P. Cash. Advert. VAT	100		345			
7	Cash. You.	40		385			
11	Chasm. Transfer*	20		405			
12	D. Cash. Life assurance policy					23,400	28,783
14	Cash. Debts				2,424		26,359
	Cash. Funeral expenses				775		25,584
20	Cash. House contents					1,297	26,881
22	Cash. Legacy. Secretary				5,000		21,881
	Cash. Legacy. Charity				1,000		20,881
	Fissure. Transfer				10,000		10,881
27	Cash. Completion					87,494	98,375
	Stakeholder. Transfer					12,000	110,375
	Cash. Estate agents. Commission				2,761		107,614
29	Costs. (Sale) 600 (Admin.) 900	1,500		1,905			
	VAT (1500 + 40 + 20 × 10%)	156		2,061			
Feb. 1	Cash. Transfer		2,061		2,061		105,553
4	Cash. Interest					108	105,661
5	Cash. Interest					194	105,885
	Fissure. Transfer				105,885		—

N.B. No double entries needed for Dec. 11   £22,923
                            Jan. 4   £12,420

** The "Cash" entry is essential, since money is being transferred from OFFICE ACCOUNT (Executors) to CLIENT ACCOUNT (Insurance Co.).

 * The question says that "the net amount" is transferred. It has been assumed that the amount due to Office Account (£482) is transferred from Client Account to Office Account and the balance of £507 transferred to the Executors Account. See the entries on the Cash Account dated Jan. 11.

Fissure. Purchase of "Epicentre" (CL.2)

Date	Details	OFFICE ACCOUNT			CLIENT ACCOUNT		
		DR	CR	BALANCE	DR	CR	BALANCE
1987 Dec. 1	Balance			104			
1988 Jan. 21	Cash. Survey fee	276		380			
	P. Cash. Search	24		404			
22	Executors of Chasm. Transfer					10,000	10,000
	Cash. Deposit				10,000		—
Feb. 5	Executors of Chasm. Transfer					105,855	105,855

Cash

Date	Details	OFFICE ACCOUNT			CLIENT ACCOUNT		
		DR	CR	BALANCE	DR	CR	BALANCE
1988 Jan.							
5	Executors of Chasm. Adverts		40				
	VAT		4				
7	Executors of Chasm. You	482			4,876	482	
11	Chasm. Transfer*				12,000		
13	Stakeholder. Re Goodinvest					2,424	
14	Executors of Chasm. Debts					775	
	Executors of Chasm. Funeral expenses						
20	Executors of Chasm. House contents				1,297		
21	Fissure. Survey fee		276				
22	D. Cash. Executors of Chasm. Transfer				13,000		
	Executors of Chasm. Legacy. Secretary					5,000	
	Executors of Chasm. Legacy. Charity					1,000	
	Fissure. Deposit					10,000	
27	Executors of Chasm. Completion				87,494		
	Executors of Chasm. Commission					2,761	
28	D. Cash. Executors of Chasm. Transfer					80,000	

2. Jack and Jill

Profit and Loss Account for the year ending December 31, 1987

INCOME	£	£	£
Costs	324,786		
less Work in hand at 1/1/87	32,874		
	291,912		
plus Work in hand at 31/12/87	44,862	336,774	
Interest Receivable		22,946	
Miscellaneous Income		1,129	
			360,849
EXPENSES			
Administrative & General			
Expenses	268,567		
plus accounts outstanding	1,242		
	269,809		
less transferred to Jack	200	269,609	
Depreciation			
Motor Cars	6,000		
Library, Furniture			
& Computer	8,500	14,500	
Bad Debts		240	
			284,349
NET PROFIT			76,500

Appropriation Account for the 6 months ending June 30, 1987

	£
Profits due to Jack	38,250

Appropriation Account for the 6 months ending December 31, 1987

Interest on Capital	£	£	
Jack (10% 60,000 ÷ 2)	3,000		
Jill (10% 25,000 ÷ 2)	1,250	4,250	
Salary			
Jill (8,000 ÷ 2)		4,000	
Profit			
Jack ($\frac{2}{3}$)	20,000		
Jill ($\frac{1}{3}$)	10,000	30,000	
			38,250
			76,500

Jack and Jill

Balance Sheet as at December 31, 1987

EMPLOYMENT OF CAPITAL

		£	£	£
Fixed Assets				
	Leasehold Property		34,000	
	Motor Cars	24,000		
less	Depreciation	18,000	6,000	
	Library, Furniture & Computer	34,000		
less	Depreciation	17,000	17,000	
				57,000
Current Assets				
	Work in hand		44,862	
	Debtors		9,765	
	Cash in bank*		6,712	
	Cash in hand		84	
Current Liabilities			61,423	
	Creditors	5,423		
	Accounts Outstanding	1,242	6,665	
Net Current Assets				54,758
Client Account				
	Cash in bank: Deposit Account	350,000		
	Current Account	34,876	384,876	
less	Due to Clients		384,876	—
				111,758

*6,952	
− 240	
6,712	

CAPITAL EMPLOYED

		£	£
Capital Accounts			
	Jack	60,000	
	Jill	25,000	85,000
Current Accounts			
	Jack	22,508	
	Jill	4,250	26,758
			111,758

Movements on Current Accounts

	Jack	Jill
Profit to 30/6/87	38,250	
Interest to 31/12/87	3,000	1,250
Salary to 31/12/87		4,000
Profit to 31/12/87	20,000	10,000
	61,250	15,250
Drawings	(38,542)	(11,000)
Adjustment	(200)	—
	22,508	4,250

Test Five

1.

1 Apr. £20,000 on deposit. Removed Apr. 28.

Aspen

Date	Details	OFFICE ACCOUNT			CLIENT ACCOUNT		
		DR £	CR £	BALANCE £	DR £	CR £	BALANCE £
Apr.							
1	Balance						20,232
11	P. Cash	14		43			
27	Cash. Horse Chestnuts. Completion			57		49,500	69,732
	Stakeholder					5,500	75,232
	Cash. Estate agents				770		74,462
28	Costs	400		457			
	VAT	40		497			
	D. Cash. Interest					83	74,545
	Cash. Transfer Interest					106	74,651
	Cash. Transfer		497	—	497		74,154
	Cash. You				74,154		—

Larch

Date	Details	OFFICE ACCOUNT			CLIENT ACCOUNT		
		DR £	CR £	BALANCE £	DR £	CR £	BALANCE £
Apr. 1	Balance						600
7	Maple Insurance. Premium					250	350
May 3	Cash. Transfer*	650		650	1,000	650	1,000
	Cash. Rowan*		400	250			
	Cash. You		250	—			
	Cash. You. Indorsed cheque			250			—
9	Cash. Cheque dishonoured	250		250			

* Another way of dealing with this would have been

(1) Pay £1,000 to Rowan out of OFFICE ACCOUNT

(2) Transfer the £350 from CLIENT ACCOUNT to OFFICE ACCOUNT

Mapel Insurance Ltd.							
Date	Details	OFFICE ACCOUNT			CLIENT ACCOUNT		
		DR £	CR £	BALANCE £	DR £	CR £	BALANCE £
Apr. 7	Larch. Premium					250	250
29	Commission	37		37			
	Cash. Transfer		37	—	37		213
	Cash. You				213		—

Mr. and Mrs. Poplar							
Date	Details	OFFICE ACCOUNT			CLIENT ACCOUNT		
		DR £	CR £	BALANCE £	DR £	CR £	BALANCE £
Apr. 12	P. Cash. Search	14		14			
18	Cash. You					4,000	4,000
25	Cash. V's solicitors. Deposit				4,000		—

Stakeholder							
Date	Details	OFFICE ACCOUNT			CLIENT ACCOUNT		
		DR £	CR £	BALANCE £	DR £	CR £	BALANCE £
Apr. 11	Cash					5,000	5,000
27	Aspen. Transfer				5,500		—

Willow

Date	Details	OFFICE ACCOUNT DR £	CR £	BALANCE £	CLIENT ACCOUNT DR £	CR £	BALANCE £
Apr. 1	Balance						1,500
15	Cash. Willow & Co. Disbursements	100		100			
	Costs	1,200		1,300			
	VAT	120		1,420			
20	Cash. Transfer		1,420	—	1,420		80
	Cash. Transfer. Interest					42	122
	Cash. You				122		/

2.   Sherry & Brandy

Profit and Loss Account for year ending April 30, 1988

INCOME	£	£	£
Costs	367,455*		
less Work in hand at 30/4/87	21,426		
	346,029		
plus Work in hand at 30/4/88	11,432	357,461	
Interest received		24,562	382,023
EXPENSES			
Administrative and General			
Expenses	264,896		
plus Outstanding accounts	18,567	283,463	
Depreciation			
Cars	6,000		
Furniture etc.	1,460		
Computers	2,100	9,560	
			293,023
NET PROFIT			89,000

Appropriation Account

	£	£	£
Salary—Brandy			24,000
Interest on Capital			
Sherry (10% 80,000–6 months)	4,000		
(10% 95,000–6 months)	4,750	8,750	
Brandy (10% 30,000–6 months)	1,500		
(10% 35,000–6 months)	1,750	3,250	12,000
Profit			
Sherry $\frac{3}{4}$		39,750	
Brandy $\frac{1}{4}$		13,250	53,000
			89,000

Sherry & Brandy

Balance Sheet as at April 30, 1988

EMPLOYMENT OF CAPITAL	£	£	£
Fixed Assets			
Freehold Premises			100,000
Furniture Library and			
Equipment	14,600		
less Depreciation	8,760	5,840	
Motor Cars	30,000		
less Depreciation	24,000	6,000	
Computer and Ancillary			
Equipment	8,400		
less Depreciation	4,200	4,200	16,040
			116,040
Current Assets			
Work in hand	11,432		
Debtors	53,567		
Cash in bank	6,197*		
Cash in hand	123		
		71,319	
Current Liabilities			
Creditors	11,890		
Accounts outstanding	18,567	30,457	
Net Current Assets			40,862
Client Account			
Cash in bank:			
Deposit Account	700,000		
Current Account	65,987	767,987	
less due to clients		765,987	—
			156,902
CAPITAL EMPLOYED		£	£
Capital Accounts			
Sherry		95,000**	
Brandy		39,000**	
			134,000
Current Accounts			
Sherry		8,516	
Brandy		14,386	22,902
			156,902

Answers: Test Five

Current Account Movements

	Sherry £	Brandy £
Balance	8,342	654
Salary	—	24,000
Interest	8,750	3,250
Profit	39,750	13,250
	56,842	41,154
Drawings	(47,326)	(22,768)
To Capital Account	—	(4,000)
Adjustment*	(1,000)	—
	8,516	14,386

Workings

* Adjustment of £1,000

Cash				Sherry—Current Account			
Balance	7,617	Sherry Current Account	1,000	Cash	1,000	Balance	8,342
		Balance	6,617				
	7,617		7,617				
Balance	6,617						

Instead of using Sherry's Current Account, his Drawings Account could have been used.

* Adjustment of £420

Cash			
Balance	6,617	Client X	420
		Balance	6,197
	6,617		6,617
Balance	6,197		

Client X				Costs			
Cash	420	Costs	420	Client X	420	Balance	367,875
				Balance	367,455		
					367,875		367,875
						Balance	367,455

* *Revaluation of Premises*

Old Value	£ 80,000
New Value	£100,000
GAIN	£ 20,000
Sherry ($\frac{3}{4}$)	£15,000
Brandy ($\frac{1}{4}$)	£ 5,000

Capital Account—Sherry		*Capital Account—Brandy*	
Old Balance	80,000	Old Balance	30,000
Revaluation	15,000	Revaluation	5,000
		Current Account	4,000
	£ 95,000		£ 39,000

Test Six

1.   Statement

Cayenne. Sale of "Pailecroft". Purchase of "Stillsand" and flat in France

SALE of "PAILECROFT"

Receipts	£	£	£
Deposit	20,000		
Completion	180,000	200,000	
Payments			
Estate agent's commission	2,200		
Costs	500		
VAT	50		
B.S. Costs	22		
Mortgage redemption	30,263	33,035	166,965

PURCHASE OF STILLSAND

Search	16		
Survey fee	300		
Deposit	10,000		
Completion	90,000		
Costs	400		
VAT	70		
Stamp duty	1,000		
L.R. Fees	160	101,946	

PAYMENT TO YOUR GRANDSON		6,000

PURCHASE OF FRENCH FLAT

Payment to French law firm		52,301	160,247
RECEIPTS			6,718
Received on account			1,000
Interest			424
BALANCE DUE TO YOU			8,142

CLIENT: CAYENNE
MATTER: Sale of "Pailecroft". Purchase of "Stillsand"

Date	Details	OFFICE ACCOUNT DR £	CR £	BALANCE £	CLIENT ACCOUNT DR £	CR £	BALANCE £
Oct. 3	Cash. You					1,000	1,000
6	P. Cash. Search	16		16			
10	Cash. Survey fee. VAT	300		316			
17	Cash. V's solicitors. Deposit	10,000		10,316			
Nov. 9	Costs	900		11,216			
	VAT (900 + 300 × 10%)	120		11,336			
	Cloves B.S. Transfer	22		11,358			
15	Cash. Completion Sale.					180,000	181,000
	Cloves B.S. Transfer				30,263		150,737
	Stakeholder. Transfer					20,000	170,737
	Cash. Completion. Purchase				90,000		80,737
	Cash. Stamp duty				1,000		79,737
18	Cash. Estate agent				2,200		77,537
	Cash. Grandson				6,000		71,537
20	Cash. L.R. fees				160		71,377
	Cash. Transfer		11,358	—	11,358		60,019
Dec. 15	Cash. Law firm				52,301		7,718
16	Cash. Interest					424	8,142
	Cash. You				8,142		—

CLIENT: CLOVES BUILDING SOCIETY

Date	Details	OFFICE ACCOUNT			CLIENT ACCOUNT		
		DR £	CR £	BALANCE £	DR £	CR £	BALANCE £
Nov. 9	Costs	20		20			
	VAT	2		22			
	Cayenne. Transfer						
15	Cayenne. Transfer		22	—		30,263	30,263
	Cash. You				30,263		—

2. Water and Air

Profit & Loss Account for the year ending December 31, 1988

INCOME	£	£	£
Costs	442,563		
less Work in hand at 1/1/88	38,693		
	383,870		
plus Work in hand at 31/12/88	24,240	408,110	
Interest Receivable		27,422	
Miscellaneous Income		5,000	440,532
EXPENSES			
Administrative and General	355,389		
plus bills due	5,755		
	361,144		
less adjustment	400	360,744	
Bad debts		300	
Depreciation			
Furniture & Library	1,220		
Motor Cars	7,268	8,488	369,532
NET PROFIT			71,000

Appropriation Account for the 6 months ending June 30, 1988

Water 35,500

Appropriation Account for the 6 months ending December 31, 1988

Interest	£	£
Water	6,000	
Air	2,000	8,000
Salary		
Air		10,000
Profit		
Water ($\frac{3}{5}$)	10,500	
Air ($\frac{2}{5}$)	7,000	
		17,500
		35,000
		71,000

Water and Air

Balance Sheet as at December 31, 1988

EMPLOYMENT OF CAPITAL	£	£	£
Fixed Assets			
Freehold premises		120,000	
Furniture and Library	12,200		
less Depreciation	6,100	6,100	
Motor Cars	36,340		
less Depreciation	29,072	7,268	
			133,368
Current Assets			
Work in hand		24,240	
Sum due in respect of remuneration		4,000	
Debtors		48,956	
Cash		14,423	
Petty cash		60	
		91,679	
Current Liabilities			
Creditors	16,342		
Accounts outstanding	5,755	22,097	
Net Current Assets			69,582
Client Account			
Cash in bank			
Deposit Account	500,000		
Current Account	23,425	523,425	
less Due to clients		523,425	—
			202,950
CAPITAL EMPLOYED			
Capital Accounts			
Water		120,000	
Air		40,000	
			160,000
Current Accounts			
Water		1,000	
Air		1,950	2,950
Bank Loan			40,000
			202,950

Appendix

Current Accounts Movements

	Water	Air
Profit for 6 months ending 30/6/88	35,500	—
Interest for 6 months ending 30/12/88	6,000	2,000
Salary for 6 months ending 30/12/88		10,000
Profit for 6 months ending 30/12/88	10,500	7,000
	52,000	19,000
	(51,000)	(17,500)*
	1,000	1,950

*Drawings	15,650
Adjustment	400
Appointment	1,000
	17,050

Index